COLLECTING RARE COINS FOR PROFIT

Books by Q. David Bowers

Collecting Rare Coins for Profit

Value Guide of Automatic Musical Instruments

How to Start a Coin Collection

Put Another Nickel In

How to be a Successful Coin Dealer

Encyclopedia of Automatic Musical Instruments

Early American Car Advertisements

Guidebook of Automatic Musical Instruments, Vol. II

Guidebook of Automatic Musical Instruments, Vol. I

COLLECTING RARE COINS FOR PROFIT

Q. David Bowers

HARPER & ROW, PUBLISHERS

NEW YORK, EVANSTON, SAN FRANCISCO, LONDON

1817

Photographs on pp. 208 and 209 courtesy
of John Evans Photography Ltd., Ottawa.

 For information address Harper & Row, Publishers, Inc., 10 East 53rd Street, New York, N.Y. 10022. Published simultaneously in Canada by Fitzhenry & Whiteside Limited, Toronto.

FIRST EDITION

Designed by Sidney Feinberg

Library of Congress Cataloging in Publication Data

Bowers, Q. David.
Collecting rare coins for profit.
Bibliography: p.
1. Coins, American. 2. Mumismatics—Collectors and collecting. 3. Coins as an investment. I. Title.
CJ1830.B63 737.4′9′73 74–5788
ISBN 0–06–010426–0

To Wynn and Lee

Contents

Acknowledgments ix

1. The Romance of Coins 1
2. Collecting Coins for Pleasure and Investment 8
3. How Coins Are Made 22
4. Coins of Colonial America and Continental Currency 35
5. United States Copper, Nickel, and Silver Coins 44
6. United States Gold Coins 122
7. United States Commemoratives, Patterns, and Territorial Gold 137
8. Coinage of the Confederate States of America 171
9. Other United States Series—Coins, Tokens, Medals 177
10. United States Paper Money 195
11. Coins of the World 207
12. Coin Grading 238
13. Building a Coin Collection 254
14. Investing in Coins 261

15. Rare Coin Investment—Questions and Answers 268

16. Building an Investment "Portfolio" of Rare Coins 280

Afterword 288

Appendix A: Selected Coin Prices, 1946–1974 291

Appendix B: Numismatic Magazines and Newspapers 306

Glossary 309

Bibliography 317

Index 319

Acknowledgments

The author expresses thanks to the following persons who helped in the ways indicated: Kenneth Bressett of Western Publishing Co. for permission to use statistics and data from *A Guide Book of United States Coins* by Richard S. Yeoman; H. J. Chase (photography); John Evans Photography, Ltd.; George L. Osborn (sketches of United States mints); K. E. Prince of the Royal Canadian Mint, Ottawa (photography).

Also to the following Bowers and Ruddy Galleries, Inc., staff members who helped in various ways: Robert Budinger, Judy Cahn, Lorraine Gillman, Don Hauser, Nancy Kane, John Murbach, James F. Ruddy, Nancy Ruddy, Phil Starr, Karl Stephens, and Beryl Williams. A special thanks to my secretary, Glinda Vallow, who typed the manuscript.

1

The Romance of Coins

In 1859, at the New Orleans Mint a number of twenty-dollar gold pieces were struck, 9,100 of them to be exact. Containing nearly one ounce of gold each, these large and heavy coins—called "double eagles" in popular parlance—were mainly used for large commercial transactions and in bank-to-bank clearings. Twenty dollars was a lot of money back in 1859, and a coin of this value was seldom seen in everyday circulation.

Over the years nearly all the 9,100 1859-O (each piece bears a tiny "O", the mintmark designating the New Orleans Mint) pieces disappeared. Some were lost, some became so worn that they were redeemed by the Treasury and were melted down to be remade into other coins, and others met unknown fates. In March, 1933, when public ownership of gold coins was declared illegal by the Treasury, most citizens, banks, and others dutifully turned their gold coins in for redemption. (Happily, the Government order exempted numismatists who had prize pieces in their collections.)

By 1933, there weren't many 1859-O double eagles around. Most of those that remained fell victim to the Treasury recall order and were destroyed. The result is that in the 1970's the 1859-O double eagle is a rarity in any condition. Even a well-worn one is likely to bring $500 to $1,000.

As chance would have it, one of the 1859-O double eagles was acquired sometime around the year it was minted by a wealthy plantation

1859–O DOUBLE EAGLE. Buried for years on a Mississippi plantation, this 1859–O double eagle was discovered recently by treasure hunters. Sold at auction by Bowers and Ruddy Galleries in 1974, the piece, one of the finest known examples of its type, brought $7,250!

owner who lived near Vicksburg, Mississippi. Keeping large sums of money in bank notes or paper currency was considered risky at the time, so "hard money," particularly gold coins, offered an attractive alternative. In 1863, this Southern gentleman left his plantation to join the Confederate forces. Before doing so he buried in the ground some of his most valuable possessions—including several five-dollar gold pieces, a number of ten-dollar gold pieces, and a twenty-dollar gold piece, which was an 1859-O. Subsequently the plantation house was burned by the advancing Union army. The mansion owner was killed in battle.

My story might end here except for one interesting thing: For years the rumor persisted that before his death the Mississippian had buried some treasure on the plantation grounds, though many dismissed the tale as fancy. A few years ago two treasure hunters, working with a metal detector, were crisscrossing the old plantation site hoping to find an interesting artifact or two. Suddenly the indicator on their detector went wild! A buried treasure—or was it just something ordinary like an old horseshoe? No time was lost in finding out! Soon a glittering handful of gold coins was unearthed, including—you guessed it—the 1859-O double eagle, nearly as bright and perfect as the day it was minted!

Now I enter the story: In February, 1974, my firm—Bowers and Ruddy Galleries of Los Angeles—cataloged and offered for sale the magnificent Stanislaw Herstal Collection and other important properties. Among the "other important properties" was the golden treasure cache from Mississippi.

What would the 1859-O double eagle bring? In Uncirculated (new) condition the coin was cataloged for $1,400 in the standard reference book used by most collectors, *A Guide Book of U.S. Coins*. But, the catalog price of rarities often lags behind the true market simply because rarities do not trade often, and a catalog listing may represent a sale which took place several years ago. When the 1974 sale took place there was standing room only on the auction floor. The event, which included some of the rarest American coins to be auctioned in recent years, attracted bidders from all over the world. In spirited, almost frantic, bidding the 1859-O twenty-dollar gold piece soared to $7,250—over five times the catalog price!

The life of a coin dealer is an interesting and enjoyable one. The process of buying and selling coins has its exciting moments—and the buried treasure story is a good example—but the greatest pleasure is in the coins themselves.

If you think about it you will realize that coins are unique among collectors' items. Coins are "footprints on the sands of time." Virtually every event of world importance during the past 2000 years has been recorded on coins and metallic tokens.

When World War I ended, Americans sighed with relief. The great conflict at last was over! Soon afterward, a new silver dollar design was proposed for use in the United States. The reverse motif? An eagle with its wings folded and at rest, a peaceful pose. Beneath was the word PEACE. When President John F. Kennedy was killed in 1963, the nation felt a tremendous loss. As a tribute, a new half-dollar design was prepared. From 1964 to the present, the Kennedy half dollar has served to perpetuate the memory of one of our most popular Presidents.

When George Washington died in 1799, Americans grieved. A number of commemorative tokens and medallions were produced to perpetuate the memory of the Father of Our Country. One of the most sentimental of these, a small token issued by silversmith Jacob Perkins of Newburyport, Massachusetts, bears the portrait of Washington surrounded by the legend: HE IS IN GLORY, THE WORLD IS IN TEARS. Certainly no finer tribute to our first President could be imagined!

Happier events have been recorded on coins, too. Beginning in 1971, Eisenhower "silver dollars" (still called this from tradition, although the coins now contain metals other than silver) have been issued. The reverse, adapted from the official Apollo 11 insignia, features an American eagle landing on the crater-pocked moon with stars and the earth in the background.

Postage stamps have been with us only since the 1840's. Books, newspapers, and other mass-produced printed material date back just a few centuries earlier. Coins, however, recorded the triumphs, tragedies, and personalities of the ancient Greeks and Romans, the despotic monarchs of the Middle Ages, the infamous Nazi regime, and are still recording history today. Other fields have recorded events of mankind for many centuries—paintings and sculpture, to name just two. However, only the very wealthy can obtain a representative collection of great art from centuries ago, whereas great and famous coins are available to anyone. As surprising as it may seem, beautiful examples of the coinage of the ancient Romans are available today for just a few dollars each.

What makes a coin valuable? As the preceding example shows, age alone does not necessarily make a coin expensive. Indeed, one rare variety of 1955 Lincoln cent, the so-called Double Die with blurred lettering on the obverse or front of the coin, is worth hundreds of dollars, despite the fact that it is scarcely twenty years old! Many factors contribute to a coin's value, and age is just one of them. Others include rarity, demand, condition, and any romance or special historical interest which might be attached to the piece.

Why do people collect coins? This is another popular question—and one which will be answered in detail in this volume. "I collect coins because they are interesting," is certainly a good answer, just as one might aspire to climb Mount Everest "because it is there." Another reason, and a major one, is for their performance as an investment. Few could argue that coins have not done spectacularly well. Indeed, coins have been one of the most fantastic investments imaginable. As a dealer since 1954, I have seen at first hand many investment successes. Many of my clients have made fortunes in the rare coin market, and it is my hope that many more will make fortunes in the future. Nothing is quite so satisfying as having a customer say, "Thank you for making a lot of money for me!"

The true collector or *numismatist* has the best of both worlds at his fingertips: He can carefully gather together an important and historically significant collection, one which brings him many years of pleasure, and then sell it for a profit years later. Thus his favorite hobby has been at the same time his best investment. This happens time and time again.

On the other hand many investors are interested in coins for the sake of investment alone.

Still others are coin investors without realizing it! An interesting case in point is the family of Lord St. Oswald. This family's collection, sold at auction by Christie's in London in 1964, was one of the largest treasure troves of American coins brought to light in recent years.

In 1795, one of Lord St. Oswald's ancestors visited the United States. When he returned to his homestead in Wakefield, Yorkshire, England, he brought back about $10 face value of United States coins. After all, the new nation had been a British colony only a few years earlier, and these newly minted coins would be interesting to show to friends. Soon the coins were put away and forgotten.

In 1964, Lord St. Oswald decided to sell the family coin collection. He brought the pieces to Albert Baldwin of A. H. Baldwin & Sons, renowned London rare coin dealer, for cataloging. According to Mr. Baldwin, the collection consisted of early English pieces, all properly attributed and ticketed, of the years of Oliver Cromwell and of Queen Anne and other British monarchs. Years ago someone had very carefully assembled a nice coin collection depicting British history. In a separate pasteboard box were the United States coins—the $10 worth brought over from America years earlier—all jumbled together! Mr. Baldwin queried Lord St. Oswald about the value of the United States coins. The owner said that he was not aware that they had great value but decided to bring them along anyway.

Those United States coins appeared as 33 separate lots in Christie's Oct. 13, 1964, auction of the Lord St. Oswald Collection. The 33 lots consisted of two magnificent Uncirculated 1794 silver dollars, several Uncirculated 1795 half dollars, and over twenty 1794 one-cent pieces, each virtually as nice as the day it was minted! The 33 lots sold for record prices. The 1794 silver dollars brought $11,400 each, from an American collector and a British dealer. Quite a few of the 1794 one-cent pieces sold for several thousand dollars each, and one actually fetched $8,400! When all was said and done, the little pasteboard box of miscellaneous United States coins—the box which represented an investment of less than $10 in 1795—brought Lord St. Oswald the princely sum of $72,000! Quite a fantastic return on an investment!

This is not the end of the story. Nine years later, in 1973, one of the 1794 silver dollars—which had sold for $11,400 at the Christie's sale—came on the market again. My business partner James F. Ruddy, who had attended the 1964 Christie's sale, attended the 1973 sale to again bid on the 1794 dollar. In 1964, Jim Ruddy was the underbidder at Christie's, and he lost both pieces by just a few hundred dollars. Now he was *sure* he would get the 1794 the second time around. While he dared not to whisper his bid, given to him by a leading Illinois collector, to anyone, the customer's words were sharp in his mind: "You can go to $100,000 for the coin, or a bit more if you have to."

The bidding for the 1794 started at $60,000, and Jim Ruddy had his hand up as the price went up bid by bid. Finally, at $108,000 he stopped, and the coin was awarded to another bidder for a record-breaking $110,000!

The "record price" for the 1794 silver dollar was $11,400 when it was sold in 1964. As is often true of record prices, today's record price is tomorrow's bargain—and the 1973 price of $110,000 proved that the record of nine years earlier was an *incredible* bargain.

A somewhat similar situation occurred with the famous 1804 silver dollar. This coin, one of America's most famous rarities, has long been considered a fabulous showpiece and fortunate the collector who owns one. Only 15 specimens of the 1804 dollar are known to exist.

In 1960, Jim Ruddy attended the auction sale of the Fairbanks Collection held by Stack's in New York. In that auction was an 1804 silver dollar. No silver dollar of this date had appeared on the market for some years prior to 1960, and speculation was rife as to what this specimen would sell for. In talking with a number of other dealers before the sale, Jim Ruddy learned that most thought a price in the $15,000 to $20,000 range would be realized. "The coin's going to be mine. I am prepared to pay $18,000," said one dealer, a gentleman from New Jersey.

With a confidential $27,000 bid from one of our clients, an industrialist from upstate New York, Jim Ruddy was confident that he would soon be the coin's owner. On the auction floor the action commenced. The 1804 dollar went quickly to $20,000 as a number of bidders raised their hands. After $20,000 there were but two bidders, Jim Ruddy and Samuel Wolfson, the latter a well-known collector from Jacksonville, Florida. Within a few moments the coin was at $21,000, then $22,000, and then by a succession of raises between the two bidders, up to $27,000. Mr. Wolfson took the coin for $28,000, the next bid.

After the sale Jim approached Samuel Wolfson and asked him how far he would have gone to obtain the rare dollar. Jim would not have been happy to learn that $28,000 or so was Wolfson's top bid, and that the coin could have been his for one or two more bids beyond that. "I was prepared to pay *any* amount. I wanted that coin," was Mr. Wolfson's reply. Such are the thrills of collecting!

Here, again, the story is not ended. As it turns out, $28,000 was a tremendous bargain. In 1973, Jim Ruddy did purchase an 1804 dollar. Obtained in a private transaction, Jim had to write out a check for well over $100,000 to obtain it.

However, coins do not have to be expensive to be interesting or to be good investments, for that matter. Many inexpensive pieces have done very well over the years and, equally important, have been good investments. An example of this is the 1883 Liberty nickel without CENTS on the reverse. From 1866, the first year that nickel five-cent pieces were made for circulation, through 1883, the pieces of this denomination were of the design with a shield on the obverse or front of the coin and a ring of stars on the reverse. In the latter year, the design was changed to the classical-appearing Liberty head. The obverse featured the portrait of Miss Liberty facing to the left and surrounded by a partial circle of thirteen stars. The reverse bore as a value the Roman numeral V within a wreath. The coin's designers thought that this numeral V, meaning 5, would suffice to indicate value. They overlooked one thing: The nickel five-cent piece was approximately the same diameter as the five-dollar gold piece. Some ingenious American citizens quickly discovered a surefire way to make money: They took the new Liberty nickels and gold-plated them. Since the coins did not say 5 CENTS but, rather, just had the numeral V, they were given to unsuspecting shopkeepers by unscrupulous persons as a new design of five-dollar gold pieces! The Mint quickly realized its error, and within a short time the important CENTS was added to the reverse design. In the meantime approximately 5,500,000 nickels without CENTS were minted. Today, a worn example can be obtained for just a few dollars, and an Uncirculated piece can be purchased in the $50 range.

2

Collecting Coins for Pleasure and Investment

"Coins are money, and everyone likes money" would be one simple answer to the question of why people collect coins. Indeed, chances are that in an old desk drawer somewhere in your home, among family papers, or perhaps in a safe deposit box you have put away a few special coins—not intentionally but just because they were interesting to you or to someone in your family in the past. Did you save a few Kennedy half dollars when they were first released in 1964? Millions of Americans did; so many, in fact, that despite the fact that more than two *billion* of these have been made it is still not common to find one in everyday pocket change. Two billion? Yes. Figured out another way that is nearly ten pieces for every man, woman, and child in the United States. Soon new coin designs commemorating the 1976 bicentennial of our country's founding will be with us. It will be a rare person, indeed, who upon seeing one of these for the first time will pass it along in circulation. My guess is that billions of these will be saved also—as sentimental souvenirs.

Considering coin collecting in its broadest sense, it is safe to say that tens of millions of Americans have set aside coins for one reason or another. Of this number, probably eight to ten million are serious enough about the hobby to write to the Treasury to inquire about ordering Proof sets (special sets made for collectors each year), to fill out albums from coins found in pocket change, and to otherwise collect in a serious manner.

Among this eight to ten million are several hundred thousand people who are advanced collectors—numismatists who carefully study coins, keep up to date with coin prices, and spend money with coin dealers and others to acquire pieces needed for their collections. In addition to collector interest, there is great investor interest in coins—and hundreds of thousands of people are attracted to the field for the potential profit to be made by carefully investing in coins over a period of time.

Coin collecting indeed combines many fascinating appeals.

An important appeal is history. Farran Zerbe, a prominent American numismatist of the early 20th century, once said that the "coin outlives the throne." Since the 7th century B.C., coins have been a necessary instrument of commerce. During the past 2,000 years, literally hundreds of historical events—some important, others obscure—have been recorded on coins. Today such coins, items which recorded history, help us now to understand it better. The economic rise and fall of ancient nations can be traced through their coins, as can the triumphs of war, the blessings of peace, and other events. The Caesars of Rome are indelibly represented on coins as are the religious and mythological figures of ancient Greece.

One of the Seven Wonders of the Ancient World was the Colossus of Rhodes, the gigantic statue of Helios, God of the Sun, that stood with beacon in hand at the entrance to the ancient harbor of Rhodes. The civilization of Rhodes is but a subject for history books, the Colossus is gone forever, but the coins from that ancient time remain. For less than $100 you can purchase a beautiful silver coin of Rhodes, with the portrait of Helios as its main design.

The implements used by the legions of Rome are museum pieces, as are statues, pottery, and other artistic relics from that period of civilization. Coins from Roman times are museum pieces, also—but the supply is sufficiently plentiful that, for $10 or $20 each many, many fascinating varieties can be obtained by the collector. In today's era of high prices it is almost incredible to think that 2,000-year-old "pieces of history," completely authentic and in excellent condition, can be purchased for such low sums. Yet it is true.

The reason is actually the financial conditions of the time in which they were issued. Paper money was not in use, and coins—particularly larger-value pieces of gold and silver—were the main store of value. A wealthy citizen of ancient Rome had no bank in which to deposit his coins for safekeeping. Rather, he secreted them in a vault in his home, buried them someplace that only he knew of, or otherwise hid and protected them. This has had a fortunate consequence for modern-day archaeologists: Tens

ANCIENT COINS. Ancient coins form a fascinating field of study for the numismatic scholar. Struck from hand-cut dies, most pieces depict real or mythological persons and events. Despite the rarities among ancient coins, many issues which are 2,000 years old or older can be obtained for just a few dollars.

of thousands of coins of ancient times have come to light when such long-forgotten treasure troves have been unearthed.

Many United States coins vividly tell of our history. In 1943, the shortage of copper, a vital material for war needs, was so acute that zinc-coated steel one-cent pieces were produced. These "white pennies" used to be seen in circulation until the 1950's. In some distant era, a student of money and finance will understand better the American monetary system of the 20th century when he reviews its coinage and finds that gold coins were last made in 1933 and heavy silver-content coins were last produced in 1964—clear indications of the Government's leaving the intrinsic-value concept behind and relying only upon cheaper-metal coins and paper money backed by the "full faith and credit of the government" (whatever that is).

Throughout history many special coin issues called *commemoratives* have been produced. The signing of a peace treaty, the discovery of a new land, a military victory, and similar events are typical reasons for the production of such pieces. In the United States, commemorative coins were first issued in 1892; in that year special souvenir half dollars were made for the Columbian Exposition. In the following year, commemorative quarters and half dollars were made for the same event. When the 1892 and 1893 Columbian half dollars were produced there was a problem regarding the design: It was desired to represent Christopher Columbus on the obverse or front of each piece. However, search of historical records revealed that no contemporary portrait of Columbus existed! Columbus was not the monarch of any country, so his pioneering discoveries were not recorded upon Spanish or Italian coins of his time. A "typical likeness" of what Columbus *might* have looked like was quickly devised—and this saved the day.

Of course, many other things besides coins record history—stamps, newspapers, and even paintings. However, when you consider that stamps have been regularly issued only since the 19th century, that printing for the general public extends back only to the 15th century, and that art from early periods is so elusive or so high priced that only the wealthy or museums can afford it, coins stand alone as everyman's contact with days and ages of long ago.

Art furnishes another reason for collecting coins. "Art" takes many forms throughout the history of coinage. Sculptors of ancient and medieval times often made their work available to posterity by creating coins or medals. In our own time the artistic concept continues. While many American coin designs have been simply created by staff members of the Mint, others have been selected by design competition. For example, in 1938 when it was decided to replace the traditional (made since 1913) buffalo nickel with a new design, a nationwide competition was announced. The winner was Felix Schlag, who captured the first prize of $1,000 in a contest of approximately 390 entrants. Felix Schlag's design of the Jefferson nickel, first minted in the year of his award, 1938, is still with us.

In 1974, an artistic competition was announced for the 1976 bicentennial coinage. Several thousand entrants were narrowed down to 12 semifinalists. In March, 1974, three winning designs for new commemorative reverses to be used on bicentennial quarters, half dollars, and one-dollar pieces were shown to the public.

The high-water mark for art in American coinage occurred in 1907 when noted sculptor Augustus Saint-Gaudens prepared beautiful designs for the American ten-dollar and twenty-dollar gold pieces. In 1905, President Theodore Roosevelt commissioned Saint-Gaudens to design a medal for his inauguration. Pleased with the design, Roosevelt was inspired to have Saint-Gaudens improve regular American coinage designs. A coin must be useful, Roosevelt reasoned, but why can't it be truly artistic at the same time? In 1905, Roosevelt wrote to Saint-Gaudens:

How is the gold coinage design coming along? I want to make a suggestion. It seems to me to be worthwhile to try for a really good coinage; though I suppose there will be a revolt about it. I was looking at some gold coins of Alexander the Great today, and I was struck by their high relief. Would it not be well to have our coins in high relief, and also to have the rims raised? The point of having the rim raised would be, of course, to protect the figure of the coin; and if we have the figures in high relief, like the figures on the old Greek coins, they will surely last longer. What do you think of this?

By return mail Saint-Gaudens replied:

You have hit the nail on the head with regard to the coinage. Of course the great coins (and you might say the only coins) are the Greek ones you speak of, just as the great medals are those of the 15th century by Pisani and Sperandie. Nothing would please me more than to make the attempt in the direction of the heads of Alexander, but the authorities on modern monetary requirements would I fear "throw fits," to speak emphatically, if the thing were done now. It would be great if it could be accomplished and I do not see what the objection would be if the edges were high enough to prevent the rubbings. Perhaps an inquiry from you would not receive the antagonistic reply from those who have the say in such matters that would certainly be made to me . . .

The result of this correspondence was the production of two beautiful coins, the Indian head ten-dollar gold piece of 1907 and the high-relief twenty-dollar gold piece of the same year. The latter coin carried out Roosevelt's and Saint-Gaudens' ideas and featured the standing figure of Liberty on the obverse, in very high relief, almost like a sculpture. Protecting the design was a high rim. The reverse depicted a sculpted-appearing eagle flying over a radiant sun. In keeping with the classical theme the date 1907 was given in Roman numerals: MCMVII.

Unfortunately, objections soon arose. For purposes of mint production efficiency it is necessary that a coin be struck quickly. But, *three* distinct and carefully aligned impressions from the dies were necessary to strike each blank disc to bring up the high-relief details of the new design to their proper sharpness. Obviously, such a piece could not be made on a high-production basis. The second objection was that the average citizen was not familiar with Roman numerals.

So, the beautiful Saint-Gaudens design was modified to a shallower relief which could be struck with one blow of the coining press. The MCMVII was quickly changed to the Arabic numeral system: 1907. However, before these changes were effected, some 11,250 pieces of the high-relief design with Roman numerals were made. Today these are very popular with collectors.

AMERICA'S MOST BEAUTIFUL COIN. The 1907 twenty-dollar gold piece or double eagle designed by Augustus Saint-Gaudens is considered by numismatists to be the most beautiful American coin ever produced for circulation. The obverse and reverse are in high relief, almost like a sculpture. The date is in Roman numerals. The sculptured appearance of this coin presented great difficulties in mass production, so the design was soon made shallower. Also, MCMVII (1907) confused the public, so this classic concept was abandoned. Only 11,250 of these beautiful pieces were struck before the design was modified. Today such coins are highly prized.

Investment has been another main reason for collecting coins. In recent decades selected rare coins have sharply outperformed such other popular indices of monetary growth as stock averages, compounded rates of return on savings accounts, and so on. In my own business, I have stressed the investment aspect of coins, for I feel that coins are truly a hobby in which the joys of collecting can be combined with solid financial planning. This is indeed a rare combination!

Time and time again I have seen people of modest means retire with a small fortune—simply because they collected choice coins over a long period of years. About ten years ago I was summoned to make a bid on the contents of a safe deposit box in a small town in upstate New York. The owner of the collection, who operated a meat market as his business, collected coins as a hobby. He was careful about it, or at least it seemed so from his coins, for his collection contained the finest examples of each type: choice specimens in Uncirculated and Proof grade, scarce varieties, and so on. It was apparent that he did not collect with investment foremost in mind, for his coins were carefully arranged in date series—one each of every variety of nickel five-cent piece made from 1866 through 1883, a complete set of Lincoln cents from the first year of issue in 1909 on down to present times, and so on.

Following his death, the collector's coins were almost forgotten. Then one day the son of the collector was talking with his banker, who suggested that he contact several coin dealers. The result was that this modest group of coins resulted in a check amounting to nearly $100,000 being given to an otherwise moderately well-off family!

Often when someone asks me about the advantages of coins as an investment I recommend that investing be combined with collecting, for the combination of the two can lead to a fuller and richer life, both from an enjoyment viewpoint and a financial viewpoint. I frequently cite the example of the life of Oscar G. Schilke, a Connecticut collector who was a friend of mine and an adviser for many years. I began collecting coins in 1953 and dealing in rare coins in 1954, and it was shortly thereafter that I first met Oscar at one of the early coin shows held annually in New York City. At the time I was an advertiser in *The Numismatic Scrapbook Magazine* and *The Numismatist*. In addition I put out small periodical catalogs. From the very beginning of my interest, I read voraciously on the subject; in the early years I spent money just as avidly for books as I did for coins. I soon found that there was a wealth of information in print and that most collectors and dealers were generally unaware of it, limiting their interests to current catalogs and price lists. I began spicing my coin descriptions with historical information.

Oscar approached me at a coin convention and showed me a small box containing several hundred dollars' worth of coins, each in its own envelope. If I remember correctly, most of the pieces were large American cents and early colonial issues, pieces of the 18th and 19th centuries. In retrospect, I think that Oscar probably had read my catalogs and wondered if I "knew what I was talking about" with all my "fancy" descriptions.

Since Oscar never put a price on anything, I had to make offers for each individual piece. He handed me one coin at a time, watching my reaction to each. Interspersed among easily recognizable issues were some scarcer varieties which only the advanced collector might be expected to pick out. I picked them out! Soon Oscar and I became good friends.

At the time I regularly attended most of the major conventions in the eastern part of the United States. Oscar Schilke also attended these shows, and at most events he would have a number of coins—from a half dozen to a dozen—for me to see before he showed them to any other dealer. He liked to test my knowledge and to surprise me, so he would always include something special in each group. One of his surprises was a 1794 token, the size of a United States one-cent piece, issued in 1794 by the firm of Talbot, Allum & Lee, New York merchants specializing in trade with India. The piece offered was examined by me fairly carefully, or so I thought, and then I made an offer of $30 for it. The coin retailed for about $40 at the time.

"Look at that one again and give me another offer," Oscar said with a twinkle in his eye. I looked at it again, and again, and still did not see why I should make a higher offer. In a fatherly fashion, Oscar then showed me the page in his copy of *A Guide Book of U.S. Coins* on which 1794 Talbot, Allum & Lee cents were listed. The one he showed me, it turned out, was an exceedingly rare variety with the words NEW YORK omitted, in contrast to the common issues which had this feature. Instead of being worth $40, the coin was worth in the $200 to $300 range. A bit embarrassed, I paid the $200 or so for the token and resolved to study coins harder than ever. Soon early American coins became my specialty, and they are to this day.

Mr. and Mrs. Schilke and I became good personal friends in addition to our business relationship. Soon I was making yearly pilgrimages to their tranquil lakeside home in Connecticut. Each visit would last several days. The first day or two would be spent talking about coins and things in general. I have always liked numismatic history, so I would ask Oscar endless questions about his experiences in the coin market during the 1930's and 1940's. Often I would take notes on what he had to say, with the idea in mind of publishing them someday. Most of Oscar's stories are still quite vivid in my mind. One which I particularly like concerned his purchases from one of New York City's leading dealers, Wayte Raymond. Mr. Raymond, who is now deceased, would ask Oscar a certain price for a desired coin and then grant a discount if Oscar could tell him, before buying the piece, of its background and history! In a way this was the same type of game that Oscar would play with me.

Oscar Schilke really enjoyed his coins. To aid in appreciating what he purchased and also to learn about coins in general, he built up a large numismatic library, much of which simply "grew" as he saved periodicals, auction catalogs, and other reference books. Soon the library occupied one wall of his study.

During the 1940's and 1950's, Oscar had an interesting arrangement with several banks in Connecticut. He would display on a bank's premises sample exhibits from his vast collection of United States coins, tokens, and paper money, usually arranged in attractive frames with historical information printed under each item. The bank would then advertise that members of the public could bring in their old coins for a free appraisal. Oscar could then negotiate to buy any pieces of interest, if he wished. In this way he acquired many desirable pieces.

Once a lady came to Oscar with a set of United States Proof coins made in 1842. Proof coins—coins with special mirrorlike surfaces and struck from polished dies—coins minted especially for collectors, were not generally available to the public until 1858, when 80 sets were sold. During the 1840's and early 1850's, such sets were made to the extent of just a dozen or two each year and were used for presentation to visiting foreign monarchs, government dignitaries, and so on. The lady in question had just fallen heir to a large mansion full of furniture and other household items. In the back of a bedroom dresser drawer was this set of 1842 Proof coins containing a glittering specimen of one each of the copper and silver coins made that year, from the half cent through the silver dollar. The set evidently had been presented to a former owner of the home, a Governor of Connecticut. The lady was surprised when Oscar told her of its significance and value—and offered her several thousand dollars for the set. The group of coins was subsequently sold by Oscar Schilke to a Midwestern dealer for a profit of about $500. In 1961, I purchased just one coin from that set, an 1842 Proof quarter with the date in very small numerals, a rare variety for most quarters of this year had the date in large numerals. I paid $10,000 for this single coin—three times what Oscar had sold the entire set for ten years earlier! Today the set would be worth far, far more.

Oscar enjoyed fraternizing with collectors and dealers. Regularly he would take the train to New York City to attend meetings of the New York Coin Club where he would buy and sell coins, trade duplicates, and keep up to date on the latest coin news and gossip. This was a vital part of collecting to Oscar and his wife, and many of their social gatherings included collectors.

During the late 1950's and early 1960's, James F. Ruddy and I purchased many of Oscar Schilke's coins and sets. He delighted in telling me that "I paid $1 for that 1875 twenty-cent piece in 1939" as he accepted my offer of $40 for it.

Numismatics made Oscar Schilke's life richer in many ways. From a personal pleasure viewpoint, he really enjoyed the company of other collectors and dealers, many of whom still recall his warm hospitality and his deep love for the coins which passed through his hands. From a financial viewpoint, his coin collection made a nice nest egg, an investment whose performance would have been hard to duplicate in any other financial medium. Oscar was a successful businessman, and over a period of years he tried many investment areas. Finally he decided—and this in an era when few people had ever heard of coin investment—that the best investment of all was to spend money on his own coin collection. He had had some unsuccessful investing experiences elsewhere, mainly by relying upon other people's advice. So, he followed his own heart! His interests knew no limits, and he formed fine collections of United States one-cent pieces, colonial coins, quarter eagles ($2.50 gold pieces), colonial and U.S. paper money, California gold, and other series.

Coins were very good to Oscar. His life story is a very interesting case in point: Coins can be a *wonderful investment* in combination with a *fascinating hobby*. Literally Oscar had the best of two worlds! To paraphrase Ben Franklin: "Mind your collection carefully, and the investment will take care of itself." By carefully selecting choice coins you can build a financial treasure for the future. In the meantime you will have lots of enjoyment in the search for the pieces you need!

Coin collecting is challenging, and the thrill of the chase is another reason the hobby has been so popular. The crossword puzzle fan knows what it means to fill in the last space after working for a long period of time. Likewise it is an exciting moment when a set of Lincoln cents is completed by filling in the last hole, perhaps a 1914 cent from the Denver Mint, or a collection of silver dollars reaches its end when the super-rare 1895 is finally acquired, perhaps in spirited bidding competition at auction. Coins can be neatly arranged in various series—collections by date and mintmark, collections by general design types, or in any of many other ways. Once a collector formulates his objective, then a "want list" of pieces still needed is made up. Once the set is complete, then interest can be directed to another set. A complete set is always a showpiece. Another collector looking at, say, a set of silver dollars is bound to exclaim, "What a beautiful 1895!"

Closely related to this is the concept of prestige. Prestige and pride of

1804 SILVER DOLLAR, THE KING OF AMERICAN COINS. Enlarged illustrations of the 1804 silver dollar, a coin considered by numismatists to be the most famous coin issue. Only 15 specimens are known, and most of these are permanently impounded in museum collections. The specimen shown here was offered by Bowers and Ruddy Galleries in 1974 at $200,000.

ownership are rewards for possessing something rare. Indeed, for some they are important reasons to acquire a valuable object. Coin clubs, major conventions, and other places provide a forum for exhibiting prize pieces. Each year at the American Numismatic Association convention, for example, trophies and prizes are awarded to outstanding exhibits in each of several categories. When William Donlon's complete collection of United States Proof sets from 1858 to date was sold at auction by Abe Kosoff in the 1950's, it was billed as a "prizewinning collection of Proof sets"—simply because the superb grouping had been exhibited at many coin shows and had won many blue ribbons as a result! During the 1950's and 1960's, Art Lovi and Irving Moskowitz, both owners of outstanding

collections, built special showcases, electrically illuminated exhibits, and other accessories so that their collections could be seen to their best advantage when exhibited at major conventions. Both collectors were successful businessmen in their own right, but I am sure that business was forgotten when the opportunity to exhibit their collections arose.

Often an individual coin can bring great prestige to its owner. The late J. V. McDermott owned a 1913 Liberty nickel, a coin valued at $200,000 or more today. He generously made it available for exhibit at coin shows and conventions. This had a two-way benefit: It made his 1913 nickel one of the most famous specimens in existence and, for the show exhibiting it, the coin often attracted crowds.

In 1973, Bowers and Ruddy Galleries acquired one of the finest known examples of the 1804 silver dollar, one of America's greatest rarities. Over the years a great aura has built up around the piece. B. Max Mehl, a well-known Texas dealer, described a specimen he offered in 1941 by saying:

In all the history of numismatics of the entire world there is not today and there never has been a single coin which was and is the subject of so much romance, history, comment, and upon which so much has been written and so much talked about and discussed as the United States silver dollar of 1804.

While there may be coins of greater rarity (based upon the number of specimens known), no coin is so famous as the dollar of 1804! This is due to the fact that this great coin was the first coin of the United States mintage to have been recognized as the rarest coin of the United States from the very beginning of American numismatics more than 100 years ago. And it is today, as it always has been, the best known and most sought-after coin, not only among collectors, but among the public in general as well.

My firm's specimen of the 1804 dollar traces its pedigree through several collections back to the middle of the 19th century. Carrying B. Max Mehl's thoughts further, I described our firm's coin in part as follows:

It is with great pleasure that we offer for sale what is undoubtedly one of the most famous and finest-preserved specimens of "The King of American Coins," the United States silver dollar of 1804.

The coin here offered has achieved a fame accorded to few, if any, other United States coins. In recent years it has appeared on the cover of *Coin World, Numismatic News*, and numerous other numismatic publications. It has been on nationwide television, it has been featured in news stories, and it has attracted the admiration of countless thousands of viewers when it has been exhibited at conventions. There is no alert numismatist anywhere in the world who has not heard of this famous coin!

Over the years we have had many wonderful coins pass our way. Included have been unique and extremely rare coins—virtually every issue listed in the *Guide Book*, as a matter of fact. No coin has given us a pride of ownership greater than the magnificent 1804 silver dollar offered here. In the past other dealers and prominent collectors have shared our feelings. The ownership of an 1804 silver dollar has in the past been a sure way to register its possessor in the "numismatic hall of fame." The inclusion of an 1804 dollar in the sale of a collection has invariably made that sale a landmark event to be commemorated for all time.

I wrote the preceding description and included it in one of our catalogs and in a news release distributed by our firm. A month or two later I was window-shopping in Copenhagen during a visit there. On Vesterbrogade, one of Copenhagen's main streets, together with Claes O. Friberg I own the Mekanisk Musik Museum, an exhibition of antique player pianos, music boxes, and other relics from years ago. Walking up Vesterbrogade from the Town House Square, I did not pay much attention to the various things for sale, Royal Copenhagen plates and porcelain, souvenirs, then an exhibit of cameras—and then I saw it! There prominently displayed in the window of a small shop which sold coins and curios was a picture of my 1804 silver dollar together with a lengthy description in Danish concerning it! A few weeks later, back in my Los Angeles office, a prominent Swiss banker asked me, "Having read so much about your 1804 dollar, may I see it?" The fame of a rare coin knows no international boundaries!

3

How Coins Are Made

Today coins are made in modern mints employing thousands of people and turning out pieces at the rate of millions of coins each day. Such institutions are showplaces of efficiency and production.

It was not always so. In ancient Greek and Roman times, coins were generally made by impressing a seal or portrait on one side of the piece, perhaps by hammering a blob of metal against an anvil or matrix in which a design was cut. Such coinage was performed entirely by hand, from the cutting of the die to the preparation of the metal used, to the striking of the piece with a hammer. As a result, the finished coins often differed widely from each other with respect to the sharpness of striking, deepness of impression, and even size and shape.

Making coins by hand continued on down through the centuries. In 1652, when the Massachusetts Bay Colony decided to produce its first coins, the colonists did the best they could with the materials on hand. Silver metal in the form of bullion was obtained from the West Indies and other sources. Blank discs, called *planchets*, were made by heating and flattening out a piece of silver and then cutting it into a circular shape. The *intrinsic-value concept* was important at the time, so a shilling (worth 12 pence) was made with a weight equal to 12 pence' worth of silver. If a Massachusetts shilling planchet was slightly overweight, it was carefully filed to bring it down to the correct weight of silver.

The intrinsic-value concept pervaded the monetary system of nations until recent times. Years ago no one would consider accepting a silver coin worth only half its weight in metal, any more than one would accept a five-dollar check in settlement of a ten-dollar account. This concept has been replaced by the government-backed or *fiat* system.

At his iron works at Saugus, Joseph Jenks made up the punches for this early American coinage. For the shilling, two punches were required. One had NE, the abbreviation for New England, engraved on one side. The other side had the Roman numeral XII, representing a shilling or 12 pence.

Coinage was accomplished in a simple manner. The silver disc was placed against an anvil or other hard surface. The NE punch was carefully placed near the top of the disc and then struck with a hammer. The planchet was then turned over. On the other end of the coin (so as not to obliterate the NE on the first side) the XII punch was then stamped. The result was a useful, if crude, coin—a piece, by the way, now worth between $5,000 to $10,000 to a collector!

These crude coins invited an insidious practice known as clipping. Anyone with a scissors or tinsnips could carefully trim a bit of silver the size of a fingernail clipping from the edge of one of these pieces. If this was done to several thousand pieces, the result would be a nice pile of silver metal—worth a good sum in those days! This practice was not unique to colonial Massachusetts; it was a problem all over the world. Actually, the problem had been solved to a degree by European and other mints working with fairly sophisticated equipment compared to what was available in colonial America.

The so-called *security edge* ended the practice of clipping. Milling—giving a coin a distinctive edge (such as found on American dimes, quarters, half dollars, and dollars today), lettering, or some other design—made it very apparent if metal was removed. Edge ornamentation is applied in two main ways. The usual way practiced until the early 19th century was to take the planchets and roll them edgewise through a set of dies which contained lettering, geometric ornaments, or other devices. The planchet, which would have had its diameter reduced slightly in the process, would then emerge with the appropriate design on the edge. From there it went to the coinage press to be placed between two dies (one for the obverse or front of the coin and the other for the reverse or back) and struck. No collar or restraining device was put on the coins. If such a piece was struck under high pressure, it might squeeze outward and be slightly larger in diameter than if it was struck lightly.

The more modern method is to do all this in one operation, by fitting the obverse and reverse die with a restraining collar which contains vertical lines or milling, or perhaps lettering. The coin is then struck between the two dies, and the metal is forced out into the collar and impressed into it, where it acquires the appropriate edge. In the case of modern-day cents and nickels the collar has no design, so the coins emerge with a smooth edge. On larger denominations the edge is milled or reeded. In all instances coins with a uniform diameter can be produced.

How Dies Are Prepared

In early days dies were prepared entirely by hand. Dies were usually made of soft steel which, after engraving, was hardened by the annealing process. Working from a design or from another coin, the engraver would then cut the various features into the die by means of engraving tools. Usually the head or portrait would be put on the obverse first. Then surrounding letters or inscriptions would be added. On the reverse a crest, shield, or whatever would be put in first and then inscriptions would come later. As such dies were made by hand, no two dies were ever alike. Of course, every part of the design had to be prepared in a mirror image of the finished product—with the letters reversed and so on, so that the resultant coin would read correctly.

Beginning in the 18th century, various punches came into wide use. From that time onward an engraver would have a set of letter and numeral punches to aid him in making the dies. In addition, certain main features were made up into punches—the portrait of a monarch, an emblem, and so on; thus the preparation of a coin die was simplified. The engraver would punch in the central portrait, then grind the die slightly so that the other surfaces would remain flat (removing in the process any metal which had been pushed up when the portrait die was stamped into it). By means of individual punches the date would be cut into the die as would be the inscription. Often small details were finished or touched up by hand. Coins from dies made in this manner are still distinctive, because like earlier products, no two dies were made precisely alike.

An interesting example of the hand production of dies can be found in the coinage of Connecticut. Beginning in 1785 and continuing through 1788, this state produced its own copper coins. Production was accomplished at several mints owned by private individuals and contractors who had special agreements with the state government.

Collectors today recognize well over 300 varieties of Connecticut copper coins produced during these four years! A small difference in the

CONNECTICUT CENTS. From 1785 through 1788 Connecticut issued its own copper coins. More than 300 varieties have been identified. Shown are specimens of 1787 and 1788. The dies were crudely cut by hand, and primitive coinage methods were used. The result is that each variety has its own special charm. Collecting colonial coins of all types is popular with numismatists. More varieties of Connecticut cents exist than of any other state.

placement of a letter, numeral, or treatment of a design constitutes a different variety. Sometimes the differences are great and other times they are not. The guidelines given to the Connecticut coiners were simple: Each piece should bear on the obverse a stylized portrait. Surrounding it should be the legend AUCTORI CONNEC ("by the authority of Connecticut"). On the reverse was to be a seated figure surrounded by the legend INDE ET LIB ("independence and liberty"). The date was to be below. The use of a portrait on the obverse and a seated figure on the reverse was in imitation of the countless British halfpennies which were in great circulation throughout Connecticut at this time. The United States Government had not yet produced its own coinage, and coins in circulation were a mixture of English, French, Spanish, and other issues. Most copper coins were British, so it was thought that if the new Connecticut pieces had designs somewhat similar to the British they would be readily accepted in the channels of commerce. In these early days when monetary systems were uncertain, a startlingly new design was apt to be rejected; in fact, this happened numerous times.

The private contractors were interested in turning out as many coins as possible in the shortest time possible, so little attention was given to artistic perfection. The portraits and seated figures on some early issues were entirely cut by hand. Later, prepared punches were used. Within those four years there are many fascinating varieties. Portraits vary from the large "African Head" resembling an inhabitant of that continent to tiny figures looking like a Roman emperor. One portrait has a supercilious grin and is called the "Laughing Head" variety. Another is called the "Muttonhead" variety, and still another is the "Hercules Head."

One would think it would have been a fairly simply matter to spell the inscriptions correctly on the dies, but that apparently was not the case. Instead of AUCTORI we have such variations as AUCIORI, AUCTOPI, and AUCTOBI. Instead of ET LIB we have such misspellings as ET LIR and ET IIB. These resulted, of course, from impressing the letter punches in the wrong sequence.

One die was made in error with the date 1877 rather than 1787, by transposing the two center numerals. This error was discovered before coins were actually struck from the dies, and was corrected by overpunching the figures with the correct ones. However, using a magnifying glass the numismatist can readily see the original figures under the correct ones.

The study of such varieties is a challenging pursuit for the inquiring mind. Over the years many students have collected these pieces, each of which has its own "personality." One cannot help but wonder what the long-ago Connecticut engraver was thinking when he punched in a date backwards and misspelled the simple legends which he had spelled correctly many times before.

Almost all early American state and colonial coins have been studied by die varieties. Such research often provides clues as to how they were made and by whom. For instance, by comparing the style of letter punches used on various coins, Eric P. Newman was able to determine that certain coins of Connecticut, Vermont, New Jersey, and a United States Government contract issue, the Fugio cent, were all engraved by the same person. Adding to the fun of such research is the fact that these private mints did not worry about the legality of coins they were striking.

An example of such unconcern for legality is the "manufactory of hardware," as he called it, established by Capt. Thomas Machin, on the shores of Orange Pond near present-day Newburgh, New York. This mint was going in full swing during the late 1780's. Earlier, Captain Machin had distinguished himself as an officer in the American Revolutionary War by constructing a heavy battleship chain across the Hudson River at West Point, a tactic intended to prevent the passage of British ships.

The captain's mint, called Machin's Mill by collectors today, officially made certain coins of Vermont and perhaps had another contract or two. However, this did not deter the fertile minds of Machin and his colleagues. Surveying the coins in circulation—copper pieces issued under the authorities of New Jersey, New York, and Connecticut; earlier issues of Great Britain, and so on—the Machin's Mill operators decided to make these as well. Particularly popular, so it seems, were British halfpennies. After all, Britain had lost the war with its colonies a few years earlier and, although British coins were still very actively in circulation, certainly no agents of the British Crown were around watching for counterfeiters.

To make counterfeit British coins did require some thinking—not much, but nevertheless a little bit. By 1787 and 1788 (apparently the years of Machin's greatest production), many British copper coins in circulation had a slightly worn appearance, for they had been circulating for a number of years. It would not be wise to make sharp and bright-appearing pieces, for they might be looked upon with suspicion. So, when the engravers prepared dies for these counterfeits they took care to make the dies appear worn on the higher spots of the design. The result was that the coins looked as if they had been in circulation for several years. Presumably the coins were also toned or artificially aged before they were released into circulation. The venture was tremendously successful, and tens of thousands of pieces entered the channels of commerce. Today these products of Captain Machin's enterprise are avidly collected by numismatists who call them "imitation halfpennies."

An interesting blunder was made one day at Machin's Mills. At this time in 1787 the mint was busily producing coins of Vermont, Connecticut, Great Britain, and others as well. Somewhere along the line a careless employee combined the obverse of a Vermont coin with the reverse of a counterfeit British coin! The result is the curious piece known today as the BRITANNIA variety. The obverse bears a Vermont design and has the inscription VERMON AUCTORI (by the authority of Vermont). The reverse, a seated figure with the British inscription BRITANNIA surrounding, is very worn-appearing, for it was intended for making counterfeit British halfpennies. In another instance the obverse of a British halfpenny bearing the inscription GEORGIVS III REX was combined with the reverse intended for a Vermont coin.

Major die varieties occur among the early coins produced at the Philadelphia Mint (which the U.S. Government opened in 1792). Sometimes a detailed study can be made of coins bearing just one particular date. An example is provided by the cents of 1794. These are of a rather simple design and have on the obverse the portrait of Liberty in the form of an attractive young woman's head. Above is the word LIBERTY and below is the date 1794. The reverse depicts a wreath with UNITED STATES OF AMERICA on the outside and ONE CENT within. At the bottom of the wreath is the fraction 1/100 indicating that the value is 1/100th of a dollar.

In 1869, a Philadelphia numismatist, Dr. Edward Maris, produced a small pamphlet entitled "The Cents of 1794." He described in detail 39 varieties. Not content with scientific descriptions which might be construed as lifeless or, at the very least, unromantic, the good doctor drew upon his knowledge of human anatomy and classical art and provided future generations of numismatists with such terms as "Roman Plica," "Diana," "Young Head," "Coquette," "Venus Marina," and "Patagonian." Each term was intended to describe Dr. Maris' impression of how the head of Miss Liberty appeared to him.

One of the most interesting varieties of 1794 is the so-called Starred Reverse. On the reverse of the piece is a circle made up of ninety-four

STARRED REVERSE CENT. One of the most interesting varieties of early American coins is the curious Starred Reverse cent of 1794 (shown in two-diameter enlargement). The close-up of the reverse clearly shows the circle of 94 tiny five-pointed stars near the edge.

tiny five-pointed stars which are close to the outer edge and which are best seen with a magnifying glass. The purpose of these stars, the counterparts of which appear on no other one-cent piece reverse, is unknown. Dr. William H. Sheldon, a prominent student of early United States one-cent pieces, is of the opinion that they were made up as a whim by some Mint employee who had some time to kill. Don Taxay, another prominent authority, believes that the piece may have been intended as a special pattern issue. It is the mystique that such pieces possess—the fact that we can never know their true intent or origin—that gives them much of their charm. Indeed, this mystique is so great that an Uncirculated example of the 1794 Starred Reverse—a coin as sharp as the day it was minted and one which is the finest known example of its variety—sold for $25,000 at auction in 1972. This was the world's record price paid for an American one-cent piece of any date.

There are many other fascinating varieties among early United States one-cent pieces. The very first American cent is itself one of the most interesting. The initial design produced in 1793 differed slightly from that used in 1794. The reverse, rather than portraying a wreath, showed an endless chain made up of thirteen links, symbolizing the thirteen colonies. The reverse read UNITED STATES OF AMERI. The engraver, fearful that

THE FIRST AMERICAN CENT. This is the very first variety of cent, issued for circulation by the United States Mint in 1793. The engraver, fearful that "AMERICA" would not fit on the die, abbreviated it to "AMERI." Subsequent issues spelled America in full. The chain design was criticized as being unrepresentative of a country dedicated to freedom, and the figure of Miss Liberty on the obverse was described as "being in a fright." Such comments led to a revision of the design shortly after it was first issued. The illustration is enlarged two diameters.

AMERICA would not fit on the die, stopped short of the last two letters and abbreviated it! The release of these new cents was awaited with anticipation. However, public comment was not favorable. The *Boston Argus* of March 26, 1793, reported: "The American cents (says a letter from Newark) do not answer our expectations. The chain on the reverse is but a bad omen for Liberty, and Liberty herself appears to be in a fright. . . ." Soon the chain device was abandoned, and a wreath was used on later issues of that year as well as cents of subsequent years.

Before leaving early American cents I will mention just one more variety—a coin which is perhaps the most outstanding instance of a blundered die in all of American numismatics. This is the 1801 Three Errors Reverse. The fraction, instead of being 1/100, is a mathematically meaningless 1/000. The attractive wreath, which normally has two large stems, has the stem omitted from the left-hand side, thereby giving it a lopsided appearance. As if that were not enough, the word UNITED is spelled

1801 THREE ERRORS LARGE CENT. Among diecutting errors found on early United States coins perhaps most outstanding is the 1801 Three Errors reverse. "UNITED" is spelled as "IINITED." The left-hand stem to the wreath is missing. The fraction, rather than appearing as 1/100, appears as a mathematically meaningless 1/000.

UNITED! Needless to say, this variety is very popular with collectors today.

Beginning around 1835, the production of coin dies was modernized. Separate master dies or hubs were prepared for the obverse and reverse design. Each hub contained the entire features of a coin. The obverse hub included everything but the date. The reverse hub was complete with all details except a mintmark, which was added separately if the finished die was intended for use in a branch mint.

To make a coinage die the master hub was forced into a soft steel blank. The date was punched in separately. The die was then finished by hand, hardened by annealing, and then used for coinage.

Until 1836, coinage at the United States Mint was done by horsepower. In that year a steam coin press was installed. From that time forward, high-speed production was possible. In modern times electric presses have been used. After the mid-1830's United States coins become more standard. The only major differences within a given year are varieties caused by the hand punching of the dates in the dies. Gone are different types of portraits, ludicrous misspelling of legends, and so on. In a way this is unfortunate but then, as now, progress is supposed to be important.

The relatively simple process of punching date numbers into the dies raised its own set of complications, so it seems. Blundered dates occur throughout the 1840's. Walter Breen, who has studied the coinage of this period, attributes this to the incompetence of James B. Longacre, who obtained his position at the Mint as a sinecure. Sometimes small date punches intended for use on a ten-cent piece were used by mistake on a quarter, thus giving rise to large-date and small-date varieties within the same year. In other instances, overdates were produced by updating a die for further use by repunching the last digit in the date. This practice continued until relatively modern times. In 1846, Mr. Longacre, perhaps daydreaming, produced a half-dollar die with the six lying on its side! This was then overpunched by a normal vertical 6—and the result today is the so-called "1846 over horizontal 6 error."

Fortunately, the adoption of high-speed modern coinage processes has not signaled the end of interesting die varieties. One of the most valuable (an Uncirculated specimen is worth close to $500 today) and most interesting of all modern coin issues is a rarity in our own time: the so-called 1955 Double Die cent. In 1955 an error occurred during the preparation of an obverse die. In recent years it has been the practice to include as part of the hub die the date as well. The 1955 hub die with all of the features—the portrait of Lincoln, the 1955 date, and the legend IN GOD WE TRUST—was impressed into a soft steel blank. The hub die was then

1955 DOUBLE DIE CENT. One of the scarcest of all modern United States coins is the 1955 Double Die cent. Due to a mistake in die preparation, all the letters and numbers on the obverse are sharply doubled. Choice examples now sell for several hundred dollars per coin—a rarity in our own time!

removed to check the depths and clarity of the impression. Still more clarity was needed, so the hub die was forced into the steel blank for a second time. However, the second time around, the hub was turned ever so slightly from the first time. The result was a bizarre-appearing die in which all of the features were doubled. IN GOD WE TRUST appeared as IINN GGOODD WWEE TTRRUUSSTT, for example!

On the day these were coined, a number of presses were producing one-cent pieces. The demand for cents was great at the Philadelphia Mint, and production facilities were humming busily. As each press produced cents, the pieces were ejected from the coinage dies into a hopper. The production from a number of presses was then dumped into one large bin and taken to another room for counting and bagging. Late in the afternoon, a Mint inspector casually looked at one of the coins from the error-making press and noted that it had a rather strange appearance. Unfortunately for the Mint, by the time he noticed this more than 40,000 Double Die cents had been produced. Approximately 24,000 of these had already been mixed with the production from other presses for the day and had been taken away.

What to do? That was the question! There was no thought at the time that the piece would become a rarity or, for that matter, that anyone would even notice it. Still, the piece was an error, and when errors are discovered, it is the usual Mint practice to melt the coins down and start all over again. Production errors such as imperfect strikings, improperly prepared planchets, and so on happen all the time and are taken care of routinely. However, the 1955 Double Die cent represented another problem. Obviously it would take days and days to sort through untold thousands of cents to separate those which had slightly doubled features. It was decided to destroy the pieces that were still in the bin, but to let the others go on into circulation—a fortunate decision for collectors, for otherwise one of the most fascinating varieties of our times would never have been available!

The Mint routinely put the coins in rolls and bags and stored them. Later on they were shipped in response to orders from banks, mainly in Massachusetts and upstate New York. No official mention had been made of the situation and no collectors knew about the variety. In fact, the one or two people at the Mint who knew about it had probably forgotten about the pieces.

Late in the same year 1955 Double Die cents were first discovered by collectors. By this time nearly all had been in circulation for a few weeks or months. No original bank-wrapped rolls of Uncirculated pieces were ever found, to my knowledge. The first public notice given the piece was in *Numismatic News.* As the features of the coin appeared to be shifted, at first this variety was called the 1955 Shift Cent. Later the 1955 Double Die nomenclature was used. Immediately a small demand began for the pieces. Coins sold for 25¢ to 50¢ apiece, and then a dollar.

In the Johnson City area of upstate New York a cigarette vending machine firm had apparently received a bag or two of coins containing many 1955 Double Die cents. At this time a pack of cigarettes cost 23¢. A quarter put in a cigarette vending machine resulted in the patron receiving a pack of cigarettes and, under cellophane within the pack, two bright Lincoln cents. You guessed it! Fortunate cigarette smokers in the area were often rewarded with Brilliant Uncirculated examples of the 1955 Double Die. Word of this spread, and James F. Ruddy, my business associate, who was living in upstate New York at the time, was able to buy quite a few dozen pieces in this manner.

In Springfield, Massachusetts, a location in which additional pieces were released, sisters at a convent started a local campaign to look for these and were rewarded by finding several dozen. By this time the price had risen so that they were able to sell them for $40 each.

Believe it or not, in 1972 the same thing happened again! This time the shifting or doubling of the die was not quite so pronounced as it was in 1955, but it was still distinctive enough that it constituted a major variety for collectors. Immediately the rush to buy these was on—and interest spread like wildfire. *Time* magazine carried a feature story on these, as did newspapers across the country. Within a matter of months the price rose from the face value of one cent per coin to approximately $100 each! My friends John Hamrick and Warren Tucker told me that after they read about the 1972 Double Die cent they decided to check a few bags (containing 1,000 coins per bag) of "ordinary" 1972 cents they had purchased a few weeks earlier. Searching began early in the evening. Soon a 1972 double die cent was found! Then another! Then still another! By 6 o'clock the next morning several hundred pieces had been found. Here truly is a treasure story from our own time—it could have happened to anyone.

While not many people had the good fortune to find hundreds of 1972 Double Die cents, many people found one, a few, or a dozen—and suddenly found themselves hundreds of dollars richer. It is such stories—and such possibilities—that make coin collecting forever fascinating!

4

Coins of Colonial America and Continental Currency

America was settled by colonists from many lands—Spain, England, Holland, and others. During the 17th and 18th centuries there was no official American coinage—or at least not until 1792, when the first mint was established at Philadelphia. Even then, it took a few years until production reached a sufficient volume to satisfy the needs of commerce. The coins in circulation were a mixture of pieces issued primarily by European governments, and by other authorities as well. Prominent in the monetary systems were coins of England and Spain.

The Spanish milled dollar was valued at 8 reales. In pirate and treasure lore such early Spanish "silver dollars" are called "pieces of eight." The larger doubloons, equal in value to sixteen of the dollar-size coins, were the monetary standard of Central America and Mexico, and to a degree of the United States as well. Fractional pieces of the eight-reales coin were known as "bits" and were valued at 12½¢ each. Our present-day term "two bits" for a twenty-five-cent piece traces its ancestry to these Spanish coins of years ago.

Also prominent in circulation, particularly along the Atlantic seaboard, were coins of England—halfpennies, shillings, crowns, guineas, and so on. Commercial transactions of the day were reckoned either in dollars (meaning Spanish dollars) or pounds (British pounds). The United States decimal system of coinage did not come until much later.

The British Crown looked unfavorably upon production of coins by its colonists. Nevertheless, as noted earlier, in response to an acute shortage of coins in circulation, the Massachusetts Bay Colony began preparing crude pieces stamped with NE on one side and the value on the other. The clipping of edges and counterfeiting soon became problems, so the designs were made more complex. Following the Willow Tree coinage from 1653 through 1660 and the Oak Tree coinage produced from 1660 through 1667, the famous Pine Tree pieces were made. These bore on one side the design of a pine tree and on the reverse the date 1652. Beneath the date was the denomination—III for the threepence, VI for the sixpence, and XII for the shilling. All were dated 1652, whereas in actuality Pine Tree coins were minted from 1667 through 1674. An explanation is that the early crude Massachusetts coinage of 1652 was called to the attention of authorities in England. Official disapproval was expressed, and to evade this disapproval, all following issues were dated with the 1652 year—so that "officially" the colonists could say that coinage had stopped many years earlier!

PINE TREE SHILLINGS. Among the most famous American coins are the 1652 Pine Tree shillings of the Massachusetts Bay Colony. Representative examples are shown. The more worn piece appears to have been bent at one time, perhaps as a precaution to ward off the witches believed prevalent in Salem and other Massachusetts communities.

Pine Tree shillings are among the most interesting and romantic of American coins. Over the years many legends have arisen concerning them. Sydney P. Noe, whose writings about early Massachusetts silver coins are the standard works on the subject, tells of "witch pieces"—Pine Tree shillings which have been bent one or several times. For a number of years the significance of these bent pieces puzzled numismatists. Noe's explanation is enlightening:

Witch pieces: One of the tragic episodes in the early history of the Bay Colony —the witch frenzy—has an indirect bearing on this coinage. A wave of hysteria seems to have swept over the colonists in 1692, centering in Salem, although Boston was not unaffected. The cruel punishments after trials that were grossly unjust still bring amazement to anyone who examines the carefully kept records.

The epidemic was not confined to the ignorant or the illiterate. Cotton Mather attended one of the trials and spoke in justification of the verdict. He also made his opinion clear in print. Judge Samuel Sewall, later Chief Justice, 20 years after made a public confession of penitence for his judicial acts.

We are told that it was the superstitious belief of the time that wearing a bent coin afforded protection against the power of "witches." Some of our Pine Tree coins show evidence of having once been bent even though as we see them now they have again been flattened. Some show dents which imply that teeth must have been the means of bending them initially. The thinness of the Pine Tree coins made bending an easy operation, and some with holes for suspension may have seen service in the same manner as those which were bent.

Sydney P. Noe further observes that it may have been a "witch piece" that is mentioned in "Mother Goose":

> There was a crooked man
> And he walked a crooked mile
> And he found a crooked sixpence
> Against a crooked stile.

Yet another legend concerning Massachusetts Pine Tree pieces avers that it was customary for a bride's parents in colonial times to give the girl's weight in Pine Tree shillings as a dowry. Even for a small girl this would have cost well over $1,000 in those times, so it is doubtful such a practice occurred. In any event, when the subject of American colonial coins comes up most people immediately recall Pine Tree shillings.

Pine Tree pieces were last made around 1674. More than a hundred years later Massachusetts again entered the coining business. By this time Massachusetts was a state and no longer had to contend with what England thought. In 1786, the Massachusetts General Court passed an act for the establishment of a mint to produce coins made of gold, silver, and copper. In the following year, coinage began. No silver or gold coins were ever produced. A modest coinage of half cents and cents was made, each piece bearing on the obverse a standing Indian with a bow in one hand and an arrow in the other. The reverse depicted an eagle. Joshua Witherle was appointed mintmaster and set about acquiring supplies of copper, erecting coining equipment, acquiring suitable premises, and so on. The dies from which the coins were made were cut by two independent engravers, Joseph Callender and Jacob Perkins, the latter being among the most famous early American silversmiths. All went well until an accounting was made of the finances of the mint. It was learned that each 1787 and 1788 half cent cost one cent to produce, and each one cent cost two cents to produce. The mint came to an abrupt halt.

As noted earlier, the state of Connecticut produced a wide variety of copper coins, more than 300 die varieties in all, from 1785 through 1788.

New Jersey produced coins with a horsehead on one side and a shield on the other. These were minted from 1786 through 1788, inclusive.

Among early state copper coins some of the most interesting were produced by the Green Mountain State, Vermont. In 1785, Reuben Harmon, Jr., obtained the state coinage contract to produce copper pieces. A mint was established at the side of Millbrook, a small stream in Rupert, Harmon's hometown. Water provided the power to strike the pieces. Dies for the first issues were made by a New York engraver. Soon, Harmon made

COLONIAL AND STATE COINS. During the 18th century many types of coins served in the channels of commerce. Most popular were the issues of England, Spain, France, and other world powers. Also circulating, however, were pieces issued in America or elsewhere for specific use in the thirteen colonies and bearing appropriate inscriptions to this effect.

(1) 1734 Spanish milled dollar (struck at the Mexico City Mint), called the "pillar dollar" as the obverse depicts the mythological Pillars of Hercules. Coins such as this served as the basic currency in America during the early 18th century. Usually contracts and legal obligations were expressed in terms of Spanish milled dollars. (2) 1723 Rosa Americana twopence piece struck in England for circulation in America. (3) 1723 Hibernia (Ireland) halfpenny. Struck on a private contract basis by William Wood, an English businessman, these pieces were intended for circulation in Ireland. They met with little favor there, so large quantities were shipped to America where they saw limited service in circulation. (4) 1786 copper coin of Vermont. From 1785 through 1788 Vermont issued copper coins in a wide variety of designs. (5) 1787 copper half cent of Massachusetts. (6) 1787 cent of Massachusetts, one of the first coins of the world to bear the word "cent" on it. The coinage of Massachusetts copper half cents and cents, which lasted for two years—1787 and 1788—was discontinued because the venture was unprofitable: each piece cost twice face value to produce. (7) 1787 Fugio cent, one of the first official United States coins. Fugio cents were struck privately by James Jarvis on a contract awarded by Congress. Hundreds of thousands of pieces were made. (8) 1789 token or store card issued by William and John Mott, importers and dealers of fancy goods in New York City. This piece, collected by numismatists today as part of the early American series, is one of the first merchants' tokens distributed in this country.

an alliance with Machin's Mills, located across the Vermont border near Newburgh, New York. This mint, which unofficially counterfeited coins of many states, did officially make Vermont coins.

The first issues of Vermont bore the motif of an early morning sun peeking over a stony ridge forested with pine trees. The legend VERMONTS RES PUBLICA surrounded the design. The latinization of Vermont was never decided upon officially, and various Vermont coins have such diverse spellings as VERMONTS, VERMONTIS, VERMON, and VERMONTENSIUM. The reverse of the early issues depicts an all-seeing eye with stars and rays surrounding. Near the border is the legend STELLA QUARTA DECIMA, which means "the fourteenth star" and is a reference to Vermont's status as the fourteenth state in the Union. It was soon found that this design was not readily accepted by citizens who were accustomed to the British halfpennies then in common circulation. To make Vermont pieces more popular, the design was changed to an obverse portraying King George II (later it was changed to King George III) and a reverse depicting a seated figure. Now familiar-looking, Vermont cents were readily accepted by the public. As noted, among later pieces produced at Machin's Mills there were some interesting mistakes made by combining Vermont dies with dies for counterfeit British halfpennies.

A number of New York copper coins circulated during 1786 and 1787. Although some of these bear the official state seal and the official state EXCELSIOR legend, it is not known whether these were produced as a private venture or under Government contract. No record indicating an official contract has been found. It is known, however, that some of them were produced by Machin's Mill in Newburgh.

The most famous of all American colonial coins was produced in New York by Ephraim Brasher, a goldsmith and jeweler. This piece, called the Brasher Doubloon, is made of gold, weighs approximately 408 grains, and had an original value equivalent to that of a Spanish doubloon—16 dollars. The Brasher Doubloon was once the subject of a fictional mystery movie bearing the same name.

During the 1600's and 1700's most of the Atlantic seaboard was under British rule. The colonies were considered fair game for all sorts of coinage issues and experiments, often devised across the ocean in England by someone who had obtained a special patent or other profitable agreement with the reigning British monarch.

In 1658, Cecil Calvert, the second Lord Baltimore, produced a coinage for the Maryland colony. The copper penny or *denarium*, as it was called, was produced only as a pattern. The larger silver issues of fourpence, sixpence, and shilling were produced for circulation in modest numbers.

Made specifically for the colonies were the Rosa Americana issues produced by William Wood, an Englishman who obtained a contract from King George I to produce coins for America and Ireland. Thought was given to making the coins as interesting as possible for the American colonies. The obverse bore the portrait of King George, an understood requirement of the time. The reverse, however, was distinctively American and bore the legend ROSA AMERICANA ("the American rose") and UTILE DULCI ("the useful with the sweet"). In the center was a large rose.

Apparently not satisfied with a nominal profit, William Wood assigned exaggerated values to his pieces. Produced in the denominations of halfpenny, penny, and twopence, each coin was only about half the size of contemporary British coins then in American circulation. For example, the piece William Wood designated as a penny was approximately the same size as a British halfpenny. These pieces were rejected by the colonists and saw little circulation here. Apparently numbers of them circulated in England or Ireland, for today most of the known examples trace their recent origins to those countries.

During the same years that Rosa Americana pieces were made—1722 through 1724—William Wood produced copper pieces for Ireland. Each bore the name HIBERNIA, the ancient name for Ireland, on the reverse. The Hibernia coins were more realistically valued and were approximately the same in size as contemporary British issues. Made in the denominations of farthing (one-fourth of a penny) and halfpenny, the Hibernia coins were rejected in Ireland, so Wood attempted to circulate them in America. This failed, and most were eventually used in England.

During the 17th and 18th centuries, to provide a medium of exchange for its colonies in North America, France shipped coins from its various mints to America. Values are contemporary French denominations of the time and are figured in sous (a sou being approximately equal to a halfpenny), deniers, and sols. None of these pieces has a distinctive American design, but they are avidly collected today by United States and Canadian numismatists for their historical associations.

While coin collecting did not become generally popular in the United States until the 1850's, it was a popular armchair pursuit in England a century earlier. During the 1780's and 1790's collecting tokens became a national pastime—a "madness," as some put it. Halfpenny-size tokens were issued privately in thousands of varieties and depicted all sorts of public and private buildings, political events, and scenes from history. The number of varieties was further increased by combining obverse dies for certain tokens with reverse dies from other irrelevant tokens, with the result that some really purposeless coin designs emerged. Many of these British-made tokens had American legends or were otherwise related to the United States. As such they are avidly collected today under the general heading of "colonial" coins. Examples are the so-called Kentucky token which bears the E PLURIBUS UNUM legend on the reverse side, the Myddelton token, the 1794 Franklin Press token, and others.

George Washington was a popular subject for contemporary tokens, most of which were made in England. Evidently the British coiners overlooked the fact that their country had lost the Revolution a few years earlier, for such items as the 1783 WASHINGTON & INDEPENDENCE token were made in large quantities and achieved wide circulation. Perhaps even more poignant was the British-made 1795 penny token depicting George Washington on the obverse and an eagle on the reverse. The edge is lettered AN ASYLUM FOR THE OPPRESS'D OF ALL NATIONS. Equally curious is another token with the well-wishing legend SUCCESS TO THE UNITED STATES on the reverse!

Among early American issues several have claim to an official or semi-official status. In 1776, the Continental dollars were produced. The obverse depicted a sundial with the legend CONTINENTAL CURRENCY surrounding. The reverse shows a continuous chain of thirteen circles with the name of a state on each circle. The motif is closely related to a Continental Currency paper money issue at the time and may have had official sanction, although precise documentation is lacking. Most specimens known today are of pewter, although a few brass and silver ones exist.

Gouverneur Morris, who had been Assistant Financier of the Confederation, was an early advocate of the decimal coinage system. It must be remembered at this time that the coins in circulation did not fit the decimal sequence. The Spanish milled dollar was divided into halves, quarters, and eighths. The British pound was divided into shillings and pence. Morris proposed a separate system—a decimal formula whereby the value of one coin could be easily calculated in relation to another. In 1783, patterns valued at 100, 500, and 1,000 units were made. These were never officially adopted, however. In the same year and also in 1785, tokens of somewhat similar design, called Nova Constellatio coppers by collectors today, were produced in Birmingham, England. It is thought that Gouverneur Morris had these struck privately. Apparently tens of thousands of these pieces circulated, for they are fairly plentiful today.

In 1787, the first official United States coins were produced. These antedated the establishment of a mint and were made under a contract given to James Jarvis. Congress authorized that 300 tons of copper coins be made. The *Guide Book of United States Coins* relates that most of the copper metal used to produce these pieces, called Fugio cents by collectors today, came from military supplies. The source is believed to have been the copper bands which held together the powder kegs sent to America by the French during the Revolution.

The obverse of each piece portrays a sun dial with the legend FUGIO ("I fly") and MIND YOUR BUSINESS. All bear the same date, 1787. The reverse of each coin shows a chain made of thirteen links enclosing the words UNITED STATES and WE ARE ONE.

Fugio cents are fairly scarce, although not extremely rare, today. A number of Uncirculated pieces have survived due to a fortunate happenstance. Sometime around the time of issue the Bank of New York acquired hundreds of pieces. These were put aside in a dusty vault and forgotten until nearly 150 years later when they came to light. At first the pieces were given away by bank officials as souvenirs and curiosities. Later additional pieces were sold. Today a choice Uncirculated piece from the Bank of New York hoard can be obtained for $200 to $300.

As the 18th century drew near its close the United States was an independent country. Coins in circulation continued to be a mixture of French, English, Spanish, and other issues—together with many copper pieces produced by the states and private minters. The stage was set for the United States to have an official mint of its own.

5

United States Copper, Nickel, and Silver Coins

In 1791, intense activity began for the founding of an official United States mint. On March 3, 1791, Congress provided for the establishment of a mint and authorized President Washington to acquire the necessary equipment and personnel. On April 2, 1792, the coinage system was formalized. It was provided "that the money of account of the United States would be expressed in dollars or units, dismes or tenths, cents or hundredths, and milles or thousands." It was further authorized that the coins appear as follows:

> Upon one side of each of the said coins there shall be an impression emblematic of liberty with an inscription of the word LIBERTY and the year of the coinage; and upon the reverse of each of the gold and silver coins there shall be the figure or representation of an eagle, with the inscription UNITED STATES OF AMERICA, and upon the reverse of the copper coins there shall be an inscription which shall express the denomination of the piece, namely, cent or half cent, as the case may require.

Ten denominations were provided for. Each piece was to be made of an alloy metal comprising eleven parts of pure metal to one part of copper which was added to improve the strength of the pieces. Copper coins—the cent and half cent—were to be struck in pure copper without alloy.

The largest coin was to be the gold ten-dollar piece or "eagle" made of 247.5 grains of pure gold which, when alloyed, weighed 270 grains "standard metal." Other denominations were the copper half cent, copper cent, silver half disme, silver disme, silver quarter dollar, silver half dollar, silver dollar, gold quarter eagle ($2.50), and gold half eague ($5).

On April 14, 1792, President Washington appointed David Rittenhouse, a leading American scientist, as first Director of the Mint. Don Taxay, in his monumental work *U.S. Mint and Coinage*, relates that Rittenhouse was in frail health when he acquired his appointment. On July 1, 1792, he took his oath of office. He served as Director for three years. A dedicated man, as Taxay relates, Rittenhouse often paid with his own funds an expenditure which he thought might incur criticism. For example, when Rittenhouse was offered an expensively crafted pair of balance scales he purchased them with his own money and then presented them to the Mint, realizing that the Mint could not afford such an extravagance.

In the summer of 1792, the Federal Government acquired property on 7th Street, near Arch, in Philadelphia. The largest and main building was of brick and three stories high. It was used for storing bullion and finished coins and also for striking gold coins. Other buildings were used for striking copper and silver coins, a blacksmith shop, a horse-driven mill for rolling out strips of metal from which planchets were made, a stable, and other functions.

In 1791 and 1792, several private engravers prepared patterns in anticipation of obtaining a Federal coinage contract. However, none was officially accepted. In 1792, the Mint produced several patterns of its own. Most bore the obverse inscription: LIBERTY PARENT OF SCIENCE & INDUSTRY. The reverse bore UNITED STATES OF AMERICA and the denomination. In 1792, the term disme was used for the ten-cent piece. Soon the silent "s" was dropped and the now-familiar dime resulted.

Thomas Birch engraved the dies for a large and handsome one-cent piece, called the Birch Cent by collectors today. This weighed 264 grains, the legal standard at the time. By way of contrast, a modern-day copper Lincoln cent weighs just slightly more than one-sixth as much. It was realized that such a heavy cent would be cumbersome to use, so experiments were conducted with smaller pieces. To maintain the intrinsic value of metal, a small amount of silver was inserted as a plug in the center of a smaller-diameter copper cent, the overall result being that the bimetallic coin would have a metal value of one cent. In another variety of pattern the silver and copper alloy were mixed together during the preparation of the metal.

Most famous of the 1792 issues is the half disme of that year. Although 1792-dated coins are regarded as patterns by collectors today, it apparently was the intent of the Government to produce the 1792 half dismes for circulation. This is evidenced by Washington's statement in his fourth annual address, on Nov. 6, 1792, in which he said: "There has been a small beginning in the coinage of half dismes, the want of small coins in circulation calling the first attention to them."

PIECES HONORING GEORGE WASHINGTON. From 1783 until the early 19th century many coins, tokens, and medals were issued to honor George Washington. Many of these were produced in England and distributed in America. Still others were produced in this country. Several varieties are shown here:

(1) 1791 "one cent" issued in England. (2) Undated (but produced in 1795) Liberty and Security penny issued in England. The lettering on the edge reads: "AN ASYLUM FOR THE OPPRESS'D OF ALL NATIONS." (3) George Washington token from the 1790's bearing the well-wishing inscription "SUCCESS TO THE UNITED STATES." (4) "HE IS IN GLORY, THE WORLD IN TEARS" reads the sentimental description on this medal issued in 1800 by Newburyport, Massachusetts, engraver Jacob Perkins in memory of the late President (Washington died on December 14, 1799). (5) In 1824, Marquis de Lafayette visited the United States. To commemorate this visit various coins (an 1822 large cent is shown) were counterstamped on the obverse and reverse with the portraits of the two heroes of the American Revolution, Lafayette and Washington.

Further evidence as to the regular-issue status of this piece is the fact that nearly all known specimens of this issue show wear, and most show a great deal of wear. Had the coins been produced as patterns, most would have survived in Uncirculated grade or close to it.

In his *U.S. Patterns*, Dr. J. Hewitt Judd quotes from a document dated April 9, 1844, acquired by Walter Breen. In this, J. R. McClintock, a Treasury official, stated:

> In conversation with Mr. Adam Eckfeldt [associated with the Mint in 1792] today at the Mint, he informed me that the half dismes . . . were struck at the request of General Washington to the extent of $100, which sum he deposited in bullion or specie for that purpose. The Mint was not at the time fully ready for going into operation—the coining machinery was in the cellar of Mr. Harper, saw-maker at the corner of Cherry and Sixth Streets, at which place these pieces were struck.

Don Taxay notes that the half dismes were apparently made on or before July 13, 1792, since Thomas Jefferson records in his account book receipts from the Mint of 1,500 of these pieces on that day. It is assumed that this 1,500, rather than the 2,000 mentioned by Eckfeldt, is the cor-

1792 HALF DISME. The 1792 half disme, of which 1,500 were issued, is considered by many to be the first coin issued for circulation under the auspices of the United States Mint in Philadelphia. According to available information, the coins were not actually struck at the mint itself, for the mint buildings were not yet ready. Rather, they were struck nearby by one Mr. Harper, a toolmaker, from official mint dies.

rect coinage figure. The coinage of 1,500 pieces coupled with the fact that present-day specimens are almost always seen in worn grades conclusively proves, in the author's opinion, that the 1792 half disme is indeed the first official issue struck for circulation by the United States Mint.

In 1793, the first United States copper coins made their appearance: half cents and cents. The following year, silver coins were produced for the first time: half dimes, half dollars, and silver dollars. The first United States gold coins made their debut in 1795, during which year eagles and half eagles (ten-dollar and five-dollar gold pieces) were made. From the

MINTMARKS ON U.S. COINS. (All illustrations enlarged two diameters.)

(1) The Philadelphia Mint has produced coins from 1792 until the present. With the exception of certain nickels dated 1942–1945, Philadelphia Mint coins bear no mintmarks. A 1942 nickel with a "P" mintmark above the dome of Monticello on the reverse is illustrated.

(2) The New Orleans Mint-produced coins from 1838 through 1909. Coins bear an "O" mintmark. The coin shown is a 1900 quarter, with the mintmark just below the eagle's tail.

(3) The Charlotte (North Carolina) Mint produced gold coins from 1838 through 1861, identified by a "C" mintmark. The 1847–C two-and-a-half-dollar gold piece has the mintmark just below the eagle and partly on the branch.

(4) The mint in Dahlonega, Georgia, produced gold coins from 1838 through 1861 inclusive. The 1845–D five-dollar gold piece has a tiny "D" mintmark just below the eagle.

(5) The San Francisco Mint has produced coins from 1854 to the present. Pieces bear an "S" mintmark. On this 1898–S quarter the mintmark is below the eagle's tail.

(6) The mint at Carson City, Nevada, produced coins from 1870 through 1893. Its "CC" mintmark is shown on an 1877–CC quarter. The mintmark is below the eagle.

(continued)

(7) The Denver mint has produced coins since 1906, identified by a "D" mintmark. The 1916–D quarter has the mintmark below the eagle's tail.

1790's until relatively recently, copper (later changed to bronze), silver, and gold were the three main coinage metals. In 1865 nickel joined the group.

By 1838, the westward expansion of the United States and the discovery of gold in certain areas of Georgia and North Carolina necessitated the opening of branch mints. In that year facilities began operations in New Orleans, Louisiana; Dahlonega, Georgia; and Charlotte, North Carolina. To differentiate these coins from those struck at the "mother mint" at Philadelphia, the branch mint issues had tiny mintmarks added to the design. New Orleans issues were given a distinctive O mintmark, Dahlonega issues a D, and Charlotte pieces a C. Later, mints were opened at San Francisco in 1854 (S mintmark), Carson City in 1870 (CC), and Denver in 1906 (D). As the Dahlonega, Georgia, mint operated only from 1838 through 1861, there can be no confusion between its D mintmark and the same letter used in later years for Denver. Today there are three mints in active operation: Philadelphia, Denver, and San Francisco.

As collectors assemble groups of coins by dates as well as mintmarks, the presence or absence of a tiny CC, S, or other mintmark can sometimes make a great difference in value.

I now will discuss each of the coin denominations produced by the United States since 1793. Some of these—the half cent and twenty-cent piece are examples—were forgotten long ago by the general public. Only collectors remember them! Today six denominations are used: the cent, nickel, dime, quarter, half dollar, and dollar. Dollar pieces are not in active circulation. About fifteen or twenty years ago it was widely thought that the one-cent piece would be soon abolished—except for a few sundry items this denomination has very little individual purchasing power. Yet today, the lowly one-cent piece is healthier than ever! In the past 15 years more one-cent pieces were made than during the entire 50 years preceding. What had happened? Virtually every state in the nation adopted a sales tax. Now a 25¢ item, for example, could not be purchased for a quarter. Usually a one-cent piece had to accompany it to pay for the tax.

United States Half Cents, 1793–1857

The lowest value or denomination produced by the United States was the half cent. These were first produced in 1793 and coined intermittently until 1857. Early specimens were made from hand-cut dies, and many interesting varieties resulted. The first year portrayed an attractive head of Liberty with a cap on a pole behind her hair. The cap-on-a-pole symbol remained a popular one throughout United States coinage. It traces its origins to ancient times during which a slave was given a ceremonial "liberty cap" when he was set free.

In 1794, the design was modified. The head of Liberty now faced to the right. Issues of 1793, 1794, and the first part of 1795 have edges lettered TWO HUNDRED FOR A DOLLAR. Beginning in 1795, a plain edge was used, although a few pieces were struck in 1797 from left-over planchets of the earlier lettered-edge style. In 1795, the head, still facing to the right, was made smaller. Half cents of 1795–1797 are almost cameo-like in their appearance, for the head and liberty cap design are very small in relation to the large field surrounding. Several interesting varieties occur. One style of 1795 has a flaw in the die which appears like a small comma, with the result that the date reads as 1,795. Varieties of 1795 and 1796 are known without a pole to the liberty cap.

Half cents of 1796 are rare in all grades or states of wear. Indeed, these are among America's great classic rarities.

No half cents were made with 1798 or 1799 dates. Beginning in 1800 a new style, the draped-bust type, was adopted. Half cents of this design were made through 1808, with the exception of 1801, during which year no pieces were struck.

From 1809 through 1836 the Classic Head type was made. Designed by John Reich, this style featured the head of Liberty facing left and with LIBERTY inscribed on a headband. Coinage of this style was intermittent, and there were many years—1812 through 1824 inclusive, for example—during which no pieces were made.

In 1840, a new style of half cent, the braided-hair type, made its appearance. From 1840 through 1848, no pieces were made for circulation. However, a few dozen were made each year for inclusion in Proof sets for presentation to government officials and others. In the 1860's, when coin collecting started to become popular, collectors realized that half cents of the rare 1840–1848 years were nearly impossible to find. The Mint obliged and restruck pieces from official dies. The practice of restriking, incidentally, was carried on from time to time during the 1860's and 1870's. The Philadelphia Mint was actually in the coin business, albeit unofficially, at the time, and various Mint officials and employees busily produced rare varieties for sale to collectors and for trading to augment the United States Mint Collection. Around 1880, there arose strong objections to this practice, and it soon died out. Collectors and scholars today have differentiated restrikes from originals in the instances in which they were made, so the collector has no trouble distinguishing one from the other. In fact, as both coins have different characteristics many collectors aspire to own one of each! For example, a serious collector of half cents might want to own both an original and a restrike (actually there are two subvarieties of restrikes) for each year from 1840 through 1848.

Half cents of the braided-hair type were made through 1857. In that year, a broad coinage act was passed by Congress. Half cents never were popular with the public, so they were abolished. Large copper cents were likewise abandoned. The legal tender status of the many foreign coins in circulation, primarily issues of England, Spain, and France, was repealed. Up until that time one could legally settle a debt in Spanish dollars or English pounds, for example, even though United States coins were very much in circulation.

United States Cents, 1793 to the Present

Legally a United States one-cent piece is a cent not a penny. However, the latter term, derived from the times when English coins were in circulation, will probably always be with us.

United States cents were first produced for circulation in 1793. As noted earlier, the first design featured a chain on the reverse, a device which was criticized as being unrepresentative of a liberty-loving land. The chain design was soon abandoned and the reverse was modified to show a wreath. In one form or another the wreath design was continued through 1857. The obverse of the second type of 1793 depicted a figure of Liberty in the form of a young lady's head. At the inception of the United States Mint it was decided to use allegorical or representative designs on our coinage rather than the likenesses of actual persons. This was followed strictly until the 1860's, when pattern pieces with Washington and Lincoln were issued. It is still general policy not to depict any living person on a coin. However, this rule has been bent several times in the case of commemorative half dollars.

Late in 1793 a liberty cap was added behind Miss Liberty's head. From late 1793 until 1857, the cents, called "large cents" by collectors today (due to their large diameter), follow the same designs as half cents, although generally the designs were used earlier on one-cent denominations.

The year 1794 saw the production of many interesting varieties, some of which were described in medical and classical terms by early researcher Dr. Edward Maris, as noted earlier. One of the most interesting varieties among early large cents is the so-called 1795 Jefferson Head. Like the 1794 Starred Reverse cent (with a circle of 94 tiny five-pointed stars around the reverse rim, for unknown reasons), the 1795 Jefferson Head has achieved a wide fame among numismatists. Not only is it rare as a variety, it has unusual features which set it apart from all other cents of this date and era, making it highly prized over the years.

Opinion concerning the origin of the 1795 Jefferson Head cent is divided. In his classic *Penny Whimsy*, Dr. William H. Sheldon notes that the Jefferson cent has been regarded as a contemporary counterfeit by some, and that other scholars have thought it more likely that the piece was the result of a whimsical experiment on the part of some early-day Mint employee who may have been caricaturing or who may have been idly "trying his hand." Dr. Sheldon is inclined to the latter view, but notes that it doesn't make much difference now, for the coin certainly circulated as a one-cent piece, most of the specimens known today being well worn. Over the years the pieces have been considered with favor by large-cent collectors, at least as a mystery and a curiosity, Dr. Sheldon observes. Now they are "members of the large cent family" and fortunate indeed is the collector who has one in his set.

Don Taxay, another prolific researcher in the field of early United States coins, considers the Jefferson Head cent to be a pattern issue. He notes that these pieces can probably be attributed to John Harper, a Philadelphia sawmaker and mechanic who had helped the Mint in various ways from its beginning, including storing some Mint equipment on his premises during the early days. In 1795, the Mint fell upon hard times. Copper was hard to obtain, and the general efficiency of operating a Federal mint was questioned by Congress. It was proposed by several that the Mint be abolished and coinage be put in the hands of private contractors. It is Don Taxay's theory that during this period Harper offered his advice on improving the Mint machinery and finally struck some pattern cents—the 1795 Jefferson Head pieces—in his own shop. The dreams of private coinage contracts never came to pass, and after a few difficult years the United States Mint flourished.

Having a private mint produce coins on contract for a government is not unusual. For instance, in Great Britain over the years private mints have been called upon many times to assist the Royal Mint with its production load. There are numerous other examples.

The general liberty cap style was used from 1793 through 1796. In the latter year the draped-bust type was adopted. The new style was continued through 1807. Throughout United States coinage, two or more styles have often been produced in the same year. For example, in 1796 liberty-cap cents as well as draped-bust cents were made.

The 1799 large cent has long been regarded as a classic rarity. Choice specimens have always commanded a premium. As far back as seventy or eighty years ago, it was a popular thing to advertise with a headline such as "$25 paid for a rare U.S. one-cent piece." The coin in question was, of course, the elusive 1799. Another scarce issue is the 1804. Particularly nice examples will sell for $1,000 or more.

The Classic Head large cents were made from 1808 through 1814. The year 1815 is significant in the history of one-cent pieces in America: It is the only year in which one-cent pieces were not made! Except for this solitary year one-cent pieces have been made continuously from 1793 until the present time. No other denomination approaches this record of completeness.

In 1816, the coronet design made its appearance. From then until 1857, the design was modified more than a half dozen times. During 1839, two distinctive heads were used. For reasons unknown to collectors today these varieties were designated years ago as the Booby Head and the Silly Head. This nomenclature is still used. While there are no major rarities among 1816–1857 large cents, several dates, particularly 1821, 1823, and 1857, can be considered scarce.

By 1857, the large cent had become an anachronism. The cost of producing these massive coins was barely a breakeven proposal for the Mint. The public liked them not a bit better, for they were large and clumsy to carry. Large cents were made for the last time in that year. The Mint immediately began to redeem the earlier issues, replacing them with newer and smaller coins. This would be the end of the story about large cents except for one thing: In 1868, well into the production of the small bronze Indian cent style, some enterprising Mint employee thought it might be interesting to make some "1868 large cents." Using a hub die from an earlier year and adding appropriate date punches a dozen or two 1868 large cents were created. These were sold to collectors as curiosities. Today these are extremely rare.

The Mint began experimenting with a new smaller cent size in 1854. A number of patterns were made in that year and also in 1855. These pieces were slightly smaller—but not much—than regular large-cent issues. In 1856, the Mint decided to go all the way. A new style cent was proposed, a cent weighing less than half of the old type and with a small diameter—the same diameter as a present-day Lincoln cent, in fact. Realizing that this radical change would require a careful introduction, the Mint struck many specimens of the 1856 pattern. On the obverse was an eagle in flight. The reverse featured a wreath of agricultural products: corn, cotton, tobacco, and wheat. The alloy was copper-nickel, a mixture made of 88 percent copper and 12 percent nickel. The resultant coins had a brassy or golden color. Samples of the new 1856 flying eagle cent were sent to newspaper editors, Congressmen, and other people of influence. The pieces were well received, and early in 1857 the new format became standard. The 1856 flying eagle cent remains today as one of the most desired coins. It is estimated that somewhere between 1,000 and 2,000 were minted. A choice Proof example sells in the $3,000 range.

In 1857, the new flying eagle cent made its general appearance before the public. A stand was erected near the Mint—and people could bring in quantities of old large cents and receive in exchange the new flying eagle cents, packed 500 into a small bag. More than 17,000,000 flying eagle cents were made in 1857, and more than 24,000,000 in 1858. In the latter year the design was discontinued, having served for only two years or, if you include the pattern issues, three years.

In its place appeared one of the most popular American coins of all times: the Indian head cent. When I began my own collecting in the early 1950's it was still possible to find an occasional one. Today they have all but disappeared. Designed by Mint engraver James B. Longacre, the obverse features Miss Liberty in an Indian headdress. Across the band of the headdress is the word LIBERTY. The reverse features a wreath design. Indian cents of 1859 have a laurel wreath. In 1860, the design was changed to an oak wreath with a shield at the top. This reverse was continued until the last year of coinage, 1909.

Indian cents from 1859 through 1864 were struck in a copper-nickel alloy which was used only for a comparatively few years. At first the Mint liked it, for the coins produced represented an attractive economic situation in comparison to the large early copper pieces. However, the new alloy was very hard—and the dies wore quickly when striking the pieces. In the early 1860's some foreign mints, notably those in France and England, began using bronze alloy to produce denominations which had been previously struck on heavy copper planchets. The prevailing feeling in the United States, at least among those who were influential in the passage of coinage laws, was that the bronze metal would not be accepted. The copper-nickel metal, in use regularly since 1857, was popular—and the public would not go for another change. The Philadelphia Mint's proposal to use bronze alloy and a lighter-weight planchet was turned down.

In 1863, a severe shortage of small change occurred as citizens hoarded all available "hard money" during this touch-and-go year of the Civil War. Few dared to prophesy whether the Union or the Confederacy would eventually triumph. In fact, at one time, Confederate notes—now worthless in terms of redemption—actually were more valuable than Union paper money! To fill the need for small change and, probably more important, to make a profit, many enterprising private firms issued tokens —pieces known as Civil War "cents" or merchant's tokens today. These pieces were, for the most part, struck on thin bronze planchets. They were enthusiastically received by the public. The ready acceptance of these thin bronze tokens was quickly noted by Mint officials and led to experimentation in this direction. A number of pattern Indian cents on thin bronze planchets were made. Part way through the following year, the bronze alloy was officially adopted. With the exception of 1943 (during which year zinc-coated steel cents were made) the bronze format has remained in use. From 1864 through 1909, Indian cents were all of the same basic design. A few varieties—the 1869/8 overdate and the 1887/8 overdate are examples—occur, but for the most part the series is fairly standard. A rarity is provided by 1877, a year in which only 852,500 were struck, a sharp drop from the millions made each year before and after that date.

The first branch mint cent made its appearance in 1908: a San Francisco product with a tiny S mintmark on the reverse. Slightly over a million 1908-S cents were produced. Only 309,000 1909-S Indian cents were made, making this issue quite a rarity today.

By 1909 the Indian cent had a long history, more than half a century of use since it was first introduced in 1859. The need was felt for a change, and the Indian cent was discontinued.

In its place came the new Lincoln cent, for 1909 was the hundredth anniversary of Lincoln's birth, and what better way could there be to commemorate this than by changing the cent design in his honor? Victor David Brenner, a noted sculptor, prepared the dies. Proud of his work, he placed his initials V.D.B. prominently at the bottom of the reverse near the edge. The new Lincoln cent caused excitement and controversy at the same time. *The Numismatist*, official journal of the American Numismatic Association, reported on the event in its August, 1909, issue:

> No new coin type has ever commanded the interest of the public and editorial reference and news space in the general press as has the Lincoln cent. Heralded long in advance, it was issued to an expectant populace on August

1909 VDB LINCOLN CENT. In 1909, the new Lincoln cent design made its appearance, thus ending 50 years of the American Indian cent motif. The first 1909 Lincoln cents bore the initials, V.D.B., of the designer, Victor David Brenner. Located at the bottom of the reverse, these tiny initials sparked a controversy. Soon the dies were modified, thus creating a variety which is popular with collectors today. The San Francisco Mint issue of the 1909–VDB cent ("1909–S V.D.B.") is particularly scarce. Philadelphia Mint issues (illustrated) are relatively common.

2nd. About 25,000,000 had been coined and distributed to various Sub-Treasuries and banks throughout the country so that the distribution could commence in all parts on the same day. As soon as it became known that a new coin had been issued places of distribution were besieged, particularly in New York, Boston, Philadelphia, Chicago, and St. Louis, where long lines formed leading to Sub-Treasuries, and continued each day with increased interest until August 5th, when the sign was displayed "No More Lincoln Pennies."

Those not content to stand in line and obtain a supply at face value (one hundred was the most that would be supplied an individual), offered to purchase at a premium, and for a few days newsboys, messengers and street fakirs had a harvest in selling the new coins at two or three for five cents. When no more were obtainable at Government supply places, stories in explanation were invented, "going to be called in," etc., and prices soared in different sections, as much as a dollar each being paid for specimens.

Favorable comment on the design, the artist and the interest of the public appeared in the first day's papers, many illustrating the new type, with lines drawn across the cut or otherwise marked or divided, so as to keep within the law prohibiting coin illustrations in the general press. But the next day, and for several succeeding days the papers turned to adverse criticism, and about everything denunciatory that is possible to say in relation to a coin was published, even to stating that you could not spend them, which was the claim of some slot machine operators.

The origin of cause for these criticisms has been traced to Philadelphia and Washington, from sources where selfish motives are not unknown when a coin type has been issued other than that produced [designed] by a government employee. Sifting all the criticisms, there was but one on which a just claim could be made, the designer's mark (initials V.D.B.) appeared a little more prominent than on the coins now in use. This was brought to the attention of the Secretary of the Treasury, who, we are informed, without question as to custom or propriety of designer's marks, ordered the coinage stopped. It was then announced that the letter B, to denote the engraver, would appear on the coins. Evidently, from the fact that the immediate demand was great and that it would require considerable time to produce dies with the letter B, properly entered or inconspicuously placed, everything to indicate the designer was removed from the dies and in a few days the coins were in plentiful supply with the initials removed.

Before the controversial V.D.B. initials were removed, nearly 28,000,000 cents had been struck at Philadelphia and 484,000 at San Francisco, the latter bearing a tiny S mintmark on the obverse. The San Francisco issue, known as the 1909-S V.D.B. cent by collectors, is a major scarcity, and an Uncirculated piece brings the best part of $300. For years, the dream of any Lincoln cent collector has been to find one of these in circulation. Even a well-worn piece will bring $100 or so!

Lincoln cents have been coined since 1909 on a continuous basis. Beginning in 1911, the Denver Mint began striking them.

Among earlier Lincoln cents there are a number of scarce issues: 1909-S V.D.B. is rare; 1909-S (without the designer's initials) is scarce; 1914-D is fairly rare, and several others are moderately scarce to rare.

An interesting variety was created in 1922. That year cents were struck only at the Denver Mint and with D mintmarks. No pieces were made at Philadelphia. During the production of cents at Denver one of the obverse dies became badly worn. Eventually the D mintmark aperture on the die became clogged with metal. The result was the production of 1922 cents without any mintmarks—almost as if they had been struck at Philadelphia! These pieces are known as 1922 "plain" cents today and are popular with collectors.

In 1943, there was a shortage of copper metal due to World War II. After experimenting with plastic, aluminum, and other substances, the Treasury Department settled on the use of zinc-coated steel for cents. With the exception of a few 1943 bronze cents which were made by error, all known pieces of this date are of steel composition. In 1944 and 1945, a slight variation on the normal alloy was used. Shell cases from military service were salvaged and the metal, slightly more brassy in appearance than bronze, was used. In 1946, the regular bronze alloy reappeared.

In 1955, the famous Double Die cent made its appearance, as noted earlier. This was followed 17 years later by the 1972 Double Die.

When the Lincoln cent was first introduced in 1909, a reverse design featuring two ears or stalks of wheat was used. This faithful motif was retired in 1958, and a new design featuring the Lincoln Memorial was introduced. This style has been continued to the present day.

One-cent pieces of all types have always been favorites with collectors and investors. In Uncirculated condition there are enough scarcities and rarities to whet the appetite of the advanced numismatist and investor. In lesser grades, pieces are sufficiently plentiful that a complete collection of Lincoln cents by date and mintmark varieties can be assembled for $200 to $300.

Two-Cent Pieces, 1864–1873

The two-cent piece made its appearance in 1864. The obverse depicts a heraldic shield with the motto IN GOD WE TRUST on a ribbon above, the first use of this motto on regular United States coinage. The reverse bears a wreath and inscription. This denomination was one of those bright ideas which seem good before they are tried, but which prove to be otherwise. During 1864, nearly 20,000,000 pieces were made. In 1865, the mintage dropped to 13,000,000. Then the mintage slumped to 3,000,000 and in a few years to below a million. By 1872, just 65,000 pieces were made, and the denomination was discontinued in circulation. In 1873, Proofs were made for collectors as part of Proof sets, but no pieces were issued for use in circulation. The public found it was easier to use two one-cent pieces than to use a two-cent piece, and the coin was unpopular from the start.

Today two-cent pieces are highly desired by collectors. Specimens of all varieties are scarce in Uncirculated and Proof condition, and even sharply defined worn ones are elusive.

Nickel Three-Cent Pieces, 1865–1889

The three-cent piece is another unusual denomination which is quite forgotten today. At one time there were two types of three-cent pieces. Those in nickel composition were struck from 1865 through 1889, inclusive, and those in silver metal were made from 1851 through 1873.

Nickel three-cent pieces are all of the same design. The obverse features the head of Liberty facing left and wearing a tiara on which the word LIBERTY is inscribed. The reverse has the Roman numeral III within a laurel wreath.

Nickel three-cent pieces were minted continuously from 1865 through 1889, inclusive. As was true of the two-cent piece, these were issued with great hopes at the beginning, but soon they proved unpopular. The first year 11,000,000 were minted, 4,800,000 the second year, 3,900,000 the third year, and so on—until in later years (with the solitary exception of 1881 in which a larger number were made) only a few thousand were produced each year, mainly specimens for sale to collectors. In 1877, 1878, and 1886 only Proofs were made, and no pieces were struck for circulation. An interesting variety is provided by the 1887/6 overdate. An 1886 die was overcut with the numeral 7 to give it extended life—and the resultant coins show traces of a 6 beneath the 7 when viewed under magnification.

Silver Three-Cent Pieces, 1851–1873

First produced in 1851, silver three-cent pieces were made continuously through 1873. Production was higher in the earlier years during the introduction of the series. Soon public interest waned, and in later years pieces were made only in small quantities for collectors. All were struck at the Philadelphia Mint with the solitary exception of one 1851 variety, the 1851-O, which bears the tiny O New Orleans mintmark.

There are three design types of the silver three-cent piece. Type I depicts a six-pointed star on the obverse and the Roman numeral III enclosed within a C-shaped ornament on the reverse. These were made from 1851 through 1853, inclusive. From 1854 through 1858, the design was modified to include three lines bordering the obverse star and to include an olive branch over the III on the reverse and a group of three arrows below the numeral. From 1859 through 1873, the third type was produced, with just two outlines to the star on the obverse. The reverse of 1854–1858 was continued. In 1873, only 600 pieces were made, all Proofs for collectors. This signaled the end of this, the smallest-diameter and lowest-valued United States silver coin.

Nickel Five-Cent Pieces, 1866 to the Present

Five-cent pieces made of nickel alloy, a denomination still with us today, were first produced in 1866. From 1866 through 1883, shield-type nickels were made. The obverse depicts a shield somewhat similar in concept to that used on the two-cent piece, but differently executed. The reverse depicts a circle of stars around the center numeral 5. On all issues of 1866 and some of 1867, there are stripes or bars between the stars. Part way through 1867 these were discontinued, and all later issues lack this feature. Nickels were popular from the outset, and although coinage has fluctuated over the years, nickels have always been made in fairly large quantities. There are some interesting exceptions. Among shield nickels there are two scarcities: the 1877 of which only 500 were made and the 1878 of which just 2,350 were made. Each of these issues was struck only in Proof condition for sale to collectors as part of sets issued that year.

In 1883, a new type of nickel, the Liberty head style, made its appearance. The obverse featured a classic head of Liberty perhaps modeled after the goddess Diana. The reverse featured a Roman numeral V within a wreath. Apart from the V no indication of the coin's denomination was given. As mentioned earlier, this was an error. Unscrupulous people gold-plated these nickels and passed them in circulation as "$5 gold pieces," for five-dollar gold pieces are of the approximate same diameter. An unsuspecting shopkeeper would be unfamiliar with the new Liberty head design and would not know that it was not a new design of a five-dollar gold piece, if indeed he even bothered to look at it carefully. To remedy this oversight the word CENTS was added later in the year.

This created an interesting situation. Approximately 5,000,000 of the 1883 nickels without CENTS were made and approximately 16,000,000 with CENTS were coined. The rumor quickly spread that the Mint made a design error (which in a way it did), and the public scrambled to hoard as many of the CENTS-less nickels as possible. The result is that today it is the nickels with CENTS that are the rarer of the two, even though three times as many were coined!

Scarce dates in the Liberty nickel series include 1885 and 1886 of which 1,400,000 and 3,300,000 were made, respectively. In 1912, nickels were coined at branch mints for the first time. In that year, 1912-D and 1912-S, coined at Denver and San Francisco, made their appearance. The San Francisco Mint Liberty nickel is elusive today, for only 238,000 were produced.

In 1912, the Liberty nickel was discontinued, or at least everyone thought so. The buffalo nickel, introduced in 1913, took its place. At the annual convention of the American Numismatic Association in 1920 a curious group of coins was exhibited: five perfect specimens of the Liberty nickel, *each dated 1913*. How were these made? Who made them? Why were they made? These questions were pondered by numismatists. In recent years the mystery has been unraveled, at least a bit. It seems that the pieces were made at the Mint for one Samuel Brown, later a resident of North Tonawanda, New York, who in 1913 was an employee of the Philadelphia Mint. Following his departure from the Mint Brown cleverly advertised to buy 1913 Liberty nickels, although none was known. Then, in 1920, he appeared with five of them, his earlier advertisements being the logical "reason" for his having them.

All five pieces were sold to Col. E. H. R. Green, millionaire son of eccentric financier Hetty Green. Colonel Green was a super collector in his time, and he spent millions of dollars on coins in the era in which a beautiful collection could be obtained for several thousand dollars. He not only desired one of each rarity; he collected two, three, or more if he could find them. Price was no objection.

Later, when the Green estate was dispersed, the St. Louis dealer B. G. Johnson came into possession of the five 1913 Liberty nickels. These were then sold one at a time to various collectors. In the meantime the fame of the 1913 nickel spread, largely abetted by B. Max Mehl. This colorful Forth Worth, Texas, dealer had an imaginative flair for advertising and spent millions of dollars selling his rare coin catalogs by full-page advertisements in Sunday newspapers around the country and even by radio programs. "I will pay $50 for a 1913 Liberty nickel if you can find me one," was a popular B. Max Mehl approach. Of course, the person buying his catalog was not apt to find a 1913 Liberty nickel, but there was no harm trying. Millions of people checked their change carefully in hopes of finding one of the treasured pieces. No others ever turned up.

In 1967, the specimen owned by J. V. McDermott was sold at public auction at the American Numismatic Association convention for the record-breaking price of $46,000. The buyer was Aubrey Bebee, who since then has made the coin available for showing at major conventions. Records are made to be broken in the coin field, and the 1913 Liberty nickel was no exception. In 1972, one was sold in a dealer-to-dealer transaction for $100,000. In 1974 the same coin, for which an offer of $150,000 was said to have been refused, had a price tag of $250,000 on it. Today the 1913 Liberty nickel remains as one of the most mysterious of all modern coin issues, and certainly one of the rarest.

Buffalo or Indian head nickels were produced from 1913 through 1938. The obverse depicts a stylized Indian facing to the right, a composite made by artist James E. Fraser who used three Indians as models. The "buffalo" on the reverse, actually a bison in proper zoological terms, is a representation of Black Diamond, a former inhabitant of the Bronx Zoo.

The first issues of 1913 had the words FIVE CENTS on the reverse on a raised mound. It was soon realized that this spot would wear quickly and the denomination would soon become invisible. So, part way through the year the design was revised and the words FIVE CENTS were relegated to a recessed area on the coin. Buffalo nickels were produced at the Philadelphia, Denver, and San Francisco mints. More than any other modern coinage design, the buffalo nickel presented great problems with striking. Both sides are in fairly high relief. That is, the pieces stand out in almost a sculptured manner. To fill the high relief portions of the Indian head on the obverse and the buffalo on the reverse great striking pressure was required. However, nickel is one of the hardest metals to work with, so even a shallow coin design is apt to present problems in this regard. With the high-relief buffalo design the problems were almost insurmountable, with the result that nearly all specimens known today, particularly those minted from 1913 through 1931, are indistinct on the higher portions. Particularly outstanding in this regard is 1926-D. An Uncirculated Denver Mint nickel of this year has very shallowly defined features and looks like a well-worn coin.

At the Denver Mint in 1918 an overdate—1918/7-D—was produced. This variety was not recognized by numismatists until many years later, after which time it was too late to look through quantities of Uncirculated 1918-D nickels in hopes of finding one. As a result only a dozen or so Uncirculated overdates of this variety are known today, and a choice one brings in the $10,000 range. A well-worn one can be obtained for several hundred dollars, however.

By 1961, I had been in the coin business for seven years, had read voraciously, and had studied tens of thousands of coins under magnification. Especially in modern United States coins I thought that I had seen everything. You can imagine my surprise when I was called upon to authenticate a startling new discovery: a 1938-D buffalo nickel which appeared to have two distinct mintmarks—both a D and an S mintmark! Impossible! No such thing had ever been heard of before! Well, under high magnification there it was—a sharp D with an unmistakable S below it. This sensational news made the front page of *Coin World* and was widely featured in other publications. It was truly one of the outstanding discoveries of modern times.

It subsequently developed that there are two varieties of this "overmintmark"—one showing the S undertype feature slightly sharper than the other. I began to think of an explanation and soon came up with it: In 1937, buffalo nickels were struck at the Philadelphia, Denver, and San Francisco mints. The following year, dies were prepared for shipment to the Western mints at Denver and San Francisco. Dies for all mints are prepared at Philadelphia—and appropriate S and D mintmarks are impressed on the dies there. The coinage dies are then shipped to the mint in question where they are used.

In 1938, the coinage order to strike buffalo nickels at the Denver Mint was received. However, it was decided to strike no pieces at all at San Francisco; a new nickel design, the Jefferson nickel, was waiting in the wings, and the buffalo nickel was to be phased out. On hand at the Philadelphia Mint were two newly prepared reverse dies with S mintmarks. Now that they weren't going to be shipped to San Francisco for use there, what was to be done with them? Why not punch over the S mintmark with a D and ship each die to Denver where it can actually be used? And this is what was done!

In 1938, Felix Schlag competed against approximately 390 other artists and won first prize! His design was selected for the new nickel to be minted. The Jefferson nickel features Jefferson on the obverse and his home, Monticello, on the reverse.

Interesting varieties of the Jefferson nickel were provided by the so-called "wartime" alloy issues of 1942 through 1945. Nickel was in strong demand as a metal for war, so a new alloy composed of 56 percent copper, 35 percent silver, and 9 percent manganese was tried. The Treasury realized that, once the wartime effort was ended, it would be desirable to quickly remove these unusual-alloy pieces from circulation; so, to distinguish them from earlier issues, each nickel of that variety was provided with an overly large mintmark above the dome of Monticello on the reverse (issues before and after had tiny mintmarks placed inconspicuously to the right of Monticello). The thought was that coin sorters at the Treasury could quickly spot these pieces and reclaim them. For the first and only time Philadelphia coins were given a mintmark—a large P which was used on the wartime-alloy nickels from 1942 through 1945 only.

There is an interesting sidelight to this situation. Sometime during the early 1950's some enterprising counterfeiters decided to make 1944 nickels. They used as a model the obverse for genuine 1944 nickels, which looks just like any other nickel except for the date. For the reverse they used a nickel of another date—but not of 1944, for the counterfeit had no mintmark whatsoever! You will remember that all 1944 nickels, including those made at the Philadelphia Mint, had larger mintmarks above Monticello on the reverse. Well, the counterfeiters certainly turned out a fine product, and many pieces were put into circulation. Then coin collectors entered the picture. From around the United States reports came in of a "new variety" of 1944 nickel—one without a mintmark! You guessed it: Collectors joined in the search for these, and soon the distribution point was located. Not long afterwards the counterfeiters were resting comfortably in jail.

Among later Jefferson nickels one of the most popular varieties is the 1950-D. During that year just 2,600,000 pieces were made at the Denver Mint, a rather low mintage for a nickel of that era. Immediately this was recognized as a potential "key date," and the scramble to buy them was on. A $2 Mint roll containing 40 pieces was selling for $5 by early 1951. Around this time my friend Kenneth Bressett, now an executive at Western Publishing Company, suggested to a friend that it might be an interesting speculation to "put away" two rolls of these nickels. His friend did this, and promptly forgot about them. Twelve or thirteen years later the price for a roll of 1950-D nickels had risen to around $700! Ken remembered his friend and telephoned him. "Do you still have those rolls of 1950-D nickels?" he asked. "Well, I suppose I do—I don't remember," was the reply. Upon hearing the new market price, he quickly found the nickels.

Beginning in 1968 the position of the mintmark on the Jefferson nickel was moved to the obverse of the coin near the date. In recent years tremendous quantities of nickels have been made. In 1964, over a billion pieces were made at each of the two mints operating that year, Philadelphia and Denver. In fact, more nickels were made in 1964 than were made of the shield, Liberty, and buffalo types from the beginning of nickel coinage in 1866 through the end of the buffalo nickel in 1938! Indeed, in nearly every series modern coinage figures are simply staggering. All early coins are rare by comparison!

Half Dimes, 1794–1873

The first half dime is the 1792 half disme, the very first issue of the Philadelphia Mint, of which 1,500 were coined. Today specimens are very rare, and a particularly nice one will sell for several thousand dollars.

In 1794, the first standard half dimes made their appearance. The design, which was continued in 1795, featured an attractive head of Liberty on the obverse with long flowing hair. The reverse depicted a delicately formed eagle perched on a cloud and enclosed within an olive wreath. Called the "flowing-hair type," the same design was used on contemporary half dollars and silver dollars. Indeed, until the 20th century, United States coin designs were standardized and it was common practice to use the same basic motif on all silver denominations. Except for the size and the identification of the denomination, there is little difference between an 1860 half dime, dime, quarter, half dollar, and silver dollar, to cite but one example.

Half dimes and other silver coins of the 1790's are often seen with what numismatists call "adjustment marks" on them. These marks were caused during the manufacture of the planchet. It was necessary for each silver coin to weigh its properly prescribed amount. It was not possible to cut circular planchets from the silver metal strips so that each planchet would be right on target. So, if an allowance was made it was desirable to make the planchet slightly heavier than need be. Metal could always be filed away from an overweight planchet, but there was nothing that could be done to an underweight planchet except remelt it and start all over again.

At the Mint a number of employees were occupied solely with weighing each planchet carefully on a balance scale and then filing the excess silver until the proper weight was achieved. The resultant planchet often had a parallel series of scraping or file marks on it. Coins struck from these planchets show traces of this custom.

In 1796 the design was changed to the draped-bust type with small eagle reverse. This was used in 1797 as well. During this period additional states joined the Union. Designs which had originally had thirteen stars were often modified to show a larger number of stars. As a result, half dimes of 1797 are found with thirteen, fifteen, and sixteen stars on the obverse. By the time sixteen stars were affixed into a design meant for thirteen, the effect was one of crowding. Realizing that many, many more states might join the Union and that more space on the coin dies was not available, the idea of adding one star for each state was dropped, and subsequent issues have just thirteen stars.

From 1800 through 1805, the draped bust design with heraldic eagle reverse was struck. The reverse of this type, also used on other silver and gold coins of the period, depicts a ceremonial eagle somewhat similar to that used on the official Presidential Seal. Within this series lies the 1802 half dime, one of America's classic rarities. Only two or three dozen examples of this date are known, and most are very worn. In fact, an Uncirculated piece does not exist, to my knowledge.

After 1805 there was a long span during which no half dimes were coined. In 1829, mintage was resumed, and the capped-bust type made its appearance. This style was used until its discontinuance in 1837. In that year the Liberty seated design, a style which was to be used on many American silver coins during the mid-19th century, made its first appearance on the half dime. Pieces made in 1837 and pieces made in New Orleans in 1838 (1838-O) have no stars on the obverse. This gives the coin a beautiful cameo-like appearance. This design, however attractive it may be to modern-day collectors, was not appreciated by the Mint—and thirteen stars were subsequently added. The design with stars was used from 1838 through 1859. A variety was created during 1853–1855 when small arrowheads were placed at the side of the date to indicate that the authorized weight of the half dime was reduced under the Congressional Act of Feb. 21, 1853.

In 1860, the Liberty seated design was modified slightly. The stars were dropped completely, and the legend UNITED STATES OF AMERICA, formerly on the reverse, was moved to the obverse where the stars had been formerly. The reverse wreath was enlarged considerably and made more ornate. Half dimes of this style were minted until 1873, at which time the denomination was discontinued.

Throughout my career as a dealer I have seen many people specialize in different series. One of my favorite memories concerns the Dr. W. E. Caldwell Collection of United States half dimes. It was the privilege of Bowers and Ruddy Galleries to offer this magnificent collection for sale at auction in 1973. The group of half dimes was sold at a very attractive profit over the price paid, but that is beside the point. Dr. Caldwell's enthusiasm is infectious, and I share his comments with you, comments he wrote to me prior to my cataloging of his collection:

It has been a pleasure to collect the half dimes which you will be selling in your November auction. My collecting of this series began quite by accident. I was convalescing from a heart attack when my maid brought in some old coins to see if they were valuable. I laid my paint brushes (my hobby to this point) aside, thank goodness, and borrowed a friend's *Guide Book of U. S. Coins.*

I evaluated the small group of miscellaneous coins and bought them. Among these pieces was a well-worn 1837 Liberty seated half dime which had been holed and plugged. This tiny coin brought back memories of an elderly uncle who gave me a nickel for the local Saturday Opera House movies each week when I was a child. I remembered that many of these "nickels" were half dimes. Why not collect half dimes and see how many different dates I could find? An interesting idea!

Soon I was off and running—buying half dimes wherever I could find them. One can "buy in haste and repent in leisure," and after a few months of fast spending I was many dollars wiser! I found it was desirable to buy from reputable dealers, large auction houses, and at major conventions. It seemed that by this method I could be more sure of getting a quality coin even though a premium price might be required. The "you get what you pay for" adage is certainly true, and I found this out!

My collection begins with the 1792 half disme, a coin which certainly is one of the most romantic issues in American numismatics. At one time I had a specimen of each and every half dime variety from 1792 to 1873, but later I traded or sold some of the very worn ones in the hope that I would be able to get top grade pieces later. It turned out that I was able to do this in some instances but not in others. It is very, very difficult to obtain true Uncirculated examples of the 1794–1850 years, and had this been an absolute requirement there would have been many dates which I would have never acquired. I feel that all Uncirculated half dimes of this era are grossly undervalued, and that examples in grades close to this grade are of extreme rarity in many instances.

Among the 1829–1837 capped bust half dimes you might find it interesting to know that the 1836 Small 5¢ and the 1837 Small 5¢ varities are much, much rarer in Uncirculated grade than catalogues indicate. The 1838-O of the Liberty seated without-stars type is also very undervalued. The specimen that you will be auctioning is the finest I have been able to buy in five years of searching.

Among later Liberty seated half dimes there are many rarities, particularly in the New Orleans pieces. Many if not most New Orleans half dimes are very weakly struck on the reverse, and to find a sharp strike, if indeed this is possible at all, many specimens must be examined. The most underrated seem to be the 1840-O without drapery, the 1842-O, and the 1844-O. The 1846 Philadelphia Mint half dime is extraordinarily rare in higher grades. Another sleeper is the 1848 Large Date in mint condition. Major rarities are 1849-O, 1852-O, and 1853-O without arrows in better grades.

A very interesting issue is the 1858. You will note that I purchased several examples of this date in order to study them. There is the "regular" date, the inverted date, and the doubled date—and I suspect that some of these may be different states of the same original die.

The 1859 transitional issue with the reverse of 1860 must rate as one of the most important of all American coin rarities. During the period I formed my collection, the present specimen, the one you will be auctioning, is the only one I was able to buy, and no others were offered for sale in price lists or auctions.

Finally, the 1869-S is an overlooked regular issue. I was only able to find a few Uncirculated pieces offered for sale, despite the fact that the catalogues treat this as a "common date."

All pattern half dimes are scarce, and most are rare. The 1794 copper half dime has been the highlight of my patterns.

I can close my eyes and see all of the half dimes in my collection. I hope that the successful bidders on the individual lots will experience the same pleasure I did from these beautiful pieces. While a monetary profit will undoubtedly be realized on the collection, I have profited in what is perhaps an even better way: five years of enjoyable collecting. . . .

The preceding comments illustrate that a person with an intelligent and inquiring mind, with no previous numismatic specialty, can build a definitive collection of a very important series. It also illustrates the advantages of combining collection with investment. After reading Dr. Caldwell's comments, it would be difficult to think of any other expenditure of his money which would have brought him more personal pleasure or more financial gain.

Dimes, 1796 to Date

Dimes or ten-cent pieces were first minted in 1796. From then through the mid-19th century, the designs are similar to those used on contemporary half dimes. The 1796 and 1797 issues are of the draped-bust type with small eagle reverse. The 1798 through 1807 dimes feature the heraldic eagle reverse style. From 1809 through 1837, the capped-bust dimes were produced. In the latter year, Liberty seated dimes without stars on the obverse, cameo-like coins similar to the half dimes of the same year, were made at the Philadelphia Mint. During the following year, similar pieces were struck at New Orleans.

Beginning in 1838, stars were added to the obverse. This style was continued until 1860, during which year UNITED STATES OF AMERICA, formerly on the reverse, was placed on the front of the coin. In its same essential form the design was continued through the end of the series in 1891.

Varieties are provided by 1853–1855 issues with arrows at the date to indicate a slight reduction in the authorized weight. In 1873, when the weight of the dime was increased again slightly, arrowheads were again placed alongside the date of the coins. These were used also in 1874.

In 1891, Charles E. Barber, chief engraver of the Philadelphia Mint,

1894–S DIME. Only twenty-four specimens were made of the 1894–S dime. The specimen shown is in Proof condition and was offered for sale by Bowers and Ruddy Galleries, Inc., in 1974.

prepared a series of new designs for the dime, quarter, and half dollar. First introduced on coins in the following year, these pieces are known as "Barber" design coins by collectors today. Barber dimes were made from 1892 through 1916, inclusive. Within that span lies one of America's most famous rarities: the 1894-S dime. Only twenty-four pieces were struck, and of that number fewer than half are known to exist today.

Why just twenty-four pieces were struck is not known. One theory holds that twenty-four pieces, equivalent to $2.40 in face value, were struck to balance the coining account ledgers for that year. Another theory—and I consider this to be the more reasonable—is that 24 impressions were struck to test the dies. At the time it was anticipated that many more 1894-S dimes, perhaps over a million, would be issued. When no further coinage order was forthcoming, the mintage remained at just twenty-four pieces.

Over the years I have handled several 1894-S dimes. The first was purchased in 1957 at an auction sale. The princely sum of $4,750 was paid for it by James F. Ruddy, soon to become my business partner, who was acting on my behalf at the time. $4,750 for one thin dime? This news was received with incredulity by the news media that lost no time in devising such catchy lines to go with the news story as "$4,750 for a cup of coffee—that is, if you spend an 1894-S dime to buy one!" Another news photo showed Jim Ruddy with a huge stack of bills to one side of him and a thin dime on the other side of him, with a caption to the effect that only Jim Ruddy would prefer to have an 1894-S dime rather than all that cash! David Garroway invited me to appear on NBC's "Today" show to tell the nation about my purchase. After our pre-show warm-up session, Mr. Garroway thought that the subject of coins was so interesting that I should not only tell about the 1894-S dime, I should tell about coins in general, which I did. The result of all this publicity was countless thousands of letters and postcards arriving on my doorstep. "I don't have an 1894-S dime, but I have one that is a year older, an 1893" was a typical statement. Of course, an 1893 dime is only worth a few dollars by comparison. Anyway, it was a lot of fun, and when I sold the 1894-S dime for a nominal profit a few months later I was sorry to see it go.

In 1961, acting on behalf of a prominent New York industrialist, I attended a California auction sale with a commission to buy the Edwin Hydeman specimen of the 1894-S dime being auctioned by dealer Abe Kosoff. The piece, possessing a magnificent prooflike surface, was one of the finest known examples.

As a dealer I often have to act as an adviser to clients. "What should I pay for the 1894-S dime?" my potential buyer asked. This was a good question. Obviously the chance to buy one at $4,750 was gone forever. The prices of great rarities in the coin field have advanced over the years, and $4,750 was just a fond memory. I suggested that a bid of $14,000 to $15,000 would win the coin. My client said he would think about it and send me instructions in the form of a coded telegram.

In the meantime I read the auction catalog description: "Although there were supposed to have been 24 coins struck, there seem to be only seven known specimens of the 1894-S dime. All are gems in Proof condition. The present market for rarities of this calibre should result in a runaway price for this offering. So seldom does it appear that advanced collectors would best reach for the 1894-S now."

The sale room was packed as the famed 1894-S dime came up for bidding. The coin opened on a mail bid of over twice what the $4,750 coin had cost me four years earlier. Soon the bidding zoomed up to $11,500, then to $11,750, then to $12,000. There was some hesitation at this point, and then the price continued upward again: $12,250, $12,500, on to $12,750—and then the final bid, mine: $13,000. The coin was mine—or, more properly, my client's! It turns out that I had estimated it just right when discussing the coin before the sale.

Making an estimate is often a touchy proposition. If I had, for example, recommended that my customer bid only $12,000, he would have missed the coin. He then would have either done without it or may have had to pay $20,000, $30,000, or even more later on. At the same time it would have been foolish for me to have suggested a bid of $20,000 or $30,000 in 1961, for in my professional opinion the coin simply was not worth that much. Such is the role of the professional numismatist.

As it turned out, the $13,000 price soon became ancient history. In 1972, dealer Jerry Cohen told me he sold an 1894-S dime to another dealer for nearly $50,000! Undoubtedly in some future year someone reading these words will say, "$50,000 for an 1894-S dime? What a bargain! I wish I could buy one for that price now."

In 1916, a new style, the Mercury dime, made its appearance. Designed by Adolph A. Weinman, the obverse depicts the winged head of Liberty, done in the style reminiscent of Mercury, the ancient winged messenger. The reverse features a fasces, an ancient symbol of military strength. It is interesting to observe that the Mercury dime was minted from 1916 through 1945, including the World War II years in which the reverse design of the Mercury dime was also the Fascist party symbol in Italy! Of course, this is just a coincidence of history. Apropos of the same type of situation, I might mention that the swastika used by the German Nazi party until its demise is but an old-time symbol found on many earlier tokens and pieces—a good luck symbol, in fact.

There are no super-rarities among Mercury dimes, but there are a number of scarce issues. Included are 1916-D, 1921, 1921-D, and two overdates, 1942/1 (Philadelphia Mint) and 1942/1-D (Denver Mint). Believe it or not, the 1942/1-D was unknown to numismatists in general until Frank S. Robinson wrote an article about it which appeared in the September, 1970, issue of the *Numismatic Scrapbook Magazine*. The overdate is not a distinct one, and careful magnification is required to discern the undertype 1 beneath the 2. However, it is there and can be found if you know what to look for. By the time the piece was discovered in 1970 the chance for finding many pieces in circulation had long passed—for untold millions of early Mercury dimes had gone to the melting pot when the price of silver rose to all time highs in the late 1960's. The 1942-D was considered to be a common date, and no one bothered to save them. Also, no one suspected that certain 1942-D dimes might really be overdates! So, here is another major rarity in our own time. In the sale of the great Terrell Collection auctioned by my firm in 1972 a choice Brilliant Uncirculated 1942/1-D dime sold for a record-breaking $2,000, thereby making it the most expensive coin of the series—a coin valued at approx-

1942/1 DIME. Close-up of the 1942/1 dime shows two distinct dates. A 1941-dated die was overpunched with figures for a 1942 die, with the result that both the 1 and 2 are visible. Such overdates exist throughout numismatics.

imately double the price of the two runners-up, the 1916-D and the regular 1942/1 (Philadelphia Mint) overdate.

Following the death of President Franklin D. Roosevelt, it was decided to honor his memory by changing the dime design to include his portrait. During his lifetime President Roosevelt had been associated with the March of Dimes campaign, so this denomination seemed particularly appropriate. The Roosevelt type dime, designed by John R. Sinnock, made its debut in 1946. This design has been continued to the present day. Roosevelt dimes from 1946 to date number several millions of pieces for each variety, so as of this writing there are no scarcities or rarities. However, hope for the collector springs eternal—and who knows but that this year or next might see a rarity produced by the Mint. It has happened before—the 1972 Double Die Lincoln cent being a recent example.

Twenty-Cent Pieces, 1875–1878

An ill-fated bright idea was the twenty-cent piece. It was reasoned that this piece would be just right for a transaction in which a quarter was too large but a dime was too small. First produced in 1875, the twenty-cent piece was somewhat similar to the quarter in size and appearance, except that the twenty-cent piece had a plain edge whereas the quarter had a

RARE 1876–CC TWENTY-CENT PIECE. One of the rarest of all American silver coins is the 1876–CC twenty-cent piece. In the enlarged (two diameters) illustration, notice the small "CC" mintmark widely spaced and below the eagle on the reverse.

This coin, formerly from the collection of noted composer Jerome Kern, was offered by Bowers and Ruddy Galleries for $59,000 in 1974 and was sold immediately. Just over a dozen examples of this rarity are known of which the Kern specimen is one of the finest.

milled or reeded edge. However, at quick glance one could not tell one from the other in pocket change. During the first year of coinage, approximately 1,400,000 pieces were made. During the second year (1876), 25,000 were made. During the last two years, just 510 and 600 pieces, respectively, were made, pieces struck especially for collectors.

It was soon realized that the twenty-cent piece was less than useful, so production came to a screeching halt. Most pieces made in 1876 were melted, including nearly all made at the Carson City Mint (1876-CC) that year. Of the 10,000 1876-CC twenty-cent pieces made, fewer than two dozen are known to exist today.

The 1876-CC twenty-cent piece is one of America's foremost rarities. Over the years my firm has handled several of these. When we sold the Armand Champa Collection at auction in 1972, the "cover coin" was a beautiful Uncirculated 1876-CC twenty-cent piece formerly owned by noted composer Jerome Kern, whose immortal melodies such as "Smoke Gets in Your Eyes" and "Ol' Man River" will always be a part of America's musical heritage. At the Champa sale, the 1876-CC twenty-cent piece sold for a new record price of $24,000 in spirited bidding competition.

In 1974, it was our pleasure to purchase the coin privately from the successful auction bidder and offer it for sale again. Our 1974 description was a lengthy one and concluded with the paragraph:

It is with great pleasure that we offer for the sale the magnificent 1876-CC twenty-cent piece owned by Jerome Kern. Certainly no finer specimen of this classic rarity does or could exist. Considering the current strength of the coin market we consider our price for this gem Uncirculated piece to be very reasonable at $59,000.

No sooner had this listing appeared than three clients telephoned to buy the coin. The first caller got it. A few days later I received an unexpected and interesting letter from one of our clients, W. Howard Hemry of Wyoming. His letter read:

I thought that the enclosed copies of your advertisements dated 1960 and 1974 concerning the 1876-CC twenty-cent piece would be of interest. The difference between $9,850 and $59,000 represents roughly a 35% annual appreciation over this period of time! Who could ask for anything more?

Mr. Hemry enclosed with his letter a copy of our $59,000 current listing together with a description from one of our catalogs published in November, 1960. In that year we mentioned that "the most important aspect of the offering of this coin is not the price asked, but the opportunity to acquire an item of this nature. The addition of this coin to your cabinet will place your collection in the class with the foremost American private and museum exhibits. We offer the 1876-CC twenty-cent piece in perfect Brilliant Uncirculated condition for $9,850."

Although few collectors can ever hope to own a specimen of the rare 1876-CC twenty-cent piece, the twenty-cent denomination in general is very popular with collectors. Numismatists view these issues as a curious and interesting denomination, which it certainly is. However, in its day a *useful* denomination it wasn't.

Quarter Dollars, 1796 to Date

Quarter dollars were first minted in 1796. Pieces produced that year are of the draped-bust type with small eagle reverse. As no further coins were minted until 1804, by which time the design had changed, 1796 stands alone as the only year of its design type. This combined with a low mintage of just 6,146 has made it a landmark with collectors. A choice Uncirculated specimen, possibly made as a presentation piece, in our Terrell Collection sale brought $17,000 in 1972. It was one of the finest known examples of this rarity.

In 1804, quarter coinage was resumed. From 1804 through 1807, the draped-bust type with heraldic eagle reverse was used. The 1804 coins provide an interesting study of coin prices and grades. In Fair condition, nearly worn smooth and just barely identifiable, an 1804 quarter is worth about $100. In Fine grade, a coin with medium wear and with design details on the higher surfaces absent, the coin fetches in the $400 range. In Very Fine grade, a step up from Fine, $750 is the approximate current valuation. There were 6,738 quarters made this year, and of that number several hundred still survive. However, most of them are in the worn grades from Fair through Very Fine. Uncirculated coins are a different matter entirely. Fewer than half a dozen are known to exist! Several years ago our dealer friend Lester Merkin sold one of these at auction for $25,000. That is quite a price range: An Uncirculated 1804 quarter is worth 250 times the price of a very worn one!

This tale also points out that when studying coins it is important to know what to expect. Mintage figures alone don't tell the story, for they don't indicate the range of condition of pieces known to exist today. Some coins are plentiful in Uncirculated condition, simply because hoards of them were discovered years ago, pieces were saved for one reason or another at the time of issue (the rumor that 1883 nickels without CENTS would become rare prompted many people to save these pieces, for example), and so on.

No quarters were made from 1808 to 1814, inclusive. From 1815 through 1838, the capped-bust type quarters were produced. This series includes several rarities, foremost of which is the 1827 original. Although Mint records state that 4,000 quarters were minted in 1827, fewer than 10 can be reliably accounted for today. Apparently all known specimens were struck in Proof condition. In 1827, young J. J. Mickley, one of America's pioneer coin collectors, visited the Philadelphia Mint and purchased four 1827 quarters for face value. Today each one of these coins would be worth in the $30,000 to $40,000 range, giving a total value of the investment of close to $150,000—all for a dollar!

In 1838 the Liberty seated design with stars on the obverse made its appearance. This design was continued until 1891. There were several modifications throughout the life of the Liberty seated series. In 1853, arrowheads were added to the date and resplendent rays were placed on the reverse of the quarter to indicate a slight reduction in weight. In 1854 and 1855, the rays were omitted but the arrows were continued. In 1873 and 1874, arrowheads were again placed alongside the date of the coin, this time to indicate a slight increase in authorized weight.

Beginning in 1866, the motto IN GOD WE TRUST was added to the reverse of the quarter. An interesting variety is provided by an 1877 San Francisco Mint issue. The mintmark on the reverse was punched in a horizontal position—lying on its side! This error was noticed and the mintmark was subsequently overpunched in the correct vertical position, the result being the so-called "1877-S over horizontal S" variety, a piece which is fairly scarce today.

Barber quarters, designed by Charles E. Barber, were produced from 1892 through 1916, inclusive. There are no great rarities in the series, but three issues, all from the San Francisco Mint, are quite scarce, particularly in higher grades: 1896-S, 1901-S, and 1913-S.

In 1916, certain silver denominations were redesigned. You will recall that the Barber dime was discontinued in this year in favor of the new Mercury dime. Likewise, the design of the quarter was changed. In place of the old Barber type appeared the Liberty standing motif. The obverse was classical in its appearance and featured Liberty in the form of a goddess draped in a sheer gown and holding a protective shield. Holding an olive branch in one hand, Miss Liberty is shown standing at the gate of a parapet. The reverse depicts an eagle in flight.

For the design by Hermon A. MacNeil, the figure of Miss Liberty was modeled by Dora Doscher, a young girl from Philadelphia. As would befit a true classical pose, the goddess Liberty was shown with her bosom undraped, and visible to all the world, at least to anyone who happened to see one of the new 1916 quarters! Morality being what it is—or was—a tremendous public outcry ensued. Midway through the following year, the goddess of Liberty was redesigned in what is probably America's greatest case of overcompensation: The second time around she wore a heavy vest of armor! Suitably protected from onlookers, the armored Miss Liberty adorned the quarter until the series was discontinued in 1930.

The Liberty standing quarter series has several interesting varieties. First there is the early variety with the undraped bust of Miss Liberty—called the Type I design by collectors today. These issues are fairly scarce due to the demand for them and due to the fact they were produced only in limited quantities in comparison to later issues. The very first year, 1916, is a rarity in its own right: only 52,000 were coined, a very low mintage for a 20th-century issue.

Among later Liberty standing quarters, the 1918/7-S overdate is scarce in all grades and is rare in Uncirculated grade. The 1921 is moderately scarce, as is 1923-S. Toward the end of the series, 1927-S has a relatively low mintage of just 396,000 pieces.

In 1932, the 200th anniversary of George Washington's birth, the quarter was redesigned to feature the portrait of the Father of Our Country. John Flanagan, a New York sculptor, modeled Washington's portrait after a bust by Houdin. On the reverse is shown a modernistic-appearing eagle.

Washington quarters, first minted in 1932, are still being produced today. As was true of the dime, silver in quarter dollars was abandoned in 1964, and later issues are made of clad metal—a sandwich composition consisting of outer layers of a copper-nickel alloy (75 percent copper and 25 percent nickel) bonded to an inner layer of pure copper.

The two scarcest issues among Washington quarters were produced the very first year: 1932-D and 1932-S. Fewer than a half million were made of each. By contrast, each and every other Washington quarter produced since that time has a mintage of over a million, with most recent issues having mintages of tens or hundreds of millions.

Quarters have always been popular with collectors. However, most 19th-century issues are scarcer than their counterparts in the denominations immediately above and below: the dime and half dollar.

The quarter has been with us since 1796 and will undoubtedly be a part of the American coinage spectrum for many years to come. There is an interesting inconsistency between United States coins and United States paper money. Today coins are produced in the denominations of one cent, five cents, ten cents, twenty-five cents, fifty cents, and one dollar. Bills are produced in the denominations of one dollar, five dollars, ten dollars, twenty dollars, fifty dollars, and one hundred dollars. To be consistent we should have either twenty-five-dollar bills or else twenty-cent pieces!

Half Dollars, 1794 to Date

Half dollars have always been avidly sought by numismatists. More so than the larger silver dollars, half dollars have been coined fairly continuously since the first year of issue, 1794. Also, many early issues were made in large quantities, so choice condition specimens can be obtained more cheaply than issues of other silver denominations from the same period.

The 1794 and 1795 half dollars are of the flowing-hair type, the same design used on the half dimes and silver dollars of the period. Over 300,000 half dollars were produced in 1795, necessitating the use of many dies. Hand-made, these dies often featured interesting blunders. One variety has the A of STATES over an original E; had the error not been noted the coin would have read UNITED STETES OF AMERICA. Another variety has the final S in STATES over a D! Still another has the 1795 date cut so low that it is partly off the edge of the coin. This error was realized, and the date was recut above it in a position 50 percent higher. On this particular variety both dates are visible, one over the other.

In 1796 and 1797, half dollars of the draped-bust type with small eagle reverse were coined. There are actually two varieties of 1796, one with fifteen stars on the obverse and the other with sixteen. Only 3,918 specimens were coined during these two years. As anyone desiring to complete a collection of different United States design types must have either a 1796 or 1797 half dollar to illustrate this type, and as the half dollar specialist has to have three issues from this range (1796 with fifteen stars, 1796 with sixteen stars, and 1797), the small available supply of perhaps 200 or 300 pieces is spread rather thin. The result is that better specimens sell for thousands of dollars each—when they can be found.

Following a lapse of coinage of several years, half dollars were again produced in 1801, this time with the heraldic eagle reverse. This style was continued through 1807.

From 1807 through 1836, the capped-bust half dollars were made. As do earlier pieces, these coins have a lettered edge which reads FIFTY CENTS OR HALF A DOLLAR. During the same span of years, no silver dollars were produced for general circulation. Thus, the honor of being the largest silver coin of the realm devolved upon the half dollar. To fill the needs of commerce, half dollars were struck by the millions during this period. Often they were shipped from the Mint in sealed bags. From there they went into bank vaults where they were stored as a convenient method of having a lot of value in a small space. The result of high mintages during this period plus the fact that many coins were spared from active circulation is beneficial to the numismatist today: Choice Uncirculated examples of many of these years can be obtained for just several hundred dollars per coin, a fraction of the price of dimes or quarters of the same general years.

Many interesting varieties occur among these early half dollars. There are quite a few overdates, the most curious of which is the so-called "1824 over various dates." Although the scrambled series of lines and curlicues is confusing, even under magnification, numismatists theorize that the die started life as an 1820, was then changed to 1822, and finally to 1824! This particular variety is not particularly rare and any collector can own one. Speaking of rarity, the prize for this among overdates of this era goes to the 1817/14 half dollar of which just five pieces are known to exist. In 1974, Bowers and Ruddy Galleries offered one of these for sale for $35,000.

In 1836, the half dollar was modified in design. Steam-powered presses were used in the Mint for the first time, and this made possible new high-speed production techniques. Gone were the lettered-edge half dollars of earlier years and in their place came the new pieces of smaller diameter and with edge reeding produced in a collar at the same time the coin was struck. The hand-prepared dies of earlier years were gone also. From 1836 onward, the main design features, except only the date, were impressed directly into the working die by the master die or hub.

Bust type half dollars of smaller diameter were produced in 1836 and 1837 with the denomination spelled as 50 CENTS on the reverse. In 1838, the style was modified somewhat, the most distinctive feature being the changing of the denomination to read HALF DOL. Such pieces were produced also in 1839.

In 1838, the New Orleans Mint opened for business. One of the first issues was the 1838-O half dollar of which just twenty specimens were struck. These pieces were produced to test the dies, and no further coinage for circulation was ever commenced. Of the twenty pieces originally produced, perhaps a dozen are known today. Of these I have had the good fortune to have handled several over the years, including a specimen which my firm offered for sale at $75,000 in 1974 and subsequently sold to a leading Midwestern collection.

The Liberty seated design, used also on other silver denominations of this era, made its debut on half dollars in 1839. This motif was continued until the last year of this design, 1891. Beginning in 1866 the motto IN GOD WE TRUST was added to the reverse above the eagle.

There are a number of varieties throughout the Liberty seated series. In 1853, arrowheads were added to the date and rays were added to the reverse, as was also done to the quarter dollars of this year, to denote a slight reduction in weight. In 1854 and 1855 the rays were discontinued but the arrowheads remained. Later, in 1873 and 1874, arrowheads were again added, this time to signify a slight increase in weight. Both known overdates, 1847/6 and 1855/4, are very rare, the earlier being the rarer of the two. One variety of 1844-O (New Orleans Mint) has a spectacularly doubled date. The first 1844 date was cut far too high and into the base of the Liberty seated figure. This was probably done by James B. Longacre, whose engraving ability was considered to be poor. Subsequently the date was recut in the proper position, giving the bizarre effect of one date overlapping the other.

There are many scarce issues in the series. In Uncirculated grades nearly all are scarce, with early Carson City issues being extremely rare. Beginning in 1879 and continuing through 1890, half dollar production was severely reduced so that an average of 10,000 pieces or less was made each year. This was because the various mints were busy turning out silver dollars in unprecedented numbers. In 1887, for example, just 5,710 half dollars—5,000 pieces for regular circulation plus 710 pieces struck as Proofs for collectors—were produced.

Charles E. Barber's distinctive design, used also on contemporary dimes and quarters, made its appearance on half dollars in 1892. Barber half dollars were coined continuously until 1915. There are no major rarities in the Barber half dollar series. In top grades there are some scarcities, 1892-O, 1901-S, 1904-S, 1913, 1914, and 1915 being examples.

In 1916, the half dollar was again redesigned. Adolph A. Weinman, designer of the Mercury dime, produced the Liberty walking half dollar. The obverse depicts the goddess Liberty with a rising sun to the left. The reverse shows a prominent eagle perched on a mountain crag. It will be noted that in 1916 the standardized Barber dime, quarter, and half dollar designs were all left behind—and new designs which for the first time in American history differed from each other, were adopted: the Mercury dime, the Liberty standing quarter, and the Liberty walking half dollar.

In 1916 and first part of 1917 branch mint issues struck at Denver and San Francisco bore mintmarks on the obverse of the coin. Midway through 1917 the mintmark position was changed to the reverse, and all later branch mint issues have the mintmark on the lower left side of the reverse.

There are no really great rarities among Liberty walking half dollars. In the early 1950's when I was a high school student in Pennsylvania, the Forty Fort State Bank in my home town was a fine friend to me. Far from being annoyed with my wanting to look through coins, the bank was actually very helpful. I fondly recall that I spent one afternoon there going through several bags ($1,000 face value—2,000 coins per bag) of mixed half dollars. By doing this I was able to complete a set by dates and mintmarks of each Liberty walking half dollar from 1916 through 1947. Today, finding even a single Liberty walking half dollar of a common date in circulation would be a rarity due to the fact that virtually all pre-1964 half dollars have disappeared from circulation because of the great rise in price of silver metal.

Scarce dates among Liberty walking half dollars include 1917-S with the mintmark on the obverse, 1921, 1921-D, 1921-S, and 1938-D. Half dollars of this style were last produced in 1947.

From 1948 through 1963, Franklin half dollars were produced. Designed by John R. Sinnock, the Franklin half dollar is of rather modernistic appearance and is not as "classical" as the earlier styles. All issues were made in fairly large quantities and none is particularly rare today.

In 1963, the world was shocked and saddened by the assassination of John F. Kennedy, certainly one of the best-loved Presidents our country has ever had. Almost immediately, thought was given to perpetuating his memory by including his likeness on a United States coin. The half dollar was selected for this purpose, and beginning in 1964 the Kennedy design was a reality. The reverse of the coin was adapted from the Presidential Seal and is reminiscent of the heraldic eagle reverse used on half dollars of more than a century earlier.

The Kennedy half dollar was an immediate hit with coin collectors and with the public at large. In the years since 1964, more than 2,000,000,000 pieces have been produced, and nearly all have found their way into dresser drawers, safe deposit boxes, and other places for safekeeping. President Kennedy was liked in foreign countries as well. When the Kennedy half dollar was first introduced, I took a number of them with me on trips to Europe in 1964 and 1965 where they made much appreciated gifts when given as tips.

The obverse of this attractive coin was designed by Gilroy Roberts, who left the employ of the Mint shortly afterwards and became a director of the Franklin Mint, one of the world's most successful private minting facilities. The reverse was designed by Frank Gasparro, who in 1959 produced the Memorial Reverse for the Lincoln cent.

The 1964 Kennedy half dollars were struck in silver. Issues from 1965 through 1970 were made of a special composition consisting of outer layers of 80 percent silver bonded to an inner core of 21 percent silver and 79 percent copper. Since 1971, the pieces have contained no silver but have been made of outer layers of copper-nickel bonded to a center of pure copper.

Silver Dollars, 1794 to Date

The large and impressive silver dollar has long been one of America's favorite coins. Silver dollars are rarely seen in circulation today. Indeed, they never were popular as a coin for hand-to-hand transactions. Rather, the silver dollar is a romantic coin, a sentimental coin associated with Christmas gifts, lore of the Wild West, and other tales.

Silver dollars have been coined intermittently over the years, and usually for special reasons rather than to fill a continuing need for commerce.

The first United States silver dollar made its appearance in 1794. Only 1,758 were minted. Of that number it is estimated that fewer than 100 survive today in all grades. Only a handful of Uncirculated specimens exist, one of which sold at auction for $110,000 in 1973. This was one of two specimens from the Lord St. Oswald Collection.

Pieces of this denomination were first made from 1794 through 1803.

The designs followed those on other silver series, with the earliest having the lovely flowing hair style and the latest having the heraldic eagle reverse. Although the official Mint records show that 19,570 silver dollars were minted in 1804, it is thought by numismatists that these pieces were actually dated 1803. In the early years, the Mint operated on a fiscal year basis rather than a calendar-year basis, and little thought was given to using dies dated a year or two earlier. If it was desired to coin several thousand silver dollars in 1804 and if some perfectly usable 1803-dated dies were on hand, then these would be the dies used. It would be poor economy to make up new dies when usable earlier ones were on hand. In later years, of course, coin collecting became very popular—and it became a matter of prime importance that coin dates match the calendar years during which they were made. However, no such thoughts occurred in 1804.

Following this last 1803-dated coinage, no silver dollars were made for many years. In 1834 and 1835, the Mint desired to prepare specimen Proof sets of United States coins for presentation to certain foreign dignitaries, royalty, and others. During these years no regular issue silver dollars were being made. In fact, none had been made since the 1803-dated coinage.

To complete the 1834 and 1835 Proof sets, it was desired to include specimens of the silver dollar denomination. The silver dollar or "crown size" piece is traditionally one of the highlights of any country's coinage, and omitting this from an American presentation set would be a serious error. The United States Mint did not want to produce silver dollars dated 1834, or 1835, for there was no authorization to make these and none were currently being made for circulation. So, it was decided to include top-grade specimens of the last date in which silver dollars were regularly issued—in this case 1804 (or so it was thought). Accordingly, the United States Mint prepared new dies with the 1804 silver dollar date. Thus, the sets contained a beautiful crown-size silver dollar coin.

It was soon realized that in the process a rarity had been created. During this time the United States Mint officials were building the National Collection of rare coins. Also, at this time the Mint actively traded coins with and sold coins to collectors—sometimes openly, other times secretly. The appeal of the rare 1804 silver dollar was immediately recognized and the Mint struck additional pieces for distribution to collectors.

The most famous and best-recorded sale of an 1804 dollar involved a coin acquired by pioneer American collector Matthew A. Stickney (1805–1894) of Salem, Massachusetts, in 1843. In their *Fantastic 1804 Dollar*,

Eric P. Newman and Kenneth Bressett quote a letter dated July 2, 1867, from Stickney to Edward Cogan, a New York dealer. We reprint part of it here:

> I was applied to by letter, July 4, 1866, by Mr. T. A. Andrews of Charlestown, Massachusetts, for the Dollar of 1804, which he understood I had in my possession and wished to obtain by purchase, for a friend in California, or information where he could get another. In reply I stated: "I have a genuine Proof dollar of the United States coinage of 1804. I do not dispose of my coins which are not duplicates, at any price. It is not likely that if I parted with this dollar, I could ever obtain another, as I have been told by a gentleman (W. Elliott Woodward, Esq.), largely engaged in selling coins at auction, that he thought it might bring one thousand dollars."
>
> On the 18th of November, 1866, Mr. Andrews wrote to me again, offering in the name of his friend "$1,000.00 in currency or the value in gold coin," saying: "I merely make the offer as requested to do, being aware that you stated that you did not dispose of coins except duplicates." I declined the offer on the 23rd of the same month.
>
> Of the genuineness of my U.S. dollar of 1804, I think there cannot be entertained a doubt, as it was handed me directly from the Cabinet of the U.S. Mint in Philadelphia, on the 9th of May, 1843, by one of its officers (Mr. W. E. DuBois), who still holds the same situation there, and can testify to it. . . .

It is evident that the United States Mint struck 1804 silver dollars on several other occasions, possibly until the late 1860's. Today only fifteen specimens are known of this rarity.

Throughout the years great publicity has been given to the 1804 silver dollar, initially engendered by the Mint itself, an institution which had a financial motive, either officially or unofficially, in promoting the piece as the most desirable, rarest, and most famous United States coin. Thus established as a tradition, the ownership of an 1804 has been the pinnacle of achievement of advanced numismatists. Indeed, any collection featuring such a coin automatically has been included in the "hall of fame" in American numismatics.

The comment of noted Texas dealer B. Max Mehl (quoted at greater length earlier) summarizes the situation nicely:

> In all the history of numismatics of the entire world there is not today and there never has been a single coin which was and is the subject of so much romance, comment, and upon which so much has been written and so much talked about and discussed as the United States silver dollar of 1804.

In 1836, the United States Mint prepared designs for a new regular issue of silver dollars. Noted engraver Christian Gobrecht designed an obverse featuring the seated figure of Liberty. The reverse depicted an eagle in flight amid a field containing twenty-six stars—thirteen small ones and thirteen large ones. The eagle, incidentally, was modeled after the Mint mascot, Peter, who was inadvertently killed one day when he perched upon a flywheel. This flying eagle design in slightly modified form was used in 1856–1858 to make one-cent pieces.

The earliest 1836 silver dollars, called "Gobrecht dollars" by collectors today, featured the raised inscription: C. GOBRECHT F. in the field of the coin between the date and the base of Liberty. C. GOBRECHT was for the designer's name and F. was an abbreviation for "fecit," Latin for "made it." Immediately objections arose to having the designer's name so prominent on the coin, and later issues omitted this feature.

Gobrecht dollars, one of America's most beautiful designs, were made only in pattern form. Most pieces were made in 1836, but some were made in 1838 and 1839 as well. Today all are extreme rarities, and a nice Proof example sells for several thousand dollars or more, depending upon the variety. Technically, Gobrecht dollars are considered as patterns, for they were made only in Proof condition (no regular or business strikes were made for circulation) and the quantities issued were small. However, collectors have traditionally adopted them as part of the regular series, and most advanced specialists in the series aspire to own at least one example of each of the 1836, 1838, and 1839 dates.

In 1840, silver dollars were once again made in large quantities for circulation, following a lapse since 1803. For some reason the beautiful flying eagle reverse design was discarded and a motif featuring a perched eagle was used. The obverse was the Liberty seated design with stars surrounding the figure of Liberty. Dollars of this style were made from 1840 through 1873, inclusive. Beginning in 1866, the motto IN GOD WE TRUST was added to the reverse.

Among silver dollar issues of this period are several rarities. Only 1,300 pieces were made in 1851 and only 1,100 in 1852 (plus a few others made as restrikes for collectors during the next decade or two). Today these are extreme rarities, as are silver dollars of 1858 of which the Mint states just eighty were made.

In 1870, the Carson City Mint produced coins for the first time. Bearing CC mintmarks, such dollars were minted of the Liberty seated design from that year through the last year of Liberty seated coinage, 1873. Carson City mintages were small in all instances. For example, in 1871 over a million Liberty seated dollars were struck at the Philadelphia Mint, but just 1,376 were issued at Carson City. Today all Carson City Liberty seated silver dollars are rare, and pieces in higher grades are particularly elusive.

1851 ORIGINAL SILVER DOLLAR. Among early silver dollars one of the rarest dates is an 1851 original. The date appears high in the field and close to the base of the seated Liberty figure. Later restrikes were made at the Mint, but the date on these appears lower and centered between the edge and the base of the seated figure.

One of America's great unresolved numismatic mysteries involves the 1873-S Liberty seated dollar. This piece is of the regular Liberty seated design, and bears a tiny s mintmark on the reverse signifying that it was struck in San Francisco. According to official Mint records, 700 pieces were produced. Yet no specimens are known to exist today, nor has any specimen ever been listed in any catalog or collection. There is always the possibility, of course, that an authentic 1873-S silver dollar might come to light someday. If so, it would be one of the finds of the century and would bring a fortune to its owner!

After 1873, silver dollar coinage was suspended until 1878. The Bland-Allison Act of Feb. 28, 1878, provided for immense coinages of silver dollars. There was no particular need for silver dollars in circulation; indeed, coinage had been suspended from time to time earlier because banks and businesses had enough to meet their requirements. And yet, in the year 1878, more than 22,000,000 silver dollars were produced—more silver dollars in this one year than had been produced during all previous years of silver dollar coinage from 1794 through 1873! Western silver mining interests influenced politicians of the time to buy silver in virtually unlimited quantities from Western mines, thus assuring a strong market for the metal. This was sort of an early price support, but on a grand scale. From 1878 through 1904, hundreds of millions of silver dollars that were neither needed nor wanted by the public were minted.

The Treasury, with its vaults bulging with these redundant coins, didn't know what to do with them all—so, in 1918, 270,232,722 silver dollars were melted down! This still left millions of dollars on hand, with the result that until the early 1960's one could still go into a bank and obtain a nice-as-new silver dollar from the 1870's, 1880's, or 1890's at face value. This had a beneficial effect for collectors, as the availability of older-dated pieces at face value spurred great numismatic interest. When the Treasury supply of older silver dollars was almost gone, the Government decided to take stock of what it had. On hand were 3,000,000 Carson City silver dollars mainly from the 1880's, pieces of fairly low original mintage. Rather than pay these out at face value, the Government decided to sell them at a premium to collectors by means of a series of auction sales held in 1973 and 1974. In this way the remaining several million pieces were dispersed, but at prices mostly ranging upwards from $30 per coin.

Silver dollars minted beginning in 1878 were designed by George T. Morgan and are known as "Morgan dollars" by collectors today. The obverse features the head of Liberty facing left. The reverse features an eagle with uplifted wings. Specimens were struck over the years at the Philadelphia, Carson City, New Orleans, and San Francisco mints. The quantities produced were immense.

Silver dollars of this era provide one field in which the numbers known today are not necessarily related to the original mintages. For example, only 228,000 1885-CC silver dollars were minted, making it one of the lowest-mintage pieces of the era. Depending upon the quality of the surface and the number of marks the coin has received, Uncirculated specimens can be obtained today for between $50 and $100 each. On the other hand, 1,200,000 1892-S silver dollars were minted, but one of these costs close to $10,000 today in choice Uncirculated condition. The explanation is that nearly all the 1885-CC silver dollars were stored by the Treasury during the time of mintage and were not released until later years. Thus, most pieces are in the hands of collectors today. The opposite was true of the 1892-S silver dollars. Most pieces were either put into circulation in or around 1892 or else were melted in 1918, with the result that few, if any, were released to collectors in later years. Thus, 1892-S in Uncirculated condition is a scarcity today.

Even more dramatic is the 1895 silver dollar situation. Mint records show that 12,000 pieces were made for circulation plus 880 Proofs for collectors. The 880 Proofs, being widely distributed among numismatists at the time, occasionally come on the market today. Such pieces are valued in the $6,000 to $8,000 range. What of the 12,000 Uncirculated pieces? Not a single Uncirculated specimen has ever come to light! It is presumed that all of these were melted in 1918.

Morgan dollars were minted from 1878 through 1904 inclusive. In the

1895 SILVER DOLLAR. The rarest date among silver dollars of the Morgan design is the 1895 issue struck at the Philadelphia Mint. Only 12,880 pieces were made: 12,000 for regular circulation and 880 Proofs. However, the regular circulation was never made, and in 1918 the coins were melted. The only specimens known to collectors are those remaining from the original issue of 880 Proofs. It is estimated that perhaps 400 to 500 examples survive. A choice Proof such as the one illustrated brings the best part of $10,000 today.

latter year coinage was suspended and was not resumed until 1921. In that year, more than 85,000,000 more Morgan dollars were produced. The folly of all this can be best appreciated when one considers that three years earlier, in 1918, the United States Government melted over 270,000,000 pieces of the same design! Politics and numismatics make strange bedfellows!

Later, in 1921, the design was changed. Anthony DeFrancisci, a sculptor and medalist, created the design. The obverse was modeled after the youthful portrait of his wife who appeared as Miss Liberty. The reverse features a perched eagle in the position of a dove with the word PEACE below, a sentiment of those post–World War I times. Peace silver dollars were struck from 1921 through 1935, but not in all years. In the latter year, coinage was suspended.

Collectors then thought that silver dollars had passed forever from the American scene. In 1964, interest was revived in making silver dollars once more. The old Peace design was resurrected, and thousands of 1964 Peace dollars were produced. However, it was decided not to release them into circulation, and it was officially stated that each and every coin went back to the melting pot. To this day, no 1964 Peace dollar is known to exist in any public or private collection. However, from time to time collectors have wistfully speculated that a few might have survived. Whether this is so remains to be seen.

In 1971, silver dollars again were produced. Although a few pieces were made in silver metal for collectors, these "silver" dollars weren't silver at all. Rather, they were made of a mixture of copper-nickel metal bonded to a core of pure copper. The obverse depicted Dwight D. Eisenhower. The reverse showed an American eagle landing on the moon. Both obverse and reverse were designed by Frank Gasparro, who earlier produced the Lincoln Memorial cent reverse (1959).

It was thought that the demand for Eisenhower dollars would be great, and in the first year over 100,000,000 pieces were coined. In the second year, 1972, the mintage climbed even further, above 170,000,000 pieces. However, once the novelty of the Eisenhower dollar passed, the pieces proved relatively unpopular and only reduced quantities have been made since then.

Indeed, the silver dollar has never been a popular coin in the channels of commerce. These large heavy pieces are too cumbersome to carry about easily, especially when compared to a paper dollar bill. However, they have always had a fascinating historical interest and souvenir value, and therein lies their greatest appeal.

Trade Dollars, 1873–1885

During the late 1860's and early 1870's, a great international trade developed with the Orient. Not wanting paper currency, Chinese merchants preferred "hard money" and their favorite was silver. The United States silver dollar weighed 412.5 grains and thus was slightly lighter than certain other crown-size coins of the world, so it was not so readily accepted. Accordingly, beginning in 1873, a special silver dollar called the "trade dollar" was minted. On the reverse was prominently stated the weight of the coin: 420 grains.

The trade dollar served its purpose fairly well, and from 1873 through 1878 approximately 35,000,000 were minted. At first, trade dollars were legal tender in the United States, but this caused confusion so this authorization was repealed and the pieces were made legal tender for export purposes only. This had strange consequences in later years. As trade dollars were not suitable for use as money within the United States, they often sold for less than face value! Indeed, coin dealers' price lists of the 1890's and early 1900's often listed common-date pieces for sale at 90¢ or 95¢ each!

Often when these pieces circulated in the Orient they would receive tiny counterstamps or "chopmarks," Chinese trademarks and figures impressed upon the coin by various banks, merchants, and others who accepted them. This meant that the institution in question accepted the coin as being genuine and of good silver. Today it is not unusual to find a trade dollar with a dozen or more counterstamps attesting to its early Oriental use.

After 1878, trade dollars were no longer made for commercial purposes. Specimens were struck in later years for inclusion in Proof sets sold to collectors, however. From 1879 through 1885 only Proofs were made. The last two years of the trade dollar—1884 and 1885—are extreme rarities. No one knows for sure how many were made; the pieces are not listed in official Mint records. However information obtained from William Idler, a Philadelphia coin dealer who had private relationships with certain Mint employees or officials, indicated just ten of the 1884 trade dollars and just five of the 1885 trade dollars were coined.

As is the case with the 1913 nickel, another unofficial coin, the true history of the 1884 and 1885 trade dollars will probably never be known. Certainly they are extremely rare—and probably the figures of five 1885 trade dollars and ten 1884 trade dollars accurately represent the numbers known to collectors today.

TYPES OF HALF CENTS

1. 1793 Liberty cap type with head facing left.
2. 1794–1797 Liberty cap with head facing right.
3. 1800–1808 Draped bust type.
4. 1809–1836 Classic head type.
5. 1840–1857 Braided hair type.

TYPES OF LARGE CENTS

1. 1793 Chain type.
2. 1793 Wreath type.
3. 1793–1796 Liberty cap type.
4. 1796–1807 Draped bust type.
5. 1808–1814 Classic head type.
6. 1816–1839 Coronet type.
7. 1839–1857 Braided hair type.

TYPES OF SMALL CENTS

1. 1856–1858 Flying eagle type.
2. 1859 Indian. Laurel wreath reverse.
3. 1860–1864 Copper-nickel. Oak wreath reverse.

4. 1864–1909 Indian. Bronze.
5. 1909 V.D.B. Lincoln type.
6. 1909–1958 Lincoln with wheat ears reverse.
7. 1943 Steel cent.
8. 1944–1945 Shell case metal cent.
9. 1959 to date. Lincoln Memorial reverse type.

TWO-CENT PIECES

1. 1864–1873 2c piece. One type issued.

NICKEL THREE-CENT PIECES

1. 1865–1889 Nickel 3c piece. One type issued.

SILVER THREE-CENT PIECES

1. 1851–1853 No outlines to star type.
2. 1854–1858 Three outlines to star type.
3. 1859–1873 Two outlines to star type.

NICKEL FIVE-CENT PIECES

1. 1866–1867 Shield type with rays on reverse.
2. 1867–1883 Shield type without rays.
3. 1883 Liberty type without CENTS.
4. 1883–1913 Liberty type with CENTS.
5. 1913 Buffalo type with raised ground.
6. 1913–1938 Buffalo type with level ground.
7. 1938 to date. Jefferson type.
8. 1942–1945 Jefferson "wartime" metal type.

HALF DIMES

1. 1794–1795 Flowing hair type.
2. 1796–1797 Draped bust; small eagle type.
3. 1800–1805 Draped bust; heraldic eagle type.
4. 1829–1837 Capped bust type.
5. 1837–1838 Liberty seated, no stars type.
6. 1838–1860 Liberty seated, with stars type.
7. 1853–1855 Arrows at date.
8. 1860–1873 Liberty seated, legend on obverse.

DIMES

1. 1796–1797 Draped bust; small eagle type.
2. 1798–1807 Draped bust; heraldic eagle type.
3. 1809–1828 Capped bust; large size type.
4. 1828–1837 Capped bust; small size type.
5. 1837–1838 Liberty seated, no stars type.
6. 1838–1860 Liberty seated, with stars type.
7. 1853–1855 Arrows at date.
8. 1860–1891 Liberty seated, legend on obverse.
9. 1873–1874 Arrows at date type.
10. 1892–1916 Barber type.
11. 1916–1945 Mercury type.
12. 1946–1964 Roosevelt type. Silver metal.
13. 1965 to date. Roosevelt type. Clad metal.

TWENTY-CENT PIECES

1. 1875–1878 20c piece. One type issued.

QUARTER DOLLARS

1. 1796 Draped bust; small eagle type.
2. 1804–1807 Draped bust; heraldic eagle type.
3. 1815–1828 Capped bust; large size type.
4. 1831–1838 Capped bust; small size type.
5. 1838–1865 Liberty seated, without motto type.
6. 1853 Arrows at date; rays on reverse type.
7. 1854–1855 Arrows at date type.
8. 1866–1891 Liberty seated, with motto type.
9. 1873–1874 Arrows at date type.
10. 1892–1916 Barber type.
11. 1916–1917 Liberty standing type I.
12. 1917–1930 Liberty standing type II.
13. 1932–1964 Washington. Silver metal.
14. 1965 to date. Washington. Clad metal.

HALF DOLLARS

1. 1794–1795 Flowing hair type.
2. 1796–1797 Draped bust; small eagle type.

3. 1801–1807 Draped bust; heraldic eagle type.
4. 1807–1836 Capped bust; lettered edge type.
5. 1836–1837 Capped bust; reeded edge; 50 CENTS reverse.
6. 1838–1839 Capped bust; reeded edge; HALF DOL. reverse.
7. 1839–1866 Liberty seated, without motto type.
8. 1853 Arrows at date; rays on reverse type.
9. 1854–1855 Arrows at date type.
10. 1866–1891 Liberty seated, with motto type.
11. 1873–1874 Arrows at date type.
12. 1892–1915 Barber type.
13. 1916–1947 Liberty walking type.
14. 1948–1963 Franklin type.
15. 1964 Kennedy type. Silver metal.
16. 1965 to date. Kennedy type. Clad metal.

SILVER DOLLARS

1. 1794–1795 Flowing hair type.
2. 1795–1798 Draped bust; small eagle type.
3. 1798–1804 Draped bust; heraldic eagle type.
4. 1836–1839 Gobrecht issues (patterns).
5. 1840–1866 Liberty seated, no motto type.
6. 1866–1873 Liberty seated, with motto type.
7. 1878–1921 Morgan type.
8. 1921–1935 Peace type.
9. 1971 to date. Eisenhower type. Silver metal.
10. 1971 to date. Eisenhower type. Clad metal.

TRADE DOLLARS

1. 1873–1885 Trade dollar. One type issued.

GOLD DOLLARS

1. 1849–1854 Liberty head type.
2. 1854–1856 Indian head type; small head.
3. 1856–1889 Indian head type; large head.

QUARTER EAGLES

1. 1796 Capped bust, no stars type.
2. 1796–1807 Capped bust right type; stars.

3. 1808 Capped bust left type; large size.
4. 1821–1834 Capped bust left type; smaller size.
5. 1834–1839 Classic head type.
6. 1840–1907 Coronet type.
7. 1908–1929 Indian type.

THREE-DOLLAR GOLD PIECES

1. 1854–1889 Three-dollar gold piece. One type issued.

FOUR-DOLLAR GOLD PIECES

1. 1879–1880 Flowing hair type. (Pattern.)
2. 1879–1880 Coiled hair type. (Pattern.)

HALF EAGLES ($5 GOLD)

1. 1795–1798 Capped bust; small eagle type.
2. 1795–1807 Capped bust right; heraldic eagle type.
3. 1807–1812 Capped bust left type.
4. 1813–1829 Capped head left; large size.
5. 1829–1834 Capped head left; smaller size.
6. 1834–1838 Classic head type.
7. 1839–1866 Coronet type, without motto.
8. 1866–1908 Coronet type, with motto.
9. 1908–1929 Indian type.

EAGLES ($10 GOLD)

1. 1795–1797 Capped bust right; small eagle type.
2. 1797–1804 Capped bust right; heraldic eagle type.
3. 1838–1866 Coronet type, without motto.
4. 1866–1907 Coronet type, with motto.
5. 1907–1908 Indian type, without motto.
6. 1908–1933 Indian type, with motto.

DOUBLE EAGLES ($20 GOLD)

1. 1849–1866 Liberty head type, without motto.
2. 1866–1876 Liberty head type, with motto. TWENTY D. reverse.
3. 1877–1907 Liberty head type, with motto. TWENTY DOLLARS.
4. 1907 MCMVII Saint-Gaudens Roman numerals issue.
5. 1907–1908 Saint-Gaudens Arabic date; without motto.
6. 1908–1933 Saint-Gaudens; with motto.

TYPES OF HALF CENTS

1. 1793 Liberty cap type with head facing left.

2. 1794–1797 Liberty cap with head facing right.

3. 1800–1808 Draped bust type.

4. 1809–1836 Classic head type.

5. 1840–1857 Braided hair type.

MAJOR DESIGN TYPES OF U.S. COINS

TYPES OF LARGE CENTS

1. 1793 Chain type.

2. 1793 Wreath type.

3. 1793–1796 Liberty cap type.

4. 1796–1807 Draped bust type.

5. 1808–1814 Classic head type.

TYPES OF LARGE CENTS

6. 1816–1839 Coronet type.

7. 1839–1857 Braided hair type.

TYPES OF SMALL CENTS

1. 1856–1858 Flying eagle type.

2. 1859 Indian. Laurel wreath reverse.

3. 1860–1864 Copper-nickel. Oak wreath reverse.

4. 1864–1909 Indian. Bronze.

5. 1909 V.D.B. Lincoln type.

6. 1909–1958 Lincoln with wheat ears reverse.

7. 1943 Steel cent.

8. 1944–1945 Shell case metal cent.

TYPES OF SMALL CENTS

9. 1959 to date. Lincoln Memorial reverse type.

TWO-CENT PIECES

1. 1864–1873 2c piece. One type issued.

NICKEL THREE-CENT PIECES

1. 1865–1889 Nickel 3c piece. One type issued.

SILVER THREE-CENT PIECES

1. 1851–1853 No outlines to star type.

2. 1854–1858 Three outlines to star type.

3. 1859–1873 Two outlines to star type.

NICKEL FIVE-CENT PIECES

1. 1866–1867 Shield type with rays on reverse.

2. 1867–1883 Shield type without rays.

3. 1883 Liberty type without "CENTS."

4. 1883–1913 Liberty type with "CENTS."

5. 1913 Buffalo type with raised ground.

6. 1913–1938 Buffalo type with level ground.

NICKEL FIVE-CENT PIECES

7. 1938 to date. Jefferson type.

8. 1942–1945 Jefferson "wartime" metal type.

HALF DIMES

1. 1794–1795 Flowing hair type.

2. 1796–1797 Draped bust; small eagle type.

3. 1800–1805 Draped bust; heraldic eagle type.

4. 1829–1837 Capped bust type.

MAJOR DESIGN TYPES OF U.S. COINS

5. 1837–1838 Liberty seated, no stars type.

6. 1838–1860 Liberty seated, with stars type.

7. 1853–1855 Arrows at date.

8. 1860–1873 Liberty seated, legend on obverse.

DIMES

1. 1796–1797 Draped bust; small eagle type.

2. 1798–1807 Draped bust; heraldic eagle type.

DIMES

3. 1809–1828 Capped bust; large size type.

4. 1828–1837 Capped bust; small size type.

5. 1837–1838 Liberty seated, no stars type.

6. 1838–1860 Liberty seated, with stars type.

7. 1853–1855 Arrows at date.

8. 1860–1891 Liberty seated, legend on obverse.

9. 1873–1874 Arrows at date type.

10. 1892–1916 Barber type.

11. 1916–1945 Mercury type.

12. 1946–1964 Roosevelt type. Silver metal.

13. 1965 to date. Roosevelt type. Clad metal.

TWENTY-CENT PIECES

1. 1875–1878 20c piece. One type issued.

QUARTER DOLLARS

1. 1796 Draped bust; small eagle type.

2. 1804–1807 Draped bust; heraldic eagle type.

3. 1815–1828 Capped bust; large size type.

4. 1831–1838 Capped bust; small size type.

5. 1838–1865 Liberty seated, without motto type.

6. 1853 Arrows at date; rays on reverse type.

7. 1854–1855 Arrows at date type.

8. 1866–1891 Liberty seated, with motto type.

9. 1873–1874 Arrows at date type.

10. 1892–1916 Barber type.

QUARTER DOLLARS

11. 1916–1917 Liberty standing type I.

12. 1917–1930 Liberty standing type II.

13. 1932–1964 Washington. Silver metal.

14. 1965 to date. Washington. Clad metal.

HALF DOLLARS

1. 1794–1795 Flowing hair type.

2. 1796–1797 Draped bust; small eagle type.

3. 1801–1807 Draped bust; heraldic eagle type.

4. 1807–1836 Capped bust; lettered edge type.

HALF DOLLARS

5. 1836–1837 Capped bust; reeded edge; "50 CENTS" reverse.

6. 1838–1839 Capped bust; reeded edge; "HALF DOL." reverse.

7. 1839–1866 Liberty seated, without motto type.

8. 1853 Arrows at date; rays on reverse type.

9. 1854–1855 Arrows at date type.

10. 1866–1891 Liberty seated, with motto type.

11. 1873–1874 Arrows at date type.

12. 1892–1915 Barber type.

HALF DOLLARS

13. 1916–1947 Liberty walking type.

14. 1948–1963 Franklin type.

15. 1964 Kennedy type. Silver metal.

16. 1965 to date. Kennedy type. Clad metal.

SILVER DOLLARS

1. 1794–1795 Flowing hair type.

2. 1795–1798 Draped bust; small eagle type.

3. 1798–1804 Draped bust; heraldic eagle type.

SILVER DOLLARS

4. 1836–1839 Gobrecht issues (patterns).

5. 1840–1866 Liberty seated, no motto type.

6. 1866–1873 Liberty seated, with motto type.

7. 1878–1921 Morgan type.

8. 1921–1935 Peace type.

9. 1971 to date. Eisenhower type. Silver metal.

SILVER DOLLARS

10. 1971 to date. Eisenhower type. Clad metal.

TRADE DOLLARS

1. 1873–1885 Trade dollar. One type issued.

GOLD DOLLARS

1. 1849–1854 Liberty head type.

2. 1854–1856 Indian head type; small head.

3. 1856–1889 Indian head type; large head.

MAJOR DESIGN TYPES OF U.S. COINS

QUARTER EAGLES

1. 1796 Capped bust, no stars type.

2. 1796–1807 Capped bust right type; stars.

3. 1808 Capped bust left type; large size.

4. 1821–1834 Capped bust left type; smaller size.

5. 1834–1839 Classic head type.

6. 1840–1907 Coronet type.

QUARTER EAGLES

7. 1908–1929 Indian type.

THREE-DOLLAR GOLD PIECES

1. 1854–1889 Three-dollar gold piece. One type issued.

FOUR-DOLLAR GOLD PIECES

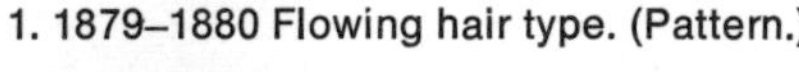
1. 1879–1880 Flowing hair type. (Pattern.)

2. 1879–1880 Coiled hair type. (Pattern.)

HALF EAGLES ($5 GOLD)

1. 1795–1798 Capped bust; small eagle type.

2. 1795–1807 Capped bust right; heraldic eagle type.

3. 1807–1812 Capped bust left type.

4. 1813–1829 Capped head left; large size.

5. 1829–1834 Capped head left; smaller size.

6. 1834–1838 Classic head type.

HALF EAGLES ($5 GOLD)

7. 1839–1866 Coronet type, without motto.

8. 1866–1908 Coronet type, with motto.

9. 1908–1929 Indian type.

EAGLES ($10 GOLD)

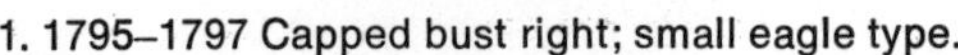

1. 1795–1797 Capped bust right; small eagle type.

2. 1797–1804 Capped bust right; heraldic eagle type.

3. 1838–1866 Coronet type, without motto.

4. 1866–1907 Coronet type, with motto.

5. 1907–1908 Indian type, without motto.

6. 1908–1933 Indian type, with motto.

DOUBLE EAGLES ($20 GOLD)

1. 1849–1866 Liberty head type, without motto.

2. 1866–1876 Liberty head type, with motto. "TWENTY D." reverse.

3. 1877–1907 Liberty head type, with motto. "TWENTY DOLLARS."

4. 1907 MCMVII Saint-Gaudens Roman numerals issue.

5. 1907–1908 Saint-Gaudens Arabic date; without motto.

6. 1908–1933 Saint-Gaudens; with motto.

6

United States Gold Coins

Gold, one of mankind's most precious metals and certainly the most romantic, was used to produce United States coins from 1795 through 1933. Pieces produced range from the tiny gold dollar, smaller than a present-day dime in size, to the heavy twenty-dollar gold piece or double eagle which contains nearly a full ounce of gold. Even larger were the massive fifty-dollar gold pieces struck in California during the Gold Rush and, later, as commemoratives at the 1915 Panama Pacific International Exposition in San Francisco.

In 1933, gold coins were minted for the last time. Legislation enacted in 1934 prohibited United States citizens in this country from owning gold coins, except for selected numismatic scarcities and rarities. Today the gold laws are a bit more liberal, but it is still illegal for citizens to hold certain modern-world gold coins (issued by countries other than the United States) and, believe it or not, it is a criminal offense to own a tiny bar of gold. All this may seem rather strange in a country famed for its freedom. To change this, laws relating to holding gold bullion were liberalized late in 1974.

Prior to 1934, it was common to have contracts payable in gold or gold coin. Certain types of United States paper money were issued with the promise that these notes could be redeemed in gold. When the United States abandoned the gold standard, it repudiated all these earlier financial commitments and invalidated all such contracts. Part of the present-day distrust of "paper dollars" is based upon such actions—not to mention that since 1933 the value of gold has increased sharply while at the same time the value of paper dollars has depreciated.

Today United States gold coins of all years and varieties can be legally held, bought, and sold by collectors and dealers. There is no restriction either as to the types of coins involved or to the quantities. As a result, gold coins have been a popular investment—an ideal way by which United States citizens can hold that precious yellow metal.

Gold Dollars, 1849–1889

One-dollar gold pieces were first minted in 1849. Coinage continued through 1889. Two basic designs were involved: the small Liberty head type minted from 1894 through 1854, the Indian princess style with small head minted from 1854 through 1856, and the Indian princess design with a larger head minted from 1856 through 1889. As can be seen, the designs overlapped in certain years.

Gold dollars were fairly popular during their original mintage period, and millions of pieces were produced, especially during the years prior to the Civil War. Later pieces were made in limited quantities, with the low water mark being reached in 1875 when only 400 pieces were made for circulation plus 25 Proofs for collectors. Contrast that with the highest mintage date, 1853, when more than 4,000,000 were made.

Interestingly, toward the end of the series three types of dollar-size coins were in circulation. Thus, in the year 1878, for example, one could have a dollar in the form of a silver dollar, trade dollar (also made of silver), or a gold dollar! In addition, not one but several varieties of paper dollar bills were in circulation!

Among the scarcest of gold dollars are issues produced by the mints at Charlotte, North Carolina, and at Dahlonega, Georgia. These mints, both opened in 1838 and closed in 1861, produced only gold coins. Each struck pieces of the one- two-and-a-half, three-(Dahlonega only), and five-dollar denominations, mainly from gold mined in Georgia and in the Carolinas.

Quarter Eagles ($2.50 Gold Pieces), 1796–1929

Two-and-a-half-dollar gold pieces, popularly called quarter eagles, were minted from 1796 through 1929. The very first 1796 quarter eagle depicts Miss Liberty on the obverse, in a plain field without stars. Just 963 of these were minted before it was decided to add stars to the obverse design for better balance. The 1796 with-stars design is even rarer—only 432 of these were minted! The same design with stars on the obverse was continued through 1807. The reverse of all pieces displays a heraldic eagle, a design similar to that used on silver coins of the period. An interesting variety is the 1804 with fourteen (rather than the normal thirteen) stars on the reverse above the eagle. This exact same reverse die with fourteen stars was used to make 1804 ten-cent pieces, coins of similar diameter.

In 1808 a new design made a brief appearance—the capped-bust left type of large diameter, of which 2,710 were minted. Although the mintage is not particularly low for a coin of this era, the fact that this design was made only in one year has sharply increased the demand for specimens, with the result that an Uncirculated piece brings well over $15,000 today.

No quarter eagles were minted from 1809 through 1820. In fact, the entire history of United States gold coinage features many lapses. Often many years would pass without pieces of some denominations being coined.

In 1821, the capped head to left design was used. The diameter was smaller than that used in 1808. This style was continued through 1834.

From 1834 through 1839, the so-called classic head type which omitted the earlier-used E PLURIBUS UNUM motto was minted. Then, in 1840, the coronet or Liberty head type made its appearance. This style was continued from 1840 through 1907, a remarkably long span of nearly 70 years without a major change, and thus a record among United States coins.

In 1908, a new type of quarter eagle made its appearance—the Indian head. Not only was the design different, the concept of the coin was different as well. With the exception of mintmarks (if the particular coin has one), these pieces have all elements incuse or intaglio in the design. The usual effect of this is that the field or plain areas of the coin's design wear first and the main features of the design such as the Indian head portrait and the eagle are the last to wear.

The Indian head design was used from 1908 through 1929, inclusive. The last year marked the discontinuance of the quarter eagle denomination.

Throughout the series there are a number of scarce and rare issues. All Charlotte and Dahlonega quarter eagles, minted (with some exceptions) from 1838 through 1860, are elusive. Among great rarities I mention the 1841. No 1841 quarter eagles were minted for circulation. Apparently a few, perhaps fifteen or twenty, were minted for inclusion in specimen presentation Proof sets. Only seven or eight 1841 quarter eagles are known today, and all are either Proofs or Proofs which show some signs of wear. This coin, one of the most famous of all American gold rarities, has been affectionately known as "the little princess" by collectors and catalogers over the years. It has been my good fortune to own several of these pieces, including one discovered in upstate New York in 1961. Part of an old estate, this 1841 quarter eagle remained unnoticed for many years. The owner was delighted to receive several thousand dollars for it, its value at the time. Since then prices have risen considerably. In 1973, we had a specimen valued at $10,000, and in 1974 another at $26,000 (the second specimen being the finer of the two).

One of the most interesting and romantic of all United States gold coins is a quarter eagle made at the Philadelphia Mint in 1848. This piece is like a regular 1848 quarter eagle in all respects except one: On the reverse the tiny letters CAL. above the eagle identify it as being from California gold.

1848 CAL. QUARTER EAGLE. Made from California gold and specifically identified as such on the coin, the 1848 CAL. two-and-a-half-dollar gold piece is one of the most historically significant of gold coins. Certainly no piece bearing the imprimatur of the United States Mint has a closer connection with the famed Gold Rush. (Enlarged illustration.)

When gold nuggets and flakes were first discovered at Sutter's Mill in Coloma, California, samples were rushed to the United States Mint at Philadelphia for testing and assay. A letter to Dr. R. M. Patterson, Director of the Mint, from Secretary W. L. Marcy read in part:

> If the metal is found to be pure gold, as I doubt not that it will be, I request you to reserve enough of it for two medals ordered by Congress and not yet

completed, and the remainder, with the exception of one or two small bars, I wish to have coined and sent with the bars to this department. As many may wish to procure specimens of coin made of California gold, by exchanging other coin for it, I would suggest that it be made into quarter eagles with a distinguishing mark on each.

The distinguishing mark was, of course, CAL. above the eagle on the reverse. The quarter eagle denomination was selected because in 1848 it was the smallest American gold denomination (the gold dollar was not made until the following year, and thus interested citizens and others could obtain one relatively inexpensively). Thus one of America's most romantic and most famous rarities was created. Also this coin can be said to be the first United States commemorative coin, for it was specifically issued to commemorate coinage from the first gold from California. Only 1,389 pieces were made. Of this number perhaps 100 to 200 exist today. An Uncirculated specimen would be valued in the range of $15,000.

Another scarce issue is the 1863 quarter eagle. No specimens were made for circulation and only 30 Proofs were made for sale to collectors. Of the 30 pieces struck, perhaps 15 to 20 exist today. By contrast, in the same year 10,800 quarter eagles were made at the San Francisco Mint (and with the tiny s mintmark on the reverse). The 1863-S quarter eagle is one of the more plentiful dates of this period. What a difference a small mintmark makes! Or, more correctly, in this instance what a difference a small mintmark *doesn't* make!

Among the Indian head quarter eagles made from 1908 through 1929, the style with the incuse designs and lettering, there are no great rarities. There is, however, one scarcity—the 1911-D of which 55,680 pieces were made. While it has a high mintage in an absolute sense, in a relative sense it is approximately ten times rarer than other issues of the period. Collecting one each of the fifteen varieties (including mintmarks) of quarter eagles from 1908 through 1929 has been a popular numismatic pursuit over the years.

Three-Dollar Gold Pieces, 1854–1889

Three-dollar gold pieces were first struck in 1854. This denomination was intended to be a convenient adjunct to the three-cent silver piece (first minted in 1851) so that a person desiring a hundred of the tiny silver three-cent pieces had but to present a three-dollar gold piece at a bank to get them. Also it was thought that three-dollar gold pieces would be a convenient way to buy sheets of one hundred three-cent stamps.

Like so many theoretical ideas throughout the history of coinage, the idea might have seemed fine originally but did not work out well in practice. Quarter eagles (two-and-a-half-dollar gold coins) were well established in commerce, and having a coin valued at 50¢ more was a redundancy—probably something like having a thirty-cent piece would be today, in view of the widespread popularity of today's quarter.

The first year, 138,618 three-dollar gold pieces were minted. Never again were mintage figures ever to touch that point. Over the years mintages declined so that by the last decade of issue, the 1880's, just a few thousand were made during most years. In some years even fewer were made—1881 with a total mintage of 554, 1883 with a total mintage of 989, and 1885 with a total mintage of 910 being outstanding examples.

Most three-dollar gold pieces were made at the Philadelphia Mint, although there are a few scattered San Francisco issues. Just one Dahlonega Mint issue occurs in the series: the 1854-D of which just 1,120 pieces were made. Likewise just a single New Orleans three-dollar gold piece was produced, the 1854-O.

The greatest rarity among three-dollar gold pieces is the 1870-S: In 1870, just two three-dollar gold pieces were minted in San Francisco. One was placed in the cornerstone of the new San Francisco Mint building completed that year, and the other was set aside, presumably by a Mint official. This second piece has been known to numismatists throughout the years and presently is a featured rarity in the magnificent collection of Louis Eliasberg of Baltimore, the owner of one of the most comprehensive collections of coins ever formed. What happened to the second piece that went into the Mint cornerstone? This remains a numismatic mystery. Years later when the cornerstone was opened, the 1870-S three-dollar gold piece was nowhere to be seen. Perhaps it will come to light again some day. Its finder will be at least several hundred thousand dollars richer!

Two other rarities among three-dollar gold pieces are the 1875 and 1876, both of which were struck only in Proof condition for sale to collectors. Only a few dozen of each were made, and surviving specimens are quite expensive today. A choice Proof 1876 is valued at the best part of $20,000, and an 1875 is valued at over $100,000.

Three-dollar gold pieces were discontinued in 1889, the same year that one-dollar gold pieces were discontinued. As a long span of years elapsed between 1889 and the discontinuance of gold coins in the American monetary system in 1933, many pieces were worn, lost, or exported, or met other fates. So, three-dollar gold pieces, never plentiful to begin with due to the low mintages, are rare in all grades today. They are highly desired by collectors, representing as they do an unusual denomination in combination with low mintages throughout the series.

Four-Dollar Gold Pieces, 1879–1880

One of the most curious denominations among American coins is the four-dollar gold piece or "Stella." Technically speaking, these coins are pattern issues. No Stellas were ever made for circulation. However, as nearly 500 pieces were made, they appear rather frequently on the coin market, and over the years they have been incorporated by some collectors into sets containing the regular series.

Today the subject of whether or not the United States should go on the metric system often makes a lively debate. It is interesting to note that the argument is hardly new—a century ago the same issue was hotly contested. The four-dollar gold piece or Stella was one of many attempts to make a coin which would be interchangeable with money used in Europe and elsewhere.

This unique denomination was proposed by John A. Kasson, United States minister to Austria in 1879, who earlier had been chairman of the Committee of Coinage, Weights, and Measures. The thought was to make an American coin which would be of the approximate value of other pieces actively circulating in Europe: the Spanish twenty peseta, Dutch eight florin, French twenty franc, and Italian twenty lira coins being examples. For the reverse design a five-pointed star was selected—hence the "Stella" nomenclature. The obverse was made in two styles: Miss Liberty with long flowing hair and Miss Liberty with tightly coiled hair. Around the obverse border was an inscription noting that the coin weighed 35 grams—30 grams of gold, 1.5 grams of silver, and 3.5 grams of copper. Instead of the English-language IN GOD WE TRUST motto commonly used on coins of that time, the Latin motto DEO EST GLORIA ("God Is Glorious") was substituted.

Of the flowing-hair design 415 pieces were made with the 1879 date and just 15 with the 1880 date. Of the coiled-hair design, just 10 pieces each were made in 1879 and 1880.

The Stella was considered unfeasible. At the time the United States was producing three-dollar and five-dollar gold pieces, so the intermediate-size four-dollar gold piece probably would have just caused confusion. The proposal was soon forgotten by everyone except coin collectors. Today numismatists consider Stellas to be rare prizes, and even the "common" 1879 flowing-hair variety will bring more than $20,000 in choice Proof condition.

Half Eagles (Five-Dollar Gold Pieces), 1795–1929

Five-dollar gold pieces saw a long and useful life in finance and commerce. Approximately the size of a present-day nickel, these pieces were perhaps the most actively circulated of all gold coins.

Half eagles were first minted in 1795. The obverse depicted the capped bust of Liberty. This style was continued through 1807. Among 1795–1807 half eagles there are two reverse types. The first has a small eagle perched on a palm branch and holding a victory wreath aloft in his beak. This style was used from 1795 through 1798. The second style, used from 1795 through 1807 (and overlapping the first style), features a heraldic eagle reverse, similar in styling to the design used on contemporary silver coins.

From 1807 through 1812 the capped draped bust to left style was used. The reverse eagle was redesigned with E PLURIBUS UNUM on a scroll in the field above the eagle.

In 1813, the half eagle was redesigned again. The head was reduced in size and the stars, rather than being arranged seven on the left side of the coin and six on the right, completely encircled the head. This motif was used through 1834, when the design was again modified. The diameter was reduced and the E PLURIBUS UNUM motto was eliminated. This style was continued through 1838.

The coronet or Liberty head style made its appearance in 1839. This design was used through 1908. In 1866, the motto IN GOD WE TRUST was added to the reverse.

In 1908, the Indian head half eagle was introduced. This style, which featured all of the designs incuse or intaglio, was similar in concept to the quarter eagle of the period. Half eagles were last minted in 1929.

The series of half eagles is studded with rarities. Particularly elusive are certain issues of the 1820's. A prime case in point is the 1822 half eagle, a coin of which just three pieces are known (two permanently impounded in the Smithsonian Institution and one in the collection of Louis Eliasberg). Mint records note that 17,796 pieces were produced this year. However, it is likely that nearly all were melted. During the 1830's the price of gold rose to the point at which all gold coins had a gold or metallic value higher than the face value. Thus, a profit could be obtained by melting down a five-dollar gold piece, taking it to the Mint, and receiving more than $5 in payment for the metal! As a result, great quantities of half eagles minted during the 1820's and 1830's were never released into commercial channels and went right to the melting pot. When the size and weight of the half eagle was subsequently reduced in 1834, the problem was solved, and coins of this denomination actively circulated once again.

Half eagles of the 1820's and 1830's are supposed to have thirteen stars encircling the head on the obverse. A curious exception is a variety of 1832 with just 12 stars. Apparently the engraver at the Mint was day-dreaming or made a mistake! No other explanation for this blunder has ever been advanced.

Liberty or coronet-type half eagles, the style minted from 1839 through 1908, have the unique distinction that they represent the only United States coin design available from all seven mints which produced coins at one time or another: Philadelphia, New Orleans, Charlotte, Dahlonega, San Francisco, Carson City, and Denver. Among Liberty head half eagles there are a number of scarce issues. Foremost in this regard is the 1841-O, a coin of which just 50 were minted and of which just 2 are known today. It is interesting to note that 15 or 20 years ago this was not recognized as a scarce date and was listed at a low value in popular reference books. Then several collectors tried to find a specimen of the "common" 1841-O and, not only found that none was to be had in the marketplace, but also that none could be traced in any auction sales or other offerings. This inspired some research, and soon it was learned that the piece was indeed a major rarity!

Also scarce is the 1854-S half eagle, a coin of which just 268 pieces were struck. The 1854-S quarter eagle is likewise rare, and only 246 were struck of this coin. Both issues were made during the first year of operation of the San Francisco Mint. By way of contrast the 1854-S ten-dollar gold piece is relatively common—123,826 were made! I mention this just to show that there are few rules in numismatics, and each coin stands on its own.

In the year 1887, just 87 half eagles were made at the Philadelphia Mint, all specimens struck in Proof grade for collectors. No pieces were made for circulation. However, on the West Coast in San Francisco in the same year, the Mint was turning out half eagles at a breakneck pace: 1,912,000 were minted! Thus, without a mintmark a Proof 1887 half eagle is worth about $5,000. With a tiny s on the back, a choice Uncirculated piece is valued at between $100 and $200.

Among Indian head half eagles, the style with the design incuse in the coin, are several scarce issues. The 1908-S and 1909-O are elusive. The last year of issue, 1929, is quite rare and a specimen will fetch several thousand dollars. It is interesting to note that 662,000 pieces were made in 1929, one of the very largest mintages in the entire 1908–1929 series. However, gold coins never circulated very actively (although half eagles circulated more actively than did certain other denominations), and most 1929 half eagles were simply stored by the Treasury after they were minted. When the use of gold coins was discontinued in 1933, the undistributed 1929 half eagles, a quantity which must have represented all but a few thousand pieces originally minted, went into the melting pot.

Eagles (Ten-Dollar Gold Pieces), 1795–1933

When the system of American coinage was proposed in 1792, the ten-dollar gold piece or eagle was designated as the highest value coin of the realm. Although the Philadelphia Mint began producing a few silver five-cent pieces in 1792 and copper coins in quantity in 1793, it was not until 1795 that the first gold coins made their appearance. In that year the first eagles and half eagles were minted. Ten-dollar gold pieces of the 1795–1804 years follow in style half eagles of this same period. The obverse features a capped bust facing right. The reverse of the earlier issues depicts a small eagle standing on a palm branch and holding aloft a victory wreath in its beak. Later issues show a larger heraldic eagle on the reverse.

All eagles of the 1795 to 1804 years are scarce. The nadir in mintage was reached with the 1798 variety with seven stars on the left side of the obverse and six on the right. Only 842 pieces were minted. In our auction of the Stanislaw Herstal Collection in 1974 a specimen of this variety sold for $13,000, a world record. Commonest of all early eagles is the 1801 of which 44,344 were minted.

No eagles were minted from 1805 through 1837, inclusive. During this period the price of gold rose to the point at which earlier-dated eagles were worth more than face value, with the result that many early pieces went to the melting pot. This compounded the rarity even further.

From 1838 through 1907, eagles of the Liberty head style were produced, with minor design changes over the years. In 1866, a major change occurred: IN GOD WE TRUST was added to the reverse. This motto was continued throughout the rest of the design until 1907.

The Indian eagle was first minted in 1907. The obverse featured Miss Liberty in the form of an Indian with a beautiful headdress. The reverse depicted a perched eagle in a defiant pose. The design was by the noted sculptor Augustus Saint-Gaudens, whose work on the beautiful twenty-dollar gold piece of 1907 was mentioned earlier. It is interesting to observe that 1907 Indian eagles and some issues of 1908 omitted the IN GOD WE TRUST motto. President Theodore Roosevelt personally believed that the name of God had no place on our coins, and the adoption of the new ten-dollar and twenty-dollar gold piece designs of this year provided an ideal opportunity to eliminate this message. However, Congress dissented and part way through 1908 the motto was restored.

Indian eagles were minted until 1933. Of this year 312,500 were minted. However, pieces were melted almost as fast as they were made due to the discontinuance of gold as a coinage metal this year. Today only one or two dozen pieces bearing this date are known to exist, and specimens are valued at about $20,000 each in Uncirculated condition.

Double Eagles (Twenty-Dollar Gold Pieces), 1849–1933

Double eagles or twenty-dollar gold pieces were first produced in 1849. James B. Longacre, chief engraver at the Philadelphia Mint, produced the first pair of dies toward the end of the year. The obverse design featured the head of Liberty and was somewhat similar in styling to that used on the tiny gold dollar also first introduced in 1849. In December, 1849, a number of double eagles bearing that date were struck. It was soon found that the relief or height of the design was too high and that pieces would not stack properly. Further, the high relief of the design made it impossible for all of the details in the higher part to be fully struck up when minted on a high-speed coining press. Thus, the coin was redesigned in lower relief.

Apparently several 1849 double eagles were struck. All were melted except one piece which is presently in the Smithsonian Institution and a second which was given at the time to Secretary of the Treasury Meredith. The location of the Meredith coin is not known today and remains as a great numismatic mystery. Should the coin ever come to light, it would undoubtedly sell for several hundred thousand dollars. Here is another lost numismatic treasure!

Beginning in 1850, double eagles were coined in large quantities for circulation. As noted, the design was in slightly lower relief. The Liberty head style was continued through 1907, but with some changes throughout the series. In 1866, IN GOD WE TRUST was added to the reverse. In 1877, the reverse indication of the denomination, formerly written as TWENTY D., was modified to read in full TWENTY DOLLARS.

One curious variety of double eagle is the so-called Paquet reverse. In 1859, mint engraver Anthony C. Paquet prepared a pattern design to

1861–S PAQUET DOUBLE EAGLE. One of the scarcest varieties of double eagles or twenty-dollar gold coins is the 1861–S Paquet reverse. Designed by Anthony Paquet, mint engraver, the reverse has "UNITED STATES OF AMERICA" and "TWENTY D." in tall, narrow letters. After dies were prepared it was realized that there would be problems concerning production of this design, so its use was countermanded. However, before word of this reached the San Francisco Mint, several thousand pieces had been struck. Today these are great rarities.

modify the reverse of the double eagle. The shield on the eagle's breast was made larger and the letters in the legend taller and narrower. In 1860, similar patterns were prepared. Finally, in 1861, it was decided to use the new Paquet style for regular coinage. Early in 1861 new double eagle reverse dies with Paquet's tall, narrow, letters on the reverse were produced at the Philadelphia Mint. Dies with O mintmarks were shipped from there to New Orleans and dies with S mintmarks were sent to San Francisco. It was anticipated that double eagles from this time forward would be of the new Paquet style.

On Jan. 5, 1861, two pieces with the Paquet reverse were struck at the Philadelphia Mint. It was noted that the reverse die was slightly too large for the obverse and that the reverse border, being too narrow, would not strike up properly. In addition, there would be abnormal wear on the dies when the coins were struck. The director immediately countermanded any further use of the die. His message to this effect was telegraphed to New Orleans and arrived before any coins were struck. The order to the San Francisco Mint was sent overland, there being no telegraph at the time west of St. Joseph, Missouri. Before the orders arrived in San Francisco in February, 1861, 19,250 1861-S Paquet double eagles had been struck. Apparently most of these were melted and then recoined into regular (pre-Paquet design) style pieces. However, some reached the channels of commerce.

The Paquet double eagles did not come to light until many decades later when numismatists began seriously studying American gold coins. It was recognized that the 1861-S Paquet was an extreme rarity; today just a few dozen coins are known to numismatists. Most pieces are in well-worn grades, for no attempt was made to set aside any at the time of issue. A piece today brings several thousand dollars.

Of the two 1861 Paquet reverse double eagles struck at the Philadelphia Mint at least one has survived. In a transaction in which I took part this piece changed hands in the mid-1960's for a figure in the $25,000 range. Today it would bring far, far more.

Liberty head double eagles include a number of other scarce issues. The 1854-O and 1856-O are quite elusive, as is 1870-CC, the latter coin being the first double eagle from the Carson City Mint. Several Philadelphia Mint issues of the period are quite rare. Double eagles were struck only in Proof condition (none were made for circulation) in 1883, 1884, and 1887, and each of these dates is highly prized today.

In 1907, Augustus Saint-Gaudens was commissioned to redesign the double eagle. The result was the magnificent high relief style with the date in Roman numerals, as mentioned earlier. These coins, bearing the date as MCMVII and considered to be among the most artistic of all coins, were minted to the extent of 11,250 pieces. Most of these were placed into circulation at the time.

I always derive pleasure from informing a client that a coin previously unsuspected as being rare is actually quite valuable. Recently an executive with the Crocker National Bank, one of California's leading banking institutions, visited my office to discuss an estate. He brought with him as a casual item, his wife's necklace. It contained, so he thought, a common-date twenty-dollar gold piece worth perhaps several hundred dollars. He was delighted when I informed him that this coin, given to his wife years ago as a gift, was actually an MCMVII high relief double eagle. So, treasures are still being found today!

After the limited coinage of MCMVII double eagles, the design was modified to a lower relief and the dates of double eagles from that point forward were expressed in the regular form. With several subvarieties, Saint-Gaudens double eagles were produced through 1933.

There are a number of interesting and scarce varieties throughout the series. One variety more interesting than it is rare is the 1909/8 overdate double eagle. A 1908 double eagle die was overpunched with the 1909 date so that it could be used in the latter year. The result is that the last digit of each coin produced from the die show traces of an 8 under the 9. The 1909/8 is the only overdate in the entire double eagle series.

The 1927-D double eagle is a major rarity. At the Denver Mint in that year 180,000 double eagles were struck. However, nearly all must have been sent to the Treasury for storage and then later melted, for fewer than a half dozen specimens are known to exist today. A specimen is now valued at close to $100,000.

Even rarer is the 1933 double eagle. In fact, this is one of the rarest and most controversial of all American coins. During the first several months of 1933, 445,500 double eagles bearing that date were struck at the Philadelphia Mint. In March, 1933, gold coinage was suspended, and in ensuing months the Treasury began to melt down its holdings. Apparently 1933 double eagles were not officially released to banks or the channels of commerce.

However, over the years several 1933 double eagles have appeared in numismatic collections. The Treasury Department, taking the stance that these pieces were never officially released, has seized such pieces when the opportunity presented itself. Today the Treasury Department's position is that 1933 double eagles cannot be legally held.

And yet there is a possibility that they can indeed be legally held. It was the practice of the Treasury Department during the early 1930's to sell coins to collectors, sometimes even coins dated several years earlier (coins which were on hand from earlier years but which were not sold to collectors at the time). Sales were made by means of mimeographed lists. Although no list or offering featuring a 1933 double eagle has ever come to light, it is theoretically possible that a collector with a strong desire for one could have purchased one at face value in January, February, or early March, 1933. In fact, it is possible that several could have been sold this way. However, to this day, no official receipts or official offers of 1933 double eagles from this time have ever come to light. Should such documentation be found in the future, then the 1933 double eagle would indeed have a legal status. Specimens in hiding, indeed if there are any, could then come out into daylight and be recognized for the rarities they are! King Farouk, the playboy ruler of Egypt, amassed many collections of various things during his reign. His coin collection was an important one, and when it was sold in 1953 it was found to contain a 1933 double eagle. Knowledge of this reached the Treasury Department, and the coin was subsequently seized.

Throughout the years, double eagles were minted in immense quantities. This large and heavy coin provided the ideal medium for bulk international transactions. From the 1890's onward, often millions of double eagles were struck in a year. The high-water mark was reached in 1928 when 8,116,000 pieces were coined.

During the latter part of the 19th century and the early 20th century,

American gold coins were shipped in huge quantities to overseas banks and other sources. Particularly popular for this purpose was the double eagle, but large quantities of ten-dollar and five-dollar pieces were sent as well. Following the discontinuance of gold coinage in 1933, America went off the gold standard. Members of the public were required to turn in gold coins (except those specifically reserved for numismatic purposes) to banks. As soon as this was done the Government raised the official price of gold from $20 per ounce to $35 per ounce, thus depriving the American public of hundreds of millions of dollars in profits. A twenty-dollar gold piece, worth just $20 in early 1933, had a bullion value of close to $35 by late 1934! It is fiscal actions such as this which have made many international bankers wary of the American monetary system. In fairness I must mention that America is not unique in this regard, and the currency policies of other countries have often made ours appear conservative by comparison!

The overseas shipments had a very beneficial effect upon coin collecting. In 1933 and 1934, foreign governments gave not the slightest thought to returning their millions of American gold coins to the United States to receive in exchange green paper dollars. Instead, they held on to their gold coins even more tightly. While the quantities of coins held by overseas banks are not known and have never been revealed, I remember one interesting incident which happened during a trip to Zurich, Switzerland, in 1961. Visiting the Swiss Credit Bank (an institution which, by the way, is one of my clients today—they have a very active numismatic department), I asked to see selections of American gold coins. After due negotiation I purchased a number of scarce dates, mainly twenty-dollar gold pieces. I then discussed the situation of American gold coins in general and asked how many double eagles the bank had available. The answer to this had to remain confidential, I was told, but the gentleman seated in the room with me at the time said that without checking elsewhere he could at that moment confirm an order for 100,000 pieces! Any larger order would have to be checked with other officials of the bank for the price might be affected slightly.

Today the gold coins available to collectors and investors have come mainly from European and South American sources so far as commoner dates in the five-, ten-, and twenty-dollar series are concerned. Scarcer dates have come from old-time collections here in the United States, for these have been highly prized by numismatists for many years and were not turned in to the government during the 1930's.

7

United States Commemoratives, Patterns, and Territorial Gold

United States Commemorative Coins

Commemorative coins have played a very important part in numismatic history. The first United States commemorative pieces were produced for the Columbian Exposition. At this event, perhaps the most famous world's fair ever to be held in our country, 1893 quarters of a special design featuring the portrait of Queen Isabella were sold as souvenirs for $1 each. Also sold for a dollar each were Columbian half dollars dated 1892 and 1893. These half-dollar coins bore a stylistic portrait of Columbus on the obverse and his flagship, the Santa Maria, on the reverse.

As both the quarter and half dollar denominations were sold for $1 each, the public considered half dollars to be a better value at the price—for a larger coin could be purchased for the same amount of money. As a result just 24,214 Isabella quarters were made whereas 2,500,000 Columbian half dollars were produced. As you might suspect, the quarters proved to be the better investment. A choice 1893 Isabella quarter is valued today at over $200 whereas a choice Uncirculated Columbian half dollar sells in the $20 range.

From 1892 to 1954, 144 varieties of silver commemorative coins were produced. Of these, 142 were half dollars, and two were other denominations: the 1893 Isabella quarter issued for the Columbian Exposition and a commemorative silver dollar issued in 1900 featuring the portraits of George Washington and Lafayette.

There was no formalized program for issuing commemorative half dollars during the early 20th century. Typically a state, community, or other group wishing to observe an anniversary or other historical event would apply to have a commemorative half dollar produced. Should Congress act favorably, authorization was then made that one or more mints would produce half dollars of a special design. These would be sold to the issuing commission at face value. The issuing commission would then sell them at a premium. Events commemorated on half dollars range from the significant to the obscure. Some examples follow:

Alabama commemorated its centennial in 1919. However, half dollars for the event were not authorized until the following year, and were not actually struck until 1921. Then, 59,038 pieces were struck and were sold at a premium. When sales began to wane, the inventive minds of the issuing commission decided to create a new variety by putting a small 2x2 on the obverse of each coin, to signify that Alabama was the twenty-second star in our nation's flag or, put another way, the twenty-second state to enter the Union. Of the 2x2 variety 6,006 were made.

The idea of making rare varieties for collectors caught on quickly, and the 1921 Missouri centennial half dollar was produced in a quantity of 15,428 pieces. Then a small 2x4 was added, and another 5,000 pieces were sold to collectors. In the same vein, 67,405 regular half dollars were struck in 1922 to commemorate the 100th anniversary of Ulysses S. Grant's birth, and then 4,256 were made of a special variety with a tiny star added to the field.

It was soon realized that issuing commemorative half dollars for collectors could be a big business. While the exact details of some of the abuses will never be known, it is certain that substantial profits were made by those associated with certain issuing commissions by withholding coins from sale to collectors and prematurely stating the issues were sold out. Later, these coins would be parceled out slowly at sharply increased prices. Perhaps an example of this is the 1936 Cincinnati set. In that year coins were struck at the Philadelphia, Denver, and San Francisco mints to commemorate the 50th anniversary of Cincinnati as "a musical center of America." Slightly more than 5,000 coins were produced at each mint. Obtained by the issuing commission at the face value of 50¢ each (for a total of $1.50 for the set), the coins were sold only by the set at $7.75 for the three. However, many collectors desiring to purchase the sets at the issue price of $7.75 found that no sets were available. Sets were available, however, from selected private sources and coin dealers for prices well in advance of the issue price—up to $50 per set in some instances. Such abuses gave commemoratives a bad name with Congress and other public officials. The last coinage of commemorative half dollars honored Booker T. Washington and George Washington Carver, and, in 1954, commemorative coinage was suspended. Commemoratives are being produced for the 1976 bicentennial of American independence, but these will be produced in large quantities and will be readily available to all who wish to order them.

The panorama of American silver commemoratives is a rich one. Such obscure events as the centennial in 1936 of Elgin, Illinois; the 150th anniversary in 1935 of the founding of Hudson, New York; the 250th anniversary in 1938 of the founding of New Rochelle, New York, and the 150th anniversary in 1936 of the city charter of Lynchburg, Virginia, are forgotten by most members of the public—but not by numismatists. They are forever commemorated on half dollars.

One of the most interesting commemorative half dollars of 1936—the year in which commemoratives were most popular in America—is the coin commemorating the 300th anniversary of the founding of Delaware. In 1638 Swedes landed in Delaware and established a settlement there. The 300th anniversary was 1938. However, the coin itself bears the date 1936, was actually struck in 1937, and also bears the date 1938!

Lest the reader think only sidelights of history were commemorated on half dollars I mention such events as the centennial of the state of Arkansas, the 75th anniversary of California's joining the United States, the 300th anniversary of Connecticut, and the 100th anniversary of Iowa as examples of more important commemoratives.

Certain commemorative silver coins were issued over a long period of years, often long after the original reason for issuance had passed. Sometimes the issuing commissions became businesses unto themselves and sought to perpetuate their existence and profits by continually selling coins to collectors year after year, almost like a small government. Usually such issues were struck at the Philadelphia, Denver, and San Francisco mints to provide, not one, but three varieties for each year. Thus half dollars commemorating the Arkansas centennial (which actually took place in 1936) can be collected from each of these three mints each year from 1935 through 1939 inclusive. The 200th anniversary of Daniel Boone's birth was commemorated in 1934 by a half dollar. However, the commemoration did not stop there as far as collectors were concerned—issues were produced through 1938. The series of half dollars commemorating the Oregon Trail was issued from 1926 through 1939, and Texas centennial half dollars from 1934 through 1938, inclusive.

Occasionally quantities of unsold commemorative half dollars were placed into circulation at face value. Examples are the 1893 Columbian Exposition, 1923 Monroe Doctrine centennial, and the 1925 Stone Mountain issues. In addition, more than a million 1952 half dollars of the

U. S. SILVER COMMEMORATIVE COINS. From 1892 through 1954, commemorative half dollars were produced in 48 designs, ultimately in 142 date and mintmark varieties. Two other silver denominations were also produced: the 1893 Isabella quarter, and the 1900 Lafayette dollar.

(1) 1893 Isabella quarter originally sold for $1 each at the 1893 World's Columbian Exposition. (2) 1900 Lafayette silver dollar. (3) 1921 Alabama half dollar, with the tiny "2x2" in the center right field above the stars; varieties exist with and without this feature. (4) 1936 Albany, New York, half dollar. (5) 1937 half dollar commemorating the 75th anniversary of the battle of Antietam. (6) Specimens of the 1936 half dollar commemorating Cincinnati as "a musical center of America" were struck at the Philadelphia, Denver, and San Francisco mints. (7) 1893 Columbian half dollar. (8) 1935 half dollar commemorating the 300th anniversary of Connecticut. (9) 1936 half dollar observing the 75th anniversary of the Battle of Gettysburg. (10) 1922 half dollar issued in commemoration of the 100th anniversary of President Grant's birth. (11) 1928 half dollar commemorating the 250th anniversary of Captain James Cook's landing in Hawaii, the most expensive of all commemorative half dollars and the most highly prized by collectors today. (12) 1935 Hudson, New York, half dollar. (13) 1921 half dollar issued for the centennial of the state of Missouri. (14) The 1921 Missouri half dollar with the numerals 2 and 4 and a star in the left obverse field above the 1821 date is a variety created for collectors. (15) 1915 half dollar issued for the Panama Pacific International Exposition held in San Francisco that year. (16) 1935 half dollar commemorates the Old Spanish Trail which extended from the coast of Florida to El Paso, Texas. (17) 1925 half dollar marks the centennial of Fort Vancouver.

1614 · CHARTERED · 1686
ALBANY · N.Y.
1936
UNITED STATES OF AMERICA
HALF · DOLLAR
4
UNITED STATES OF AMERICA
LIBERTY
IN GOD WE TRUST
HALF DOLLAR
ANNIVERSARY BATTLE OF ANTIETAM
E PLURIBUS UNUM
SEVENTY-FIFTH
1937
5
UNITED STATES OF AMERICA
HALF DOLLAR
6
CINCINNATI · A · MUSIC
1886
1936
IN GOD WE TRUST
UNITED STATES OF AMERICA
COLUMBIAN HALF DOLLAR
COLUMBIAN EXPOSITION
WORLD'S
CHICAGO
14
92
1893
7
UNITED STATES OF AMERICA
HALF DOLLAR
8
THE CHARTER OAK
CONNECTICUT
1635 – 1935
UNITED STATES OF AMERICA
BLUE AND GRAY REUNION
75TH ANNIVERSARY
1863
1938
IN GOD WE TRUST
HALF DOLLAR
BATTLE OF GETTYSBURG
9
UNITED STATES OF AMERICA
ULYSSES S. GRANT
1822
1922
HALF DOLLAR
10
IN GOD WE TRUST
E PLURIBUS UNUM
UNITED STATES OF AMERICA
CAPT. JAMES COOK DISCOVERER OF HAWAII
IN GOD WE TRUST
HALF DOLLAR
E PLURIBUS UNUM
1778
1928
11
UNITED STATES OF AMERICA
IN GOD WE TRUST
HALF DOLLAR
12
CITY OF HUDSON N.Y.
E PLURIBUS UNUM
1785 · 1935
UNITED STATES OF AMERICA
1821
1921
HALF DOLLAR
13
MISSOURI CENTENNIAL
SEDALIA

Washington–Carver commemorative issue were distributed at face value through banks. Most of these were quickly absorbed by collectors and others who desired the pieces as souvenirs.

The last commemorative silver issue, with George Washington Carver and Booker T. Washington on the obverse and the map of the United States on the reverse, were struck at the Philadelphia, Denver, and San Francisco mints from 1951 through 1954, inclusive. Toward the end of that period large quantities remained unsold, and production was stopped.

Since 1954 there have been a number of efforts to introduce new commemorative half dollars, but the abuses of the past and lack of a formal policy have precluded success.

In addition to coins officially designated as commemoratives, many issues produced as part of our regular coinage have commemorated specific events. For example, the 1932 Washington quarter, the same design in use today, was originally produced to commemorate the 200th anniversary of Washington's birth. The 1848 quarter eagle with CAL. above the eagle on the reverse was originally made as a commemorative or souvenir issue, not formally for sale at a premium to collectors, but a commemorative nevertheless.

United States Commemorative Gold Coins

Throughout our coinage history only thirteen gold commemorative coins have been issued and sold at a premium to collectors and others. In 1903, commemorative gold dollars were sold at the Louisiana Purchase Exposition held in St. Louis. There were two varieties: one with the obverse featuring Thomas Jefferson and the other William McKinley. Of each of these 17,500 were struck. During the next two years, commemorative gold dollars were struck for the Lewis and Clark centennial exposition in Portland, Oregon. Slightly more than 10,000 were struck each year.

In both 1916 and 1917, approximately 10,000 commemorative gold dollars were produced to help finance the McKinley Memorial at Niles, Ohio, the President's birthplace. The centennial of Grant's birth in 1922 was the occasion for two issues of commemorative gold dollars, a variety with a star in the obverse field and a variety without, each minted to the extent of about 5,000 pieces. The latest-issue commemorative gold coin was the 1926 sesquicentennial (150th anniversary) quarter eagle sold at the Philadelphia fair in that year.

From a mintage viewpoint, Grant commemorative gold dollars, each with a production of about 5,000 pieces, are or at least should be twice as rare as 1904 and 1905 Lewis and Clark gold dollars, each of which had a mintage of slightly over 10,000. However, this is not the case. Most of the 1904 and 1905 gold dollars were sold as souvenirs to persons who attended the Lewis and Clark centennial exposition in Portland in 1905. Most purchasers were not numismatists and gave little thought to preserving the coins carefully; hence, many sustained wear or damage or were lost. On the other hand, very few members of the general public purchased 1922 Grant gold dollars; nearly all went to coin collectors and dealers. Therefore, choice Uncirculated Lewis and Clark gold dollars are several times rarer than choice Uncirculated Grant dollars. Mintages, while important, do not necessarily tell the entire story.

From the viewpoint of commemorative coins, the most outstanding event in American history was the Panama Pacific International Exposition held in San Francisco in 1915 to celebrate the opening of the Panama Canal and, in addition, provide a showcase for art, science, technology, and the rebirth of the city of San Francisco following the earthquake of 1906. Several commemoratives were prepared. Each bore an S mintmark and was struck at San Francisco. A complete set of coins consists of a half dollar, gold dollar, quarter eagle, and two fifty-dollar gold pieces. The large and impressive fifty-dollar "slugs" (as collectors call them) were made in two shapes: round, of which 483 were sold, and octagonal, of which 645 were sold. Each of these pieces was sold for $100, or twice face value. Today each coin brings $15,000 or more! For the fairgoer who wanted the finest a complete set of coins was available encased in a glass-fronted copper frame and displayed on a velvet background, with gold lettering on purple ribbons beneath each coin. A set such as this brings more than $30,000 today!

In summary, 144 United States commemorative silver coins have been issued: a quarter dollar, a silver dollar, and 142 varieties of half dollars. There have been 13 varieties of commemorative gold coins: nine gold dollars, two quarter eagles, and two fifty-dollar gold pieces.

Commemoratives are very popular with collectors. Whether a collector chooses to collect one of each major design or one of each and every date and mintmark variety, a fascinating panorama of dates, events, persons, and places awaits him. Many numismatists hope that commemoratives will once again be produced—and sold perhaps on an unlimited basis to all buyers for a specific period of time. If sold through the Treasury Department (rather than private issuing agencies), the abuses of the past could be avoided.

United States Pattern Coins

I consider United States pattern coins to be among the most fascinating of all issues. Actually, the term "pattern" covers a wide field: designs which were proposed but which for one reason or another were never used, metals and metal substitutes which were tried and abandoned, pieces made to test dies, coins made up for purely experimental reasons, and so on. From patterns Mint officials and others selected those designs later produced in quantity for general circulation.

Edgar H. Adams, one of the most prolific researchers numismatics has ever known, and his associate, William H. Woodin, who was later to become Secretary of the Treasury under Franklin D. Roosevelt, produced in 1913 the first comprehensive book on the field, *United States Pattern, Trial, and Experimental Pieces*. For years a standard reference, the volume listed and described pieces known to these two men and illustrated specimens of prominent collections, including that of Mr. Woodin. In 1959, an updating and rewriting of the volume was done by Dr. J. Hewitt Judd and retitled *United States Pattern, Experimental, and Trial Pieces*. In his introduction Dr. Judd quoted DuBois Patterson's interesting view of pattern coins published in the *American Journal of Numismatics* in 1883:

> Open for me your cabinet of patterns, and I open for you a record which, but for these half-forgotten witnesses, would have disappeared under the finger of Time. Read to me their catalogue and I read to you, in part at least, the story of an escape from the impractical schemes of visionaries and hobbyists—a tale of national deliverance from minted evil. These are to be enjoyed as bygones, though there lingers a fear for the sparks that still smolder under the ashes. Laws have been framed for them, words have warred over them. Now, only these live to tell the tale of "what might have been." Only these remind us of what has been weighed, measured, and set aside among the things that are not appropriate, not convenient, not artistic, in short, that are not wanted.

Actually, Patterson's remarks don't cover the whole story. Collectors and historians feel that many pattern designs are more beautiful or more practical than those which were actually adopted for general use, and that the designs may have been rejected for political or personality reasons rather than reasons connected with the coins themselves. Many numismatists consider the study of patterns to be a separate subject—just like the study of commemoratives, of tokens, or of colonial coins. I consider patterns to be very closely related to the study of regular United States coinage. By studying patterns one can learn the reason why certain designs were adopted and why certain others weren't, and at the same time see some of the most beautiful coins ever to leave the United States Mint.

In 1961, James F. Ruddy and I purchased and resold the fabulous collection of United States pattern coins gathered by Maj. Lenox R. Lohr, former director of Chicago's Museum of Science and Industry. This collection, the largest ever to be priced and offered for sale in numismatic history, comprised nearly 1,500 issues. Rarities were there—sometimes in duplicate and triplicate. Particularly amusing to me was one pattern nickel which was listed in reference books as being unique. The Maj. Lenox R. Lohr Collection contained *three* of them! As I have studied patterns very carefully over the years, I have made a number of discoveries. When I am asked, "Is there opportunity for the student in numismatics today—or have all of the important discoveries been made?" I recall that in the 1840's a Congressman recommended that the Patent Office be abolished, for all possible inventions of use to mankind had already been invented! While many important numismatic discoveries have already been made, there still are many to be made in the future. I am proud to say that in more than 20 years of dealing in coins I have identified quite a few important varieties—pieces previously unknown, but now listed in standard reference books and recognized by collectors.

A recent discovery of a previously unknown pattern coin—one I made

UNITED STATES OF AMERICA
1
UNITED STATES OF AMERICA
1866
2
IN GOD WE TRUST
5
CENTS
IN GOD WE TRUST
3
UNITED STATES OF AMERICA
5
CENTS
UNITED STATES OF AMERICA
4
STANDARD SILVER
25
1869
E PLURIBUS UNUM
1882
5
UNITED STATES OF AMERICA
HALF DOLLAR
1871
6
UNITED STATES OF AMERICA
IN GOD WE TRUST
ONE DOL.
E PLURIBUS UNUM
LIBERTY
1880
7
UNITED STATES OF AMERICA
895.8 S.
4.2—G.
100—C.
25 GRAMS
ONE DOLLAR

UNITED STATES PATTERN COINS. From 1792 onward many pattern coins were produced at the United States Mint to test designs, metals, and other concepts prior to issuing coins for circulation. During the 19th century such pieces were sold to collectors. More than 1,000 varieties of patterns of the years 1792–1916 are known. Some interesting ones are: (1) 1866 pattern issue combining the obverse of a $3 gold piece with the reverse of an 1866 shield nickel—literally two coins in one—was discovered by the author in 1972 in a safe deposit box where it had lain since the 19th century. (2) 1866 pattern nickel featuring Abraham Lincoln, but no coins bearing Lincoln's portrait were issued until the Lincoln cent made its appearance in 1909. (3) 1866 nickel featuring George Washington. (4) 1869 Standard Silver twenty-five-cent piece, one of the many hundreds of pattern issues produced in the Standard Silver series during 1869 and 1870. (5) 1882 half dollar of the beautiful "School Girl" design used also for quarters and silver dollars and which is considered to be among the most beautiful designs ever made. (6) 1871 pattern silver dollar featuring Miss Liberty as an Indian princess. (7) 1880 pattern metric dollar. (8) 1872 pattern double eagle. (9) 1877 pattern fifty-dollar gold piece. Two specimens, each slightly differing from the other in design, were produced in gold and are now on view at the Smithsonian Institution. Considered the most valuable and desirable of all United States coins, they sold for $10,000 each in 1909—by far a world's record at the time. The specimen shown here is a Proof striking in copper, one of just two or three known, auctioned by Bowers and Ruddy Galleries, Inc., as part of the Austin Collection sale in 1974.

in 1973 and published in April, 1974—is listed in Bowers and Ruddy Galleries' *Rare Coin Review* No. 20 and was described in part thus:

> 1866 Unlisted pattern nickel. Found last year in a collection of coins which had been kept intact since 1882, this coin is offered here for the first time. To our knowledge, this unlisted piece was unknown to Edgar H. Adams and William H. Woodin, and later to Dr. J. Hewitt Judd and Don Taxay (who has also done research in the pattern field) when they compiled their pattern coin studies.
>
> One side of the coin is struck from the regular 1866 shield nickel die—the die used to strike regular issue Proofs. The other side is from the obverse of a three-dollar gold piece of the period. Literally, the coin has two obverses! The coin is struck in nickel composition metal. The coin is in nearly mint state. The offering of this coin is a momentous event in the field of American pattern coins. Very, very few coins have escaped the careful studies of past specialists in this field. The reason for this piece, presumably the only one known, not being published before is that it was stored away from 1882 until 1973 and was not available for study! Listed patterns which are unique (only one specimen known) have been priced in the tens of thousands of dollars—or even more in the instance of pieces of special historic value (for example, a value of $250,000 or more has been placed on a unique pattern 1907 gold coin). What the ultimate value of this unique and heretofore unlisted pattern nickel is remains to be seen—but we consider our present price to be conservative: $9,950.

In general, pattern coins are divided into several categories. Prime in importance are basic pattern issues. These are characterized by new and different designs, often one of which is finally selected for eventual mintage for circulation. Thus, before the motto IN GOD WE TRUST was regularly used on United States silver coins in 1866, patterns were issued with this motto in 1863, 1864, and 1865. Before flying eagle cents were issued for circulation in 1857, patterns were struck in large quantities in 1856. The purpose of a pattern is to familiarize Congressmen, Mint officials, and others with the artistic and practical aspects of a new design before it is actually adopted. Patterns can be struck in the intended metal of coinage or in other metals. For example, 1863, 1864, and 1865 pattern quarters, half dollars, and silver dollars with IN GOD WE TRUST were struck in silver (the intended metal of coinage) as well as in copper and aluminum.

A pattern can also represent a new denomination or value. For example, in 1879 and 1880, pattern four-dollar gold pieces or "Stellas" were produced. These never went beyond the pattern stage; no pieces were ever made for circulation.

Experimental pieces form another category. Such pieces were made to try out radical new concepts. For example, in 1852, some one-dollar gold pieces were made with large holes in the center, an idea adopted from Oriental coins. The thought was to increase the diameter of the gold dollar without sacrificing the gold content or weight. Another example is a variety of 1882 pattern nickel with five equally spaced raised bars or ridges on the edge. This coin, called the "blind man's nickel" by collectors today, was designed to enable a blind person to instantly recognize a coin by its touch.

Trial pieces are yet another category. In their usual form such coins consist of strikings from dies in metals other than those intended for coinage. An example would be a twenty-dollar gold piece of a regular design struck in copper rather than gold. Such pieces were made in many years. It was not uncommon for copper and aluminum trial pieces to be made in the gold and silver series. Sometimes such pieces were made actually to test the dies before proceeding with regular coinage. Other times they were made to provide curiosities for collectors. As an example of the latter is a rare 1885 Proof set I once owned of all the copper, nickel, silver, and gold denominations from the cent through the twenty-dollar gold piece—with each coin struck in aluminum!

Die trials are often struck in lead or copper, perhaps using just one die. Certain die trials are made from unfinished dies—without the date, without stars, or with some other finishing touches not yet added. Such pieces are made at the Mint to see how the die is "coming along" during the process of preparation. Unlike patterns, experimental pieces, and trial pieces, most die trials are one of a kind. Once a die trial is produced there is no reason to make many trials to sell to collectors or to give to legislators. Rather, the die is then worked on further and perhaps at a later state another single die trial is made.

Certain other pieces included in the pattern field have been made to show to collectors, to artificially create a rarity, or simply to make something unusual. Often a coin such as this is called a "pìece de caprice." The previously mentioned new pattern variety I discovered in 1973 is an example. Is the coin a five-cent piece or a three-dollar piece? The obverse is that of a regular 1866 shield five-cent piece; the reverse is from the obverse of a three-dollar gold piece. Certainly at the time of issue no one intended to make coins with different denomination designs on each side. Perhaps the piece was made by a Mint official as a private souvenir. Another example is a unique coin I purchased twenty years ago from my friend Oscar Schilke. In 1859 someone at the Mint took a beautiful Proof silver dollar of the regular issue, carefully held it in a coin press as it was stamped on the center of the obverse and reverse with Proof dies of the tiny 1859 half dime. The result was literally two coins in one! Such pieces fascinate collectors and are very valuable.

Let me explain here the term restrike. It describes not only certain coins in the pattern field, but also regular issue coins as well. A coin struck from official Mint dies at a date later than that which appears on the coin is a restrike. Restrikes have been made in hundreds of instances throughout American coinage. It was common practice in the early years of the Mint to produce, for example, silver dollars dated 1803 in the calendar year 1804. Technically such a piece is a restrike, but it makes little difference today.

During the mid-1960's when Lincoln cents were being hoarded by collectors and others and were rare in circulation, the United States Mint abandoned its traditional practices and produced millions of coins from dies dated a year or two earlier. Also during this period the Denver Mint dropped the use of the traditional D mintmark—so as not to make more varieties for hoarders! The restrikings just cited were done by the Mint for economic necessity and not to provide rarities for collectors or to enrich Mint officials. On the other hand, certain other restrikes, particularly those made during 1858–1875, were produced at the Philadelphia Mint to provide a stock of coins to sell and trade to collectors. Half cents of the dates 1840 through 1848, all extremely rare, were restruck and sold to collectors. Likewise, 1856 pattern flying eagle cents, always a favorite rarity, were restruck at the Philadelphia Mint during the late 1850's and early 1860's.

Sometimes restrikes are differentiated by collectors and dealers, especially when there is a difference in date placement or design. Other times whether a coin is an original or restrike is not noticed, for both originals and restrikes are nearly identical in appearance. An example of a restrike versus an original and the difference in their values is provided by the 1851 silver dollar. Original 1851 silver dollars have the numerals of the date high in the field and close to the base of the seated figure of Liberty. A decade or so after 1851 it was realized that silver dollars of that date were extremely rare. There simply were not enough to satisfy the demands of collectors. So, the Mint prepared new dies with the 1851 date, taking care to center the date numerals carefully (without realizing it was less historically accurate to do so). Today 1851 original silver dollars are several times rarer than restrikes and bring a correspondingly higher price. Really advanced silver dollar collectors aspire to own one of each variety, the original with the date high in the field and the restrike with the date centered.

During the 19th century it was often the practice to keep on hand dies from earlier years. Sometimes such dies were stolen or otherwise acquired by persons outside of the Mint—dealers and collectors—who produced restrikes. One of the silliest of all restrikes is that of the 1804 large cent. Among large cents 1804 is a rare date, and original specimens command a great premium. About 1860 some unknown individuals, either Mint employees or collectors with connections to the Mint, decided to make some more 1804 cents. They had a problem, however: No 1804 cent dies were on hand. Locating a badly rusted 1803 obverse die, they altered the date to read 1804. Apparently a reverse die of the 1804 era was not available, so the next best thing was to take what was on hand—a reverse die used in 1820. The result is a transmogrification: a strange coin with a rusted 1804 obverse and a reverse with the style from a later period. The entire piece is rather crudely struck and looks not at all like an original. Perhaps it was intended to sell such pieces to children or other unsuspecting persons. Whatever the original purpose might have been, hundreds were released and such pieces are fairly common today. They are popular with collectors who appreciate their interesting story.

The first pattern coins produced by the United States Mint were made in 1792. In that year more than a dozen varieties were produced, the most familiar being the 1792 silver half disme. Earlier I mentioned this was the first coin to be made under the auspices of the United States Mint and released into circulation. Another interesting variety of that year is the silver-center cent. It was realized that to have a full cent's worth of copper in a coin (as necessary to give full weight and measure to the coinage), the diameter would have to be large and the piece would be heavy. A compromise was thought of whereby a tiny plug of precious silver metal would be inserted in the center of a smaller-diameter copper coin, thereby making the coin easier to handle but still giving it a total intrinsic value of one cent. Examples of the silver-center cent are very rare today; fewer than a dozen are known to exist.

Among the most famous of the 1792 patterns are the Birch cents, large-diameter copper coins of full weight produced by Thomas Birch. Several varieties were produced. The obverse of each bears the inscription LIBERTY PARENT OF SCIENCE & INDUSTRY, a reference to the encouragement of advancement possible under America's new status as an independent country. The reverse bears the inscription UNITED STATES OF AMERICA with ONE CENT in the center. Most specimens have a fraction 1/100 at the bottom, but a unique variety has G. W. PT. instead, an abbreviation of "George Washington President."

Some of the most beautiful among early-19th-century patterns are those prepared by Mint engraver Christian Gobrecht during the 1830's. The beautiful Gobrecht silver dollars of this period depict the seated figure of Liberty on the obverse and a flying eagle on the reverse. From these patterns eventually came the designs used on all regular-issue silver coins from the half dime through the silver dollar. The beautiful flying eagle reverse was never used for regular silver coinage, however. It did reappear later on small copper-nickel one-cent pieces of 1856–1858.

One of the simplest coins ever produced at the United States Mint is a silver three-cent piece pattern made in 1849. Bearing an Arabic figure 3 on the obverse and a Roman numeral III on the reverse, the coin lacked any other identification and is merely a token in appearance. Some have called this the least attractive of all coin designs, Dr. J. Hewitt Judd's reference to it as an "ugly duckling" being an example. Actually the piece was never intended as a pattern of what the finished coin would look like. Rather, it was struck simply to show what the size of such a coin, a denomination then not currently in use, would be.

In 1858, dissatisfied with the flying eagle design then currently in use on the small cent, the United States Mint prepared a series of patterns with differently styled obverses and reverses. The same year regular Proof sets were first sold to collectors, some 80 sets finding buyers. The Mint was just beginning to realize that collectors constituted an attractive market and a source of profit. Accordingly, the Mint prepared pattern copper-nickel cents and sold them in sets of twelve pieces. Each set contained coins of three obverse designs: (1) the regular flying eagle style, (2) a pattern design featuring a very small flying eagle, and (3) an Indian head design similar to that adopted for use in 1859. With each of the three obverse dies there were four reverse combinations: (1) the agricultural wreath reverse as used on regular flying eagle cents, (2) the laurel wreath reverse regularly adopted in 1859 for coinage, (3) a pattern oak wreath design, and (4) a pattern oak wreath design with an ornate shield at the top. Apparently sales of these sets continued for several years after 1858, for in a study of the series I found numerous minor die varieties among these patterns and also some issues that appeared to be later strikings from dies which showed light evidences of rust.

In 1861, thought was given to including mention of God on our nation's coinage. Numerous patterns were prepared using the motto GOD OUR TRUST. In the following year, additional patterns with this motto were prepared. In 1863, the motto as we know it today, IN GOD WE TRUST, made its first appearance on patterns. Subsequently this motto was used for regular coinage on two-cent pieces beginning in 1864 and on silver and gold coins beginning in 1866.

A very interesting series of pattern coins, the Standard Silver issues, appeared in 1869 and 1870. At this time large numbers of fractional-currency notes—small pieces of currency of values ranging from three cents through fifty cents issued to meet the post–Civil War needs for circulating change—were in circulation, and it was thought desirable to issue a special series of coins to redeem the notes. The logic of this is not clear today, but at the time it seemed that a new series of designs for the dime, quarter, and half dollar would be desirable. Each piece was to be about 20 percent lighter in weight than the other regular Liberty seated coins then in circulation. It will be remembered that at the time Liberty seated silver coins of the regular design were of high silver content with the face value nearly equal to the metallic value. On the other hand, paper money had (and has) very little intrinsic value—just the scrap value of the paper it is printed on. It was thought that the Standard Silver series, being coins issued to redeem paper money with no intrinsic value, would not have to have full silver intrinsic value.

Standard Silver designs were created in a multiplicity of metals and varieties. Apparently the main motive was not the feasibility of Standard Silver coins as a new circulating medium to redeem fractional currency, but rather to provide large numbers of specially made pattern coin varieties for sale to collectors. As an example of this, Standard Silver dimes were made in 1869 in three designs, each differing only slightly from the others (but each constituting a different variety so far as collectors are concerned). In addition, pieces were struck in three different metals: silver, copper, and aluminum. To create even more varieties, each issue was available in two edge styles, plain and reeded or milled. So, to have a complete set of Standard Silver dimes of 1869, a collector would have to purchase from the Mint six examples of each of the three designs (silver with plain edge, silver with reeded edge, copper with plain edge, copper with reeded edge, aluminum with plain edge, aluminum with reeded edge), for a total of eighteen pieces. Likewise, quarters and half dollars were made in abundant varieties. The next year, even more Standard Silver coins were produced, including five-cent pieces, a value not issued in 1869. The creation of even more designs and die combinations made it necessary for the collector to assemble nearly *fifty* 1870 dimes to have a complete collection of all the Standard Silver varieties issued that year. The varieties among other denominations proliferated as well. By carelessly combining obverse dies meant for one type of coin with reverse dies meant for another, several illogical patterns were created: coins which do not have the UNITED STATES OF AMERICA on them. This situation has happened several times throughout pattern coinage history.

In 1872, Mint engraver William Barber created the Amazonian series of patterns. Outstanding are the designs for the quarter, half dollar, and silver dollar. Miss Liberty appears in the form of a goddess with her left arm resting on a shield and holding a sword. Her right arm caresses a perched eagle. This classically inspired design has long been a collectors' favorite.

Throughout American coinage history many errors have been made in coin designs—errors in spelling, the number of stars on a coin, placement of the date, and so on. From the standpoint of illogic, few errors can compare to one on certain pattern twenty-cent pieces of the year 1875. Miss Liberty is seated at a seashore. In the distance is a steamship with auxiliary sails. A strong wind apparently is blowing from left to right, for the sails of the ship are billowed forward and the ship is sailing to the east. However, in defiance of all meteorological laws a flag from the mast is flying to the *left!* Curiously enough, as far as I know this inconsistency escaped the attention of collectors until I noticed it when cataloging a collection of patterns a few years ago. The same design error was repeated on pattern silver dollars and trade dollars of the same year.

The year 1877 is remarkable for the production of some of the rarest and most beautiful pattern coins ever produced in America. Mint engravers Anthony C. Paquet, George T. Morgan, and William Barber all submitted designs and made patterns for half dollars. The designs covered a wide variety of styles ranging from motifs adapted from classic mythology and history to adaptations of other coins. In the latter category, several pattern half dollars of 1877 are identical except for size to the regular 1878 Morgan silver dollar designs. Very rarely does a single 1877 pattern half dollar appear on the market, for each variety was issued in very limited numbers. The most remarkable offering in recent history—since my firm's early offering of the Maj. Lenox R. Lohr Collection in 1961, in fact—occurred in 1972 when Bowers and Ruddy Galleries sold at auction the remarkable collection of United States coins formed over a period of years by Armand Champa, a prominent numismatist from Louisville, Kentucky. Mr. Champa specialized in patterns and over a period of years acquired twenty-one specimens of 1877 half dollars. Some of these were duplicates. At the sale itself, collectors from all over the world competed to acquire these prizes, and many sold for several multiples of their catalog value. While the prices were all-time high records in 1972, now many of them appear quite cheap, as is nearly always the case over a period of years when a collector purchases a combination of rarity and high condition.

Two of the most remarkable coins ever produced by the United States were issued in 1877, the large and impressive fifty-dollar gold pieces or "quintuple eagles." These massive coins are somewhat similar in design to twenty-dollar gold pieces of the period. Patterns were struck in two varieties, one with a slightly smaller head than the other. Specimens were struck in gold and in copper. Two or three examples of each copper variety are known to exist, and one specimen of each variety in gold is known. The gold pieces are a permanent part of the Smithsonian Institution Collection.

These pieces were inspired by the large and impressive fifty-dollar gold "slugs" which circulated in California a decade or two earlier. Senator Gwin of California presented a bill to Congress in 1854 to coin gold pieces in denominations of $100, $50, and $25 to be called the Union, Half Union, and Quarter Union, and recommended that only the Half Union should be struck to begin with. Why it took from 1854 until 1877 for the Half Union to be produced would be a good subject for numismatic research. Perhaps in 1877 a general awakening of interest in art and beauty of coin design (as evidenced by the spectacular series of 1877 pattern half dollars of many artistic designs) prompted Mint officials to re-evaluate the Gwin proposal.

The fifty-dollar pieces struck in gold have an interesting history. In July, 1909, Edgar H. Adams (who was later to write a book on the pattern series) wrote an article on these in *The Numismatist*, official journal of the American Numismatic Association. The article read in part:

THE WORLD'S HIGHEST-PRICED COINS. The two unique U.S. pattern quintuple eagles sold for $10,000 each—specialists consider them cheap at this price. . . .

The two unique United States $50 gold coins, each of different design, which have long been regarded as the rarest coins in the world by American coin collectors, were purchased a short time ago by William H. Woodin, of New York City, for $10,000 each, which figure by far exceeds all recorded high premiums paid for any coin ever sold.

The coins were bought of John W. Haseltine and Steven K. Nagy, the Philadelphia coin dealers, establishing a new world's record. The previous record was held by a specimen of the New York Brasher Doubloon in gold struck in New York in 1787, for which $6,200 was paid at the Stickney Collection sale in Philadelphia two years ago.

The newly discovered gold pieces are included in the United States series of pattern coins and represent the most interesting pieces in the American series, the denomination being equivalent to five eagles, or the "Half Union" recommended in 1854 by Secretary of the Treasury Guthrie (on the recommendation of Senator Gwin). They illustrate the single case where United States coins of this value were struck in gold. They never emerged from the experimental stage, although declared by experts to be the handsomest and most striking coins ever issued at the U.S. Mint.

These two gold pieces have not been seen since the year of their mintage, 1877, and were supposed by all collectors to have been melted up.

Therein lies a tale of sorts. Steven K. Nagy (by then in his retirement) and I had many interesting conversations in the 1950's. At that time I was researching United States patterns and asked him about his earlier transactions. It seems that Mr. Nagy had certain connections (which he declined to identify specifically) at one time with Mint officials, and certain pieces presumed to have been melted were, in fact, acquired by him and several other favored Philadelphia coin dealers. Mr. Nagy mentioned that he was able to obtain a number of rare Gobrecht dollars, restrikes of certain early American silver dollars, and other pieces. Exactly what Mr. Nagy knew will never be known, for he has since passed away and did not leave a written record of his recollections.

The United States Mint was rather upset by all of this publicity valuing the coins at $10,000 each and the statement that even this price was "considered cheap by specialists." They sought to re-acquire the coins from William H. Woodin and in doing so made an unusual bargain: In exchange for the two pieces William H. Woodin received "several trunks full of patterns" of earlier dates, a treasure trove of coins which became the source of most pattern coins now in the hands of collectors. It is estimated that these patterns today would have an aggregate value of many millions of dollars. Concerning the value of the two gold coins themselves, it would not be inconceivable that if one were sold it would bring many hundreds of thousands of dollars, certainly setting a record for any United States coin. This will not happen, however, for each piece is now the property of the American people and are on display at the Smithsonian Institution. Copper strikings of the 1877 fifty-dollar gold pieces are occasionally encountered in the marketplace. One appeared in our sale of the Austin Collection in 1974 and sold for $50,000.

In 1878, 1879, and 1880, numerous metric coins were made. The most famous of these are the 1879 and 1880 four-dollar gold pieces or "Stellas." Also produced were other denominations, including the silver dollar and twenty-dollar gold piece. All these metric designs were subsequently rejected.

The idea of the metric coinage was not new then, and over the years various proposals have been advanced. In 1874, Dana Bickford, a New York City gentleman who found that international exchange rates caused him no end of confusion on a visit to Europe, contacted the Mint and proposed a truly international coin which could be carried from one country to another without having to compute its value. Dr. Henry Linderman, Director of the Mint, was enthusiastic about the proposal and caused to be struck a number of pattern pieces incorporating Bickford's ideas. The reverse stated the weight of the coin as being 16.72 grams of .900

fine (90 percent pure) gold. To make the coin international the value was expressed in six currencies: ten dollars; two pounds; one shilling; one pence; 41.99 marks; 37.31 kronen; 20.73 gulden; and, finally, 51.81 francs. Several factors caused the rejection of the Bickford proposal. International monetary rates fluctuated then as they do now, and the standards expressed on the coin would not remain in effect for long. While a ten-dollar denomination was convenient in our currency system, in the other countries such pieces would have had awkward fractional values, certainly making them difficult to use easily.

In 1881, 1882, and 1883, many pattern nickels were produced. These eventually led to the adoption of the Liberty nickel for regular circulation. Beginning about this time the sale of patterns, officially and unofficially, by the Mint to collectors was sharply curtailed. As a result, few patterns dated past the mid-1880's are in the hands of collectors. The curtailment was the result of a tremendous uproar in the numismatic journals of the day by collectors and dealers who resented the favored treatment given to certain Philadelphia coin dealers who had access to rarities from the Mint. Some patterns were available from the Mint by direct purchase by collectors (the 1858 sets of pattern cents being examples), whereas other patterns were made only in limited quantities and were sold privately, traded for specimens needed for the Mint collection, or otherwise dispersed in small numbers. When William H. Woodin acquired his large quantities of patterns from the Mint in exchange for surrendering his two 1877 fifty-dollar gold pieces, he found among the patterns a large quantity of pattern 1896 cents and nickels of an unadopted shield design. These coins are occasionally found on the marketplace today. About twenty years ago I purchased a hoard of several dozen pieces formerly owned by Mr. Woodin and obtained by him directly from the Mint. These 1896 issues are the only post-1890 patterns which regularly appear on the market today.

Among 20th-century patterns the illustrious gold issues of Augustus Saint-Gaudens produced in 1907 are worthy of mention. Best known among these is a variety of MCMVII (the date in Roman numerals) double eagle in extremely high relief, in even higher relief than the pieces coined in limited quantities for circulation that year. Over the years James F. Ruddy and I have owned several of these, including a specimen purchased from Yale University in 1961. The sale of an MCMVII extremely high relief twenty-dollar gold piece was recorded at $200,000 in 1974. At the time, a regular MCMVII high relief piece sold for several thousand dollars in Uncirculated condition.

In 1916, several varieties of patterns were prepared for the Mercury dime, Liberty standing quarter, and Liberty walking half dollar. These were released by the Mint only in limited quantities, probably by presentation to the designers of the coins or others closely involved with their production. As a result, only a few examples of each variety are known today, and only at rare intervals do specimens appear on the market.

Since 1916, patterns have not been documented by numismatists. Occasional pieces have appeared on the market, particularly patterns and die trials of commemorative half dollars. Most of these trace their history to the estates of the designers who produced them. Thus, two trial strikings of Grant Memorial commemorative half dollars presently in the Ernest Keusch Collection and sold by Bowers and Ruddy Galleries in 1972 trace their pedigree to the family of Laura Gardin Fraser, who originally designed these pieces.

U.S. Territorial Gold Coins

Not struck by regular United States mints, but nevertheless an important part of American coinage history, are United States territorial gold coins, sometimes called "pioneer" gold issues. This field encompasses coins issued mainly in various regions where important gold discoveries were made. At the time of such discoveries there was a need for coins to serve as a medium of exchange.

Mined gold, in the form of dust, nuggets, or gold extracted from quartz or other matrices, was occasionally used as money. However, the fineness (purity) of such gold was subject to wide variation, and the necessity of having to carefully weigh gold dust at the conclusion of a commercial transaction was inconvenient, to say the least. So, in California, Georgia, North Carolina, and certain other areas bankers and assayers performed the valuable function of accepting gold dust, refining it, and then delivering to the owner a comparable value in gold bars prominently stamped with the name of assaying or banking firm, the weight, and fineness or purity of each bar. A nominal commission was deducted for performing the assaying service. Some of these firms issued coins as well.

While such coins, usually issued in values equivalent to regular American gold coins ($1, $2½, $5, $10, and $20 values were the most popular), were not issued under the auspices of the United States Government or even state and territorial governments, such pieces did find a ready acceptance with miners and merchants alike. To be sure, there were many abuses. For example, the Miners' Bank, active in San Francisco in 1849, issued ten-dollar gold pieces which contained gold heavily alloyed with copper, with the result that the gold or intrinsic value was substantially less than the $10 value marked on the coin. While this may have been profitable to the Miners' Bank for a short period of time, the public soon became aware of the discrepancy, and the firm went out of business in January, 1850. On the other hand, the issues of Moffat & Company, produced in San Francisco from 1849 through 1853, contained a high gold content and were readily accepted in the channels of commerce, and the firm prospered.

In 1830, Templeton Reid issued gold coins of the values of $2.50, $5, and $10. His private mint was located in Lumpkin County, Georgia, formerly a part of the territory of the Cherokee Indian Nation. Simple in their designs, Reid's gold pieces bear the inscription 1830 GEORGIA GOLD on one side and, on the other side, TEMPLETON REID ASSAYER and the denomination.

Very little is known about Templeton Reid or his operation. Apparently he assayed and refined gold and then minted gold coins from the resultant metal, probably with the assistance of a small staff. While all pieces are dated 1830, the business may well have continued for several years after that time. In 1849, Templeton Reid produced ten- and twenty-five-dollar gold pieces (the latter a unique denomination among territorial gold coins) bearing the imprint CALIFORNIA. It is presumed that Templeton Reid, learning of the California gold discoveries, relocated his business there. However, little documentation exists as to Reid's California operations, and only two specimens of his California gold coins are known to numismatists: a solitary example of the 1849 ten-dollar issue presently located in the Smithsonian and the 1849 twenty-five-dollar issue formerly on display at the United States Mint, but stolen from that exhibit in 1858 and not yet located.

Templeton Reid's Georgia pieces, while rare, are occasionally seen on the market. Every several years a specimen will appear. Choice examples are valued at over $10,000 each, and much more in certain instances.

During the early 19th century, America's most important native gold source was Rutherford County in North Carolina. Sometime around 1830 a German family skilled in the jewelry and metallurgy trade emigrated to Rutherfordton. Christopher Bechtler, Sr., his son August, and his nephew Christopher, Jr., soon established minting facilities. Don Taxay, who has done extensive research in this field, has written that by 1831 the Bechtlers had assembled or constructed the necessary minting equipment and were

1
ONE
CAROLINA GOLD
28G.
2
A. BECHTLER
5
DOLLARS
CAROLINA GOLD
134.G:
21
CARATS
3
C. BECHTLER
5
DOLLARS
CAROLINA GOLD
140
G.
20
CARATS
4
CALIFORNIA GOLD
WITHOUT ALLOY
FULL WEIGHT OF
N.G.&N.
1849
SAN FRANCISCO
HALF EAGLE
5
UNITED STATES OF AMERICA
TEN DOLS.
6
UNITED STATES OF AMERICA
TWENTY DOLS.
7
UNITED STATES OF AMERICA
1851
CALIFORNIA

TERRITORIAL GOLD COINS. United States territorial gold coins, sometimes called "pioneer" gold issues, were not struck by regular United States mints. This field encompasses pieces issued mainly in the various regions where important gold discoveries were made—Georgia, Carolina, and Colorado. Several dozen varieties are known to numismatists. Almost without exception, territorial gold coins are scarce; many are extreme rarities. Representative issues shown are: (1) Gold dollar struck during the 1830's by Christopher Bechtler at Rutherfordton, North Carolina. (2) Five-dollar gold piece issued by A. Bechtler in Rutherfordton during the 1830's. (3) Five-dollar gold piece issued by Christopher Bechtler after 1834 and of reduced weight in comparison to the pre-1834 issues. (4) An early (1849) California five-dollar gold piece issued by Norris, Grieg & Norris, believed to have been struck in Benicia City, though it bears the San Francisco designation. (5) 1852 ten-dollar gold piece issued by Augustus Humbert, United States Assayer of Gold, California. (6) 1852 twenty-dollar gold piece issued by Augustus Humbert. (7) A choice example of the famed fifty-dollar octagonal gold "slug"—this one issued by Augustus Humbert. These massive gold pieces are eagerly sought after by collectors, representing as they do the ultimate gold denomination from the Gold Rush era. (8) 1854 twenty-dollar gold piece issued by Kellogg & Company of San Francisco. (9) 1849 two-and-a-half-dollar gold piece issued by the Mormons in the State of Deseret (now Utah). (10) 1860 Mormon five-dollar gold piece. (11) 1849 five-dollar gold piece issued in Oregon Territory. (12) 1860 ten-dollar gold piece issued by Clark, Gruber & Company of Denver.

ready to begin operations. To secure public confidence in the Bechtler coins, great publicity was given to them. From 1831 until 1852, the Bechtler family produced a wide variety of private gold coins. Denominations were $1, $2.50, and $5. Extending for more than two decades, the Bechtler coinage encompassed a larger span that did the production of any other private minting facility producing gold coins.

Over the years the weights and purity of these coins varied. When the price of gold increased sharply around 1834, the weights of Bechtler coins were diminished. Production was made not only from gold found in Rutherford County but from gold found in nearby Georgia as well. Hence, certain Bechtler issues bear the designation GEORGIA GOLD and others CAROLINA GOLD. Still others are identified as NORTH CAROLINA GOLD.

As the Bechtler enterprise became established, the gold content of its coins was lowered slightly. Today the earlier issues, which contained a high gold content and which were thus melted down in large quantities, are rare. Later issues, while scarce, are readily obtainable on the numismatic market. In fact, certain pieces are available in the range of several hundred dollars per coin, a relatively low price for a territorial gold issue.

Of all gold rushes in history none is more famous than the California Gold Rush. Although small alluvial deposits of gold had been discovered in Southern California years earlier, it was the finding of gold at Sutter's Mill on the American River in 1848 that captured the imagination of millions of people all over the world. California, earlier consisting primarily of quiet Mexican settlements, suddenly burst into worldwide prominence. Gold had been found, and a fortune awaited anyone traveling to El Dorado, so the legend went.

The exact circumstances surrounding the discovery of gold at Sutter's Mill probably will never be known, for when the stories were first recorded there were several versions as many people sought to establish their own fame and credit. Hubert Howe Bancroft, an early California historian whose writings are more comprehensive and detailed than any of his contemporaries, described the discovery in detail. Most of the following information was obtained from Bancroft's commentary, published as part of his *History of California* in 1888.

In the 1840's John Sutter, a Swiss, had a vast agricultural empire known as New Helvetia (New Switzerland) centered at the site of present-day Sacramento. In August, 1847, Sutter made an agreement with John Marshall whereby Marshall would become a partner in a sawmill to be located on a site at Columa (now called Coloma) on the banks of the

American River. By New Year's Day, 1848, the main frame of Sutter's Mill had been erected.

Early in the morning of Monday, the 24th of January, 1848, while inspecting the work, John Marshall noticed yellow particles mingled with the excavated earth. The thought occurred to him that they might possibly be gold. Sending an Indian to his cabin for a tin plate, he washed out some of the dirt, separating out some of the golden particles. He believed he had found a gold mine. His statement was laughed at. The next morning Marshall again walked down by the race. A bright glitter from beneath the water caught his eye. Bending down, he picked from its lodgement against a projection of soft granite a larger piece of the yellow substance than any he had seen previously. He turned it over, weighed it in his hand, bit it, and then hammered it between two stones. It must be gold!

Marshall reacted rather calmly. He went to his companions and showed the gold to them. Together they collected some three ounces. Two days later he mounted his horse and rode to Sutter's Fort to announce the discovery. Late in the afternoon of Jan. 28, Marshall showed Sutter his find. Sutter examined the stuff attentively and finally agreed it looked like gold. Together they performed various tests known to identify the precious metal. The substance was definitely gold.

Sutter regarded the discovery of gold as a misfortune. He envisioned that all industry and agriculture at New Helvetia would stop and that a gold panic would ensue. Accordingly, everyone who knew of the discovery was sworn to secrecy. Secrecy did not last long, however, and soon word of the treasure spread. The California Gold Rush had begun.

Gold came pouring into San Francisco, Sacramento, and other northern California towns. Ideally, gold producers wanted to have their metal refined and paid for with United States gold and silver coins which could then be spent in the regular channels of commerce. However, the official United States mints at New Orleans, Dahlonega, Charlotte, and especially at Philadelphia were thousands of miles and several months' travel away. Few United States coins were in circulation in California.

In July, 1848, enterprising San Franciscans requested the right to privately mint coins. Col. R. B. Mason, the military governor of California, agreed at first, and then upon considering the legalities of the matter (California was about to become a state, and the minting of private coins might present complications), countermanded his earlier permission. For a number of months commerce was conducted using the few United States coins then in circulation, imported foreign coins from many lands (which often had to be purchased at a high premium in gold dust, a fact which some miners resented), and the native gold itself. The situation soon became untenable, and despite the lack of legality several firms began issuing their own coins.

The very first issues produced in California are believed to be 1849 five-dollar gold pieces made by the firm of Norris, Grieg & Norris. The company issued pieces bearing the imprint of San Francisco and Stockton. However, it is believed that most of the early pieces were actually struck in Benicia City, at one time the capital of California. Laid out with care, Benicia City was planned to become the premier metropolis in the northern part of the Golden State. However, San Francisco's more favorable location and excellent harbor changed all that, and Benicia City remained a hamlet.

In August, 1849, Moffat & Company commenced issuing coins. The enterprise was formed by John L. Moffat, an assayer from New York who, with his partners Curtis, Perry, and Ward, first produced small bars or ingots of gold. Over the next several years bars or ingots were issued by many banks. Often differing in value from ingot to ingot and not being as familiar in shape or format as coins, such ingots did not meet with ready use in everyday circulation. Also, ingots were of generally higher values. During 1849 and 1850, Moffat & Company produced a large quantity of five- and ten-dollar gold pieces. These had a intrinsic value of $9.98, according to assays later performed on them at the Philadelphia Mint.

Agitation for the establishment of a regular United States Mint at San Francisco continued. However, little sympathy was forthcoming from Congress. Finally in September, 1850, Congress passed a measure to alleviate the critical problem of the valuation of gold dust and the varying charges levied by different banking houses to assay, refine, and convert gold into bars. The United States Assay Office of Gold was conceived. It was directed that the United States Assayer, a position to which Augustus Humbert, a maker of watch cases from New York, was subsequently appointed, should work in conjunction with an already established assayer presently conducting business successfully in California. Moffat & Company solicited the right to operate the United States Assay Office of Gold.

The new Assay Office opened for business on Jan. 29, 1851 under a joint arrangement between Augustus Humbert, acting on behalf of the United States Government, and Moffat & Company. By the next month the firm was producing coins in large quantities, including massive fifty-dollar gold pieces of octagonal shape which were familiarly called "slugs."

This nomenclature was said to have been derived from the fact that several of these awesome coins, if wrapped together in a handkerchief, made a formidable weapon for "slugging" someone.

These large and impressive pieces were issued in tremendous quantities and were an ideal medium of exchange in large transactions. Prices were often very high in San Francisco and in the gold fields; even with present-day (1974) inflation, prices would have to advance considerably to catch up with those being charged then for such staple items as food and clothing. It was a case of much demand and little supply. Few who came to the gold fields thought of bringing food and provisions with them; they were interested in taking gold from the earth in large quantities. Some of the most attractive profits were made by merchants and trading companies who supplied the miners' needs.

The Assay Office also produced pieces of $10 and $20 values. The opening of this enterprise was resented by most San Francisco banks, assayers, and gold traders, many of whom were reaping windfall profits by charging high rates to assay and refine gold. Their business dwindled, as did the business of several other firms engaged in private minting of coins.

The United States Assay Office of Gold closed its doors in December, 1853, in anticipation of the opening of the new official minting facility, the San Francisco Mint. The San Francisco Mint began producing silver and gold coins in 1854, although only in limited numbers due to the difficulties of starting up operations and of securing the necessary equipment and materials. Thus there was still room for private gold coinage in California for another year or two.

The impressive octagonal fifty-dollar pieces of the United States Assay Office of Gold are among the most desired and most romantic of all American issues. Many varieties exist, all of which are scarce and some of which are quite rare.

While the Moffat–Assay Office of Gold enterprise was the largest, a number of other firms competed for miners' gold, particularly in the early years. In 1849, J. S. Ormsby & Company produced five- and ten-dollar gold coins in Sacramento. Miners and others exchanging gold dust for coins were charged a 20 percent premium. In addition to this service charge, a profit was realized by issuing ten-dollar gold pieces which contained only $9.37 worth of gold. Perhaps the large volume of business done by the firm was possible because the company's location in Sacramento placed it closer to the gold fields than was San Francisco. Only a few Ormsby pieces are known to exist today.

Pacific Company, which operated in San Francisco in 1849, was supervised or operated by the firm of Broderick & Kohler. Seeking windfall profits, the firm produced ten-dollar gold pieces containing only $7.86 worth of gold, and five-dollar gold pieces of proportionately low value. The firm met with a poor reception, and apparently its coinage ceased shortly after it had begun. All issues are very rare today.

Frederick D. Kohler, who had been associated with the firm, was appointed the official California State Assayer in 1850. This office, established the year before Congress set up the United States Assay Office of Gold, was California's effort at ending the abuses in the gold refining industry. Kohler operated in this capacity until the California State legislature, learning of the intent to open the Assay Office, discontinued the State Assayer post. During 1850 and early 1851, Frederick D. Kohler issued gold bars or ingots. Each bar bore his name and title together with the purity of the gold in the bar, its weight, and current value. As such ingots were made by pouring gold into molds, each varied slightly in weight and value. Known specimens bear imprints stating them to be worth $36.55, $37.31, $40.07, $41.68, $45.34, $50.00, and $54.09. Undoubtedly, the thousands of bars issued included many other odd values, there apparently being no control standard. Larger ingots valued up to about $150 were produced at one time. No such large pieces are known today.

In 1849, Theodore Dubosq, Sr., Theodore Dubosq, Jr., and Henry Dubosq established Dubosq & Company. The trio, formerly in the jewelry trade, may have had their dies prepared in Philadelphia by James B. Longacre, then engraver at the Mint (this information is from the research of Don Taxay). In 1850, when the Dubosq firm was in full activity in San Francisco, ten-dollar gold pieces of two varieties were struck, apparently in fairly large numbers. These pieces were of excellent weight and value, being of full $10 gold value or even slightly higher; the firm's profits were made by a service charge. However, such pieces are extremely rare today, and only infrequently do pieces appear on the coin market.

In 1850 and 1851, Baldwin & Company, a San Francisco jewelry manufacturer that purchased the machinery and equipment formerly owned by Broderick & Kohler, produced five-, ten-, and twenty-dollar gold pieces in large quantities—more than $500,000 worth in the first three months of 1851 alone.

In the same year Dunbar & Company and Schultz & Company, both firms located in San Francisco, each issued five-dollar gold pieces, examples of which are very rare today.

A fairly late arrival on the gold coinage scene in San Francisco was Wass, Molitor & Company, a firm owned by two Hungarians, Count S. C. Wass and A. P. Molitor. Contemporary accounts praise the firm for its expertise and precision in refining. Adding to the appeal of the firm was its service of assaying gold dust and returning coins to the depositor within 48 hours, one-fourth the time taken by the United States Assay Office during the same period. In addition, coins produced under company's imprint were of excellent gold value, slightly higher than the United States federal standard, in fact. Five- and ten-dollar gold pieces dated 1852 were produced in large quantities. In 1855, ten- and twenty-dollar gold pieces were issued. Perhaps the most famous of all Wass, Molitor & Company pieces are the massive fifty-dollar 1855 gold coins. Round, as opposed to the octagonal shape of the Assey Office coins of the same denomination, these pieces featured on the obverse an attractive head of Liberty copied from the United States double eagle, and a reverse bearing a wreath and suitable inscriptions. These coins were produced in tremendous quantities. However, since few were saved by coin collectors at or near the time of issue, the survival of pieces was strictly a matter of chance, and today such pieces are rare.

Another latecomer was Kellogg & Company, which did an active business in San Francisco in 1854 and 1855. This firm produced large quantities of gold coins, mostly of the $20 denomination. Dies for a round-shape fifty-dollar gold piece dated 1855 were prepared, but most specimens known today are in Proof condition, indicating that most of the pieces were struck for presentation purposes or for sale or trade to collectors. Apparently few if any actually served as a circulating medium.

Several other firms also produced gold bars, ingots, and a few scattered coin issues (mostly patterns which never reached actual circulation). The idea of opening a private mint in California was an attractive one to Easterners, and various firms were incorporated with the idea of preparing dies, gathering equipment, and establishing facilities which then could be moved to San Francisco to set up a ready-made mint. Most such ideas died aborning; their surviving relics are a curious admixture of pattern coins telling "what might have been." Few of these companies ever actually set up business or, for that matter, ever reached San Francisco.

Rounding out the story of California coinage are pieces referred to as small denomination issues—coins issued mainly from about 1852 through 1882 by jewelers, silversmiths, and private mints. Made in round and octagonal shapes in the denominations of 25¢, 50¢, and $1, these are popular with collectors. Values are nominal, and many issues can be obtained in the range of $50 to $100 per coin. In recent decades, however, hundreds of thousands, if not millions, of copies of these coins have been made up to sell as souvenirs, so the authenticity of any piece should be verified before paying a premium price for it. I might mention that the same goes for any coin of high value. California and other territorial gold coins do not fall under the protection of Federal counterfeiting laws, so many copies have been made—some in prodigious quantities. For example, scarcely a week goes by at my office in which I do not receive a letter from someone who has an "1850 Baldwin & Company $10 gold piece" or, even more aggravating (for they were issued in larger quantities), an "1855 Blake & Company $20 gold piece." Copies of both of these issues have apparently been distributed by the hundreds of thousands.

John Murbach, a member of the Bowers and Ruddy Galleries staff, became so amused with the interesting stories which accompanied fake Baldwin and Blake pieces that he started keeping a list of them. These copies were made in the 1960's for the most part, and yet people have written to us such diverse tales as "my grandfather owned it for 60 years and then gave it to me," and "this coin has been in a safe deposit box for over 100 years!" A coin is either genuine or it isn't. A fake coin accompanied by all the words a present-day Shakespeare could muster would still not be a genuine coin. On the other hand, a genuine coin can stand alone without any "pedigree." Should you encounter a "California gold piece," the best way to make an initial determination of whether further research is warranted is to take it to a local druggist or chemist and determine whether the piece is actually struck in gold. This can be done by performing a simple specific gravity test.

In the Oregon Territory, the Oregon Exchange Company in Oregon City issued five- and ten-dollar gold pieces in 1849. Both denominations are rare, the $10 value being extremely so. Each has a beaver motif on the obverse.

The Mormon community, the State of Deseret, issued an extensive series of coins in what is now Utah from 1848 through 1860. Apparently the 1848 issues were patterns or were at least struck in limited quantities, for no specimens are known today. The earliest dated issues are those of 1849 in the denominations of $2.50, $5, $10, and $20. The standard design of that year bears clasped hands on one side and a bishop's mitre above an all-seeing eye on the other. The legend HOLINESS TO THE LORD appears as the inscription.

In 1850, Mormon five-dollar pieces of a slightly differing design were produced. Gold to strike these was obtained mainly from California. In

1860, a new Mormon design bearing a seated lion on the obverse and an eagle and beehive on the reverse made its appearance. Gold for this later issue was imported from Colorado.

The gold content of the Mormon pieces was severely debased, perhaps the lowest of any territorial issue. Thus, the pieces were held in low esteem outside of the Mormon settlement. Within Mormon country, however, they were readily accepted, and this led to coinage in large quantities by the Mormon church, which operated the mint.

Gold was discovered in quantity in 1859 in the Colorado Territory. This triggered a gold rush second only to the California Gold Rush. To Colorado, particularly to the mountains immediately west of Denver and Colorado Springs, went thousands of gold seekers. This activity continued well into the late 19th century as additional important strikes were made, the gold find in Cripple Creek in the early 1890's being an example.

Several private minting facilities were established. Foremost was the firm of Clark, Gruber & Company which minted coins in Denver bearing the dates 1860 and 1861. Best known are the ten- and twenty-dollar issues with a representation of Pikes Peak on the obverse and bearing the legend PIKES PEAK GOLD. Other issues in the values of $2.50, $5, $10, and $20 were of the Liberty head obverse and eagle reverse motif, somewhat similar to contemporary United States Mint issues. Clark, Gruber & Company was an honorable firm, and its coins were of excellent weight and value, even better than those produced by the United States Mint. In 1862, the firm sold its facilities to the United States Government for a branch mint. The Government subsequently operated an assay office, but the actual opening of a mint did not occur until many years later in 1906, by which time the height of the gold rush had passed.

In Georgia Gulch, Colorado, the firm of J. J. Conway & Company struck two-and-a-half-, five-, and ten-dollar gold pieces in 1861. Undated, the coins bear inscriptions and numerals and are of simple format, lacking central figures or designs. Apparently only a few such coins were issued, for specimens are exceedingly rare today.

Also scarce are the Colorado pieces issued in South Park at the Tarryall Mines by John Parsons & Company. The obverse of each piece bears the representation of a quartz stamping mill, a device by which gold is extracted from quartz rock. The reverse depicts an American eagle. Only a few specimens of the two-and-a-half- and five-dollar gold pieces minted by this firm exist today.

Territorial gold coins of all types are in great demand by collectors. Most are extremely rare, particularly in higher grades, for at the time of production they were made for everyday use, not for presentation to important officials or for sale to collectors. Adding to the appeal of these coins is their mystique. Often produced under primitive conditions and in the "Wild West" where few journalists were on hand to keep meticulous records or write interesting stories, the backgrounds of these pieces have been lost to history in many instances. Only the coins themselves survive as tangible reminders of what in California's instance has been termed "the days of old, the days of gold, the days of '49."

8

Coinage of the Confederate States of America

In 1861 the newly formed Confederate States of America, seeking to establish its status as a nation in its own right, attempted to produce its own coins. Paper money issues were also planned. Confederate paper money was subsequently issued in tremendous quantities—by the millions of notes. However, coins were a different story, and only two issues appeared, both in small numbers. The story of these is quite interesting.

Two coin denominations were produced with distinctive Confederate designs: the 1861 cent and the 1861 half dollar.

The story of the 1861 Confederate States of America cent began early in that year when the Confederacy contacted Bailey & Company, a well-known Philadelphia jeweler, about coining on a contractual basis a supply of one-cent pieces for the South. Bailey & Company agreed to do this, and arranged with Robert Lovett, Jr., a die-sinker of that city, to prepare the pieces. In 1860, a year earlier, Lovett had produced a one-cent-size business token with an attractive classic bust of Liberty on the obverse and with his own advertisement on the reverse. Bailey & Company thought that this beautiful design would be an ideal motif to adapt for use on the Confederate cent. Lovett thus used his Liberty head motif for the Confederate States of America obverse, surrounding it with the legend CONFEDERATE STATES OF AMERICA, and the date 1861 below. The reverse depicted a wreath of tobacco, cotton, and sugar cane—all products of the South—with a cotton bale below. On the bale he added his initial as a tiny L.

Lovett struck just twelve pieces in copper-nickel, the standard coinage metal of the time. United States one-cent pieces of the era were struck in copper-nickel, and the Confederacy planned to use the same standard. Following this small beginning Lovett became fearful that his contractual assignment would be viewed as illegal by the Union authorities, so he concealed the dies and the twelve coins in his cellar. Being quite proud, however, of his beautiful little Confederate cents, he carried two of them as pocket pieces. Sometime early in the 1870's he accidentally spent one of these in a tavern. The solitary 1861 Confederate cent, as chance would have it, found its way to Capt. J. W. Haseltine, a Philadelphia coin dealer and renowned numismatic researcher. (It was Haseltine who produced a series of pioneering listings of American silver coins by die varieties, for example.) Haseltine, familiar with the Liberty design from its use on Lovett's 1860 trade token and other Lovett tokens, immediately recognized who made it. He subsequently made several visits to Lovett in an effort to learn the true story of the Confederate cent. Numismatists had not known or suspected that such a thing as a Confederate cent existed or, for that matter, was ever made.

Lovett, still concerned with the legality of his work, remained silent. However, one day Lovett had a change of heart and pulled out one of his cabinet drawers for Haseltine. There all in a tidy row were the ten remaining original 1861 Confederate cents! Lovett then told the story of the origin of the Confederate States of America pieces. He sold Haseltine the ten coins and the dies used to strike them.

Realizing the sensation that knowledge of the existence of a genuine Confederate cent would have for numismatists, and further realizing that the tiny supply of ten original pieces would hardly suffice to fill the demand, Haseltine enlisted the help of J. Colvin Randall and Peter L. Krider, both also of Philadelphia, in producing restrikes from the original dies. They were careful not to produce any restrikes in the original copper-nickel metal, thus preserving the integrity of the twelve original pieces struck in 1861 by Lovett. The story of the restriking is quite interesting and was told in an advertisement used to sell the coins:

PHILADELPHIA, April 2, 1874

Having succeeded in discovering and purchasing the dies of the Confederate Cent, we, the undersigned, have concluded to strike for the benefit of collectors a limited number, and in order to protect those gentlemen who had the [copper-nickel] pieces, originally struck in 1861, we determined to strike *none* in that metal. Our intention was to strike five hundred in copper, but after the fifty-fifth impression the collar burst and the dies were badly broken. They are now in the possession of Mr. Haseltine, and may be seen at any time at his store, No. 1343 Chestnut St., Philadelphia.

The history of this piece is probably known to most collectors (having been written up extensively in the numismatic press after Capt. Haseltine's discovery), but for the information of those who are ignorant of the facts, we will state that the dies were made by Mr. Lovett, of Philadelphia, in 1861, who says that they were ordered in that year by the South, and that he struck but twelve pieces, but probably thinking that he might have some difficulty in reference to them (having made the dies for the South), he mentioned the matter to no one until a few months since, when he parted with ten pieces, struck in [copper-nickel] which he stated were all he had, having lost two pieces. One of the said lost two pieces was the means of the dies and pieces being traced. Although the Confederacy did not adopt this piece, it will always be considered interesting as the only coinage designed for the said Confederacy. . . .

CONFEDERATE STATES OF AMERICA COINS. Two coin designs were produced by the Confederate States of America. On a contractual basis Robert Lovett, Jr., a Philadelphia diesinker, produced 12 specimens of the 1861 CSA cent. At the United States Mint in New Orleans four original specimens of the 1861 Confederate half dollar were struck. In later years restrikes were made of both issues. (1) One of the 12 original 1861 Confederate cents struck in copper-nickel. (2) Restrike of the 1861 Confederate States of America half dollar, using the original Confederate States of America reverse die which bears a distinctive design.

The notice went on to say that seven restrikes were made in gold, twelve in silver, and finally 55 in copper, and that by April 1, 1874, six of the ten original 1861 Confederate States of America copper-nickel cents had been sold. In the years since, the originals have become widely dispersed. Only rarely does one come on the market, a recent example being the specimen sold for nearly $15,000 by Bowers and Ruddy Galleries in 1974.

The story of the 1861 Confederate States of America cent goes one step further. The original dies, broken and defaced, were acquired in the early 1960's by Robert Bashlow, a New York coin dealer. Using these dies as masters, the innovative Mr. Bashlow produced thousands of copies of Confederate cents in a wide variety of metals. These were widely advertised in the numismatic press and achieved great distribution among collectors. Technically speaking, they are not restrikes, for they were not made directly from the original dies. But they did serve to make possible the ownership of an 1861 Confederate cent in a related form, albeit with the surface displaying die cracks and other defects.

The Confederate half dollar had a similar history. Following the demise of the Confederacy in 1865, it was thought by collectors that no Confederate coins were made. This omission was more than made up for by the countless worthless Confederate notes in circulation. Early in 1879, Dr. B. F. Taylor, associated with the Louisiana State Board of Health, made it known to numistatists that he possessed a very unusual item: a Confederate half dollar of distinctive design. In his 1929 book, *A Register of Half Dollar Die Varieties*, M. L. Beistle relates that in April, 1879, after some lengthy correspondence, Dr. Taylor sent his Confederate half dollar, together with the original reverse die, to Mr. E. B. Mason, Jr., a Philadelphia coin dealer, with instructions to inform the public of the existence of this coin.

It was Dr. Taylor's wish that the coin would eventually become the property of an important historical or numismatic association. This eventually came true, although not through any generosity on Dr. Taylor's part, when the coin was subsequently purchased by J. Sanford Saltus and presented to the American Numismatic Society, in whose New York City museum it is now an important treasure.

Through correspondence with officials once connected with the Confederacy the history of the 1861 half dollar was pieced together. In February, 1861, the New Orleans Mint was turned over by the State of Louisiana to the Confederate States of America. The Confederacy operated the Mint for a time and used regular United States dies (without any mark or design of the Confederacy) to produce additional coins, mainly 1861-O half dollars. The Confederacy also operated the Dahlonega (Georgia) Mint following its seizure in 1861.

In April of the same year, Mr. Memminger, Secretary of the Treasury of the Confederacy, requested that designs for a distinctive C.S.A. half dollar be prepared and submitted to him for approval. Several were subsequently sent. The approved issue bore an obverse identical to that currently being used by the United States of America: the seated figure of Liberty surrounded by thirteen stars and with the 1861 date below. The reverse was a distinctive design featuring at the center a shield with seven stars above, representing the seceding states. Above the shield was a Liberty cap on a short pole. To either side were stalks of sugar cane and cotton, products of the South. Surrounding was the legend CONFEDERATE

STATES OF AMERICA with HALF DOL. below. The dies were engraved by A. H. M. Patterson, a New Orleans engraver and die-sinker.

Dr. B. F. Taylor, who had been the Chief Coiner of the Confederate States of America, stated that in addition to his own coin three others were struck. Interestingly enough, one of these specimens, long lost to numismatics, came to light about ten years ago when John J. Ford, Jr., purchased one offered for sale as a restrike. He was delighted to find that the piece was indeed an original, as evidenced by its weight and the appearance of its surface, and was one of the greatest finds of recent times.

Following Dr. Taylor's revelation of the existence of his 1861 Confederate States of America half dollar and the original reverse die, the pieces were acquired by J. W. Scott, a prominent New York city coin dealer. Mr. Scott was one of the most active dealers in the late 19th century. Ever an entrepreneur, he had two exhibits at the Columbian Exposition in 1893 from which he sold coins, souvenirs, and novelties to the public. Thus Mr. Scott was perhaps the ideal distributor for restrikes of the Confederate half dollar.

In 1923, M. L. Beistle wrote to David Proskey, a former employee of the Scott firm, and received the following reply concerning the history of the Confederate restrikes:

J. W. Scott bought the die of the reverse of the Confederate half dollar, together with the Proof specimen of the only known Confederate half dollar, at that time, from E. B. Mason, Jr., of Philadelphia (a worn specimen of the 1861 CSA half dollar having since been found). The U.S. government had seized the obverse die as their property since 1861 and could have seized both sides, as at the close of the war in 1865 the U.S. government became the heir of the Confederacy.

Scott decided to strike impressions from his die and he sent out circulars offering silver restrikes at $2 each, agreeing to have only 500 pieces struck. Preparing for this issue, Scott purchased 500 U.S. half dollars of New Orleans mintage [these would have been regular 1861-O half dollars.—Ed.] and had the reverses drilled off. Then for fear the die would break, a steel collar was affixed, and 500 impressions in white metal were struck in order to be able to supply something should the die go to pieces, but the die held intact even after the silver pieces were struck. Each of the latter obverses (of the Liberty seated design) was placed on a blank of soft brass and then struck on a screw press. This helped to keep the obverse from flattening. [The earlier-mentioned white metal pieces were not restrikes but were simply tokens with the Confederate design on one side and an advertisement for Scott on the other.—Ed.]

The writer supervised the process, so that the workers kept no specimens for souvenirs. The die was then softened and cut across, so no more could be struck from a perfect die. The die now reposes in the collection of the Louisiana Historical Society, the gift of Mr. J. Sanford Saltus. A couple of brass impressions exist showing the ridge across. These are now in the collection of Mr. Elliott Smith, New York City.

When all were struck Scott sent out circulars with the coins to the subscribers, offering to pay 50¢ each over the subscription price for the return of any of the pieces, stating as a reason "oversubscription," which was untrue. It is doubtful if over 250 were sold, as Scott had a plentiful supply of them for over 30 years thereafter. He gradually raised the price to $15 each. The original Proof half dollar was several times placed in various auction sales, but always "bought in." Finally the writer sold it to Mr. J. Sanford Saltus for $3,000, who presented it to the American Numismatic Society.

The original circular sent to Scott's subscribers, estimated to be no more than 250 by David Proskey, noted that "the die (damaged only sufficiently to prevent restriking) is a very valuable and interesting relic and is now for sale. Price: $50." The promotion referred to by Proskey appears in the last paragraph of the circular:

Up to October 10th we received orders for 567 pieces [of the 500 restruck]; the odd 67 subscribers have been supplied from a like number of patrons who ordered two copies. This, we concluded, would be the more equitable plan for all parties concerned. Amateurs who ordered two will please remember that by this plan they certainly get one, whereas if they had drawn for chances they might have been left without any. We have received quite a number of orders since the 10th, all of which we are unable to fill, unless some of our subscribers, who get two, will kindly return one for which we will be pleased to pay $2.50. Respectfully, Scott & Company.

Restrikes of the 1861 Confederate half dollar are seen occasionally on the numismatic market and now sell in the $500 to $1,000 range, depending upon condition and sharpness of striking. The restrikes all have the milling or reeding on the edge squashed flat (due to restraining the piece in a collar while striking it) and have the obverse slightly wavy or flattened in appearance. On the other hand, originals have perfect edge reeding and have perfect obverse characteristics, as would any normally struck coin.

9

Other United States Series—Coins, Tokens, Medals

Many diverse United States series have attracted the attention of collectors and investors. Coins of Hawaii, tokens issued by various merchants, medals, and others all have devotees.

Coins of Hawaii

Take, for example, Hawaiian coins. Hawaii, now a state in the Union, was once an independent country and issued its own coins, paper money, and stamps. These have always been popular with collectors.

The Kingdom of Hawaii issued one-cent pieces in 1847. They bore a likeness of Kamehameha III and were widely circulated throughout the island chain. Originally 100,000 pieces were coined, but, as of 1862, official reports noted that only 11,000 pieces remained in circulation, the others having been recalled by the government. These coins, the approximate size of a United States large cent of the same era, are scarce today. As often happens, many rumors have arisen over the years to explain their scarcity. One tale has it that island natives disliked the pieces and threw them into the sea. Another version is that a ship containing tens of thousands of pieces was lost in a storm. Such stories make romantic reading, but they seldom are the truth.

Except for this relatively small quantity of one-cent pieces, Hawaii was without a national coinage until the 1880's. Until then coins of other

COINAGE OF HAWAII. During the 19th century the Kingdom of Hawaii circulated its own coinage. In 1847 an issue of copper cents was struck by a firm in Massachusetts to the extent of 100,000 pieces. In 1881 several varieties of pattern nickels were produced. In 1883, ten-cent, twenty-five-cent, fifty-cent, and one-dollar pieces were produced in large quantities—to a total face value of $1,000,000—for circulation. In addition twelve-and-a-half-cent or eighth-dollar pieces were made in limited numbers for Proof sets.

(1) 1847 copper one-cent piece of Hawaii.

(2) Pattern 1881 nickel five-cent piece. Only a few were made, and these are very rare today. No five-cent pieces were ever made in quantity for circulation.

(3) 1883 dime.

(4) Extremely rare 1883 twelve-and-a-half-cent or eighth-dollar piece. Fewer than thirty examples were struck of this issue, all for Proof sets sold to collectors. No specimens were made for circulation.

(5) 1883 quarter.

(6) 1883 half dollar.

(7) 1883 silver dollar.

countries were in circulation, the majority of these pieces being American silver and gold issues.

In 1883, King David Kalakaua appointed Claus Spreckels, one of the famous sugar barons in Hawaii, to contract with the United States Government for an issue of coinage. The original instructions called for silver coins bearing Kalakaua's portrait to be issued in denominations of 12½¢, 25¢, 50¢, and $1. At the last minute, the ten-cent piece or dime was substituted for the 12½¢ value, thus creating a great rarity. While several hundred thousand pieces each of the dime, quarter, half dollar, and dollar were eventually struck by the San Francisco Mint in California, fewer than thirty examples of the 12½¢ value were made. These were included in 1883-dated Proof sets produced late in 1884.

The Kalakaua silver coins were immediately accepted by the Hawaiian populace, although there were outcries about the rather secret manner in which the Kingdom of Hawaii had acquired the pieces through Spreckels.

In all, 500,000 silver dollars, 750,000 half dollars, 500,000 quarters, and 250,000 dimes—a total issue of coins amounting in face value to $1,000,000—were issued. Today all but the quarters are considered scarce in higher grades, and Uncirculated pieces of all types command good premiums. For some reason, quarters in Uncirculated condition seem to have survived in fairly generous quantities compared to the other denominations.

Hawaiian silver coins continued in general criculation until Jan. 1, 1905, when they were demonetized and United States coins officially took their place. By 1937, more than $815,000 worth of the original coins had been melted.

Throughout this period the Hawaiian government had paper money in circulation, a currency issue backed by Hawaiian silver as well as United States coins. An interesting fact is that these "certificates of deposit" were *fully backed* by silver at the Hawaiian Treasury. For every paper dollar outstanding, there was one dollar in silver representing it at the Treasury. Thus Hawaii was one of the few countries in the world ever to fully protect its currency (something other governments unwisely deemed not necessary).

All told, five types of currency were issued during Kalakaua's reign (1874–1891), these being $10, $20, $50, $100, and $500 denominations. Only 200 of the $500 bills were printed and issued. Due to their high value, they were soon found to be of little everyday use in the Hawaiian economic structure and all $500 notes were subsequently redeemed for silver and destroyed. Only a single pair of one-sided front and back Proof printings of the $500 bill remains in existence today to illustrate the highest denomination ever produced by this island kingdom. This unique pair is in the California collection of John Murbach.

The later Republic of Hawaii issued notes in various denominations between 1880 and 1899. According to official records, only eighty-nine pieces of Hawaiian currency remain outstanding and uncancelled; all others were redeemed. Of these eighty-nine notes, fewer than twenty-five are known to numismatists today!

While obtaining a complete set of Hawaiian coins and currency is an impossibility, the collector does have the opportunity to acquire various coin issues—and if he is lucky, perhaps a piece of currency or two. Then the numismatic treasures can be displayed as samples of money from the only state in the Union ever to have been a kingdom.

Tokens

Tokens have captured the interest of thousands of numismatists. Generally speaking, tokens are small coins, usually round in shape and often used in commerce, but lacking an official value assigned by the government. Such pieces were issued for many purposes: to aid in political campaigns, to advertise a merchant's wares, to serve as an admission check or ticket, and so on. Streetcar tokens, once in plentiful use throughout

America, fit into this category as do tiny tokens issued in 1864 to support the presidential election campaign of Abraham Lincoln, to cite two examples.

Years ago a group of enthusiasts banded together to form the Token and Medal Society (TAMS), which currently is the largest collectors' organization within this specialty. A periodic magazine offers for sale and trade many diverse items, not to mention research articles on various aspects of coinage history.

One of the earliest tradesman's tokens (sometimes called "store cards") issued in America was that of William and John Mott, manufacturers, dealers, and importers in the trade of clocks, jewelry, and related items. These tokens, issued in 1789, are highly prized today, and a particularly outstanding example might well bring several hundred dollars. At the opposite end of the spectrum are thousands of tokens still being produced today for use in coin-operated laundry machines, as prizes in slot machines (in areas where gambling is permitted), and so on. Many tokens collectors (and I am numbered among these) have had small tokens made for use as business cards.

Two important major categories of early United States tokens are Hard Times tokens and Civil War tokens. During the period from about 1833 through 1844 there were hard economic times in America, especially during the Panic of 1837. Also there were many political vicissitudes, one of the most prominent being President Jackson's continuing war with the United States Bank. In circulation appeared thousands of tokens, most of which were the size of contemporary United States one-cent pieces. Many of these pertained to President Jackson—a token of Jackson holding a sword in one hand and a bag of money in the other and standing within a treasure chest, surrounded by the words I TAKE THE RESPONSIBILITY, being an example. Others were issued by merchants. For example, T. D. Seaman, a butcher in Belleville, New Jersey, issued a token advertising his services as did J. Cochran, a manufacturer of bells in Batavia, New York. There are dozens and dozens of other examples.

Around the turn of the century, Lyman H. Low, a coin dealer, issued a catalog and check list enumerating varieties of the 1833–1844 Hard Times tokens. This still serves as a guide for collectors. One interesting thing about Hard Times tokens is that great rarities, pieces which are unique or nearly so and which may have immense historical significance, can be purchased for small sums in comparison to what certain other rare coins sell for. Ten or fifteen years ago my friend Don Miller, a prominent attorney, told me he had just purchased for $200 a coin which he

HARD TIMES TOKENS. From 1833 through 1844 many privately issued tokens, mostly the size of the contemporary American large cent, were issued. Today these are called Hard Times tokens, for economic conditions were uncertain during this period, particularly following the Panic of 1837.

Hard Times tokens divide themselves into two major categories: those issued by private individuals to advertise a business and those issued for political reasons. The pieces issued by Walsh's General Store in Lansingburgh, New York; by John J. Adams of Taunton, Massachusetts, by W. A. Handy of Providence, Rhode Island, and by Robinson, Jones & Company are examples of the former category. Pieces referring to Van Buren, Webster, and to the slave trade (the "Am I not a woman & a sister" token) are examples of pieces with political messages.

Today Hard Times tokens are very popular with collectors. Many varieties can be obtained for just a few dollars each.

had spent more than ten years searching for, always prepared to pay "any price" to get it if he had to. More recently, Ray Byrne, a devoted collector of tokens who has settled upon these as his main interest after having collected many other series, found after many years of searching a rare token issued in New Orleans in 1834 by the obscure firm of Peuch, Bein & Co., importers of hardware, guns, pistols, and cutlery. So intense was Byrne's search for this that he placed advertisements for it in numismatic publications over a long period of time. So proud was he of his success—and justifiably so—that he brought the coin to the 1973 American Numismatic Association convention and put it on display so that other collectors could share his treasure. And yet the value of this coin, considerable to a token collector, was but a fraction of what many regular United States coins which are just moderately rare sell for.

Often the story behind a Hard Times token can be fascinating. As such stories embody, at least for me, the essence of what numismatics is all about, let me give some examples from Lyman H. Low's research published in 1900.

A token published by Low as No. 99 in his list (Low assigned a number to each variety) features on the obverse the legend WALSH'S GENERAL STORE/LANSINGBURGH N.Y./1835. The reverse shows an agricultural plow surrounded by the inscription SPEED THE PLOUGH, IT FEEDS ALL. This particular token, the size of a United States large cent, currently retails for just a few dollars. And yet it has a really fascinating history. Low relates:

> Alexander Walsh was one of the most prominent merchants in Rensselaer County, New York, for more than 40 years. His store was widely known as "Walsh's Museum," from the extent and variety of his stock. His "plough penny," struck in 1835, circulated freely throughout all of Northern New York.
>
> Walsh participated in the ceremonies on the opening of the Erie Canal in 1825 by the invitation of Governor DeWitt Clinton, whom he accompanied on the first boat, and received with the other guests one of the silver medals struck to commemorate the event. In 1839 he entertained Henry Clay at his home in Lansingburgh. He retired from business in 1846, and died August 4, 1849. He was greatly interested in agricultural matters, and he was a frequent contributor to journals devoted to farming and horticulture. A letter written by him to the New York Horticultural Society, and published in the "American Mail," June 10, 1833, under the heading "Rural Cemeteries," led to the purchase and establishment of Greenwood Cemetery, Brooklyn, as is shown by the editorial remarks printed therewith.

The story above also refers to a silver medal issued to commemorate the opening of the Erie Canal. Is this another collectors' item? It certainly is! And the story of this medal is given in fuller detail in the section on medals a little later in this chapter.

One of the most prolific issues of tokens during the 1833–1844 Hard Times period was made by Dr. Lewis Feuchtwanger. Of the erstwhile doctor, Lyman H. Low relates:

FEUCHTWANGER COINS. Dr. Lewis Feuchtwanger, a merchant and metallurgist, produced many tokens during the 1837–1864 period. Made of Feuchtwanger's composition, the metal is gray in appearance and is similar to so-called German silver.

Dr. Lewis Feuchtwanger's first business location appears to have been at 377 Broadway, where he remained from 1831 to 1837. Thereafter, until 1857, his changes were numerous—and considering the limits of New York City within that period, he may be said to have roved widely. He is listed over the years at twelve different addresses in various directories, ranging from number One Wall Street to 21 White Street, three addresses of which are in Maiden Lane.

Feuchtwanger was the inventor of an alloyed metal resembling "German silver," which he hoped to induce the United States government to adopt for use in minor coinage. He was a druggist and chemist. In 1832 in addition to this business he also sold natural curiosities such as rare minerals, gems, preserved reptiles, and so on—a large collection of which he placed on exhibition at Peale's Museum and the New York Lyceum of Natural History.

At his Broadway store, advertised as being "one door below White Street," he advertised "Nurembergh Salve" and "Kreosote, a recent German discovery for preventing toothache." These nostrums seem to have been highly esteemed in their time.

From the token collector's viewpoint, Feuchtwanger is forever memorialized by the thousands of tiny "Feuchtwanger cents" issued in 1837. These pieces bear a defiant eagle killing a snake on the obverse, with the date 1837 below. The reverse reads FEUCHTWANGER'S COMPOSITION, and then within a wreath, ONE CENT. In addition, a limited number of the three-cent pieces were made. The one-cent pieces were made in vast quantities, and today attractive specimens can be obtained in the range of $10 to $30 each.

CIVIL WAR TOKENS. During the Civil War there was a great shortage of coins in circulation, particularly during the years 1862 and 1863 when the outcome was quite uncertain. To fill the need for circulating pieces many thousands of privately issued tokens appeared. Some bore political messages, others commercial advertisements. Most pieces were of the size of the diameter of the contemporary American Indian cent, but there were exceptions.

More than 10,000 die varieties of Civil War tokens have been identified by collectors. Many are quite common and can be obtained for just a few dollars apiece.

Civil War tokens are another major collecting interest within this field. The *Guide Book of U.S. Coins* estimates that during the years from 1860 through 1864 more than 50,000,000 pieces were issued. Numismatic researchers—Dr. George Fuld and his father, Melvin H. Fuld, prominent among them—have identified nearly 10,000 die varieties, some extremely rare and others very common. Most specimens were struck in bronze with the date 1863.

Civil War tokens are divided into two general categories: store cards, which are pieces issued advertising specific businesses or professions, and political pieces, which bear sentiments of patriotism, peace, and so on. During the middle years of the Civil War the outcome was in doubt. In fact, at one time on the world currency exchanges Confederate paper money—later completely worthless—was valued higher than was paper money of the Union! Because of fluctuating rates for paper money the public hoarded all types of "hard money"—including copper, silver, and gold coins. To fill the need for small pieces in circulation thousands of merchants and other individuals produced what we now know as Civil War tokens.

There are many fascinating varieties among Civil War tokens. One variety bears a flag motif and has the inscription IF ANYONE ATTEMPTS TO TEAR IT DOWN SHOOT HIM ON THE SPOOT. Another misspelling resulted in the legend THE UNION MUST AND SHALL BY PRESERVED.

Other issues bear the legend ONE CENT on the reverse with a tiny NOT above it just to keep everything legal, for the pieces had no official currency status so far as the government was concerned. Others had such sentiments as THE HORRORS OF WAR, THE BLESSINGS OF PEACE, and MILLIONS FOR CONTRACTORS, NOT ONE CENT FOR WIDOWS.

So vast is the field of Civil War tokens that no one can possibly hope to collect them all. Usually the numismatist specializes, preferring, for example, to collect only the issues of Wisconsin or perhaps Cincinnati, Ohio, or perhaps only tokens issued by taverns and saloons. The possibilities in this regard are almost endless. Best of all, the pieces are inexpensive. Several dollars each is the going rate for most, and even great rarities can be purchased for less than $10.

Outside of the fields of Hard Times tokens and Civil War tokens are many other specialties. Several years ago, seeking a numismatic diversion and a challenge, I endeavored to collect one each of as many different tokens—mostly the size of a nickel—once used to operate electric pianos (nickelodeons) and orchestrions, the automatic self-playing orchestras. At one time colorful nickelodeon pianos manufactured by the Rudolph Wurlitzer Company, the J. P. Seeburg Piano Company, and others were a familiar sight in taverns, hotels, amusement parks, and even red-light districts all over America. While such instruments usually were played by dropping a nickel or a dime in a beckoning coin slot, often the establishment housing such a machine would issue special tokens which could be used for this purpose. Some of these were given as prizes in slot machines or games of chance. Others were issued as advertisements.

I quickly learned that a small and inexpensive token can often have a really fascinating history. At a coin convention I purchased for $2 a small bronze token bearing the inscription ATLANTIC GARDEN/50 BOWERY/NEW YORK, 1863 on one side, and on the other GRAND CONCERT EVERY NIGHT/ADMISSION FREE. Research soon established that this token, actually a

INTERESTING AMERICAN TOKENS. Over the years many private businesses and individuals have issued tokens. The author has made a specialty of collecting such pieces which refer to automatic musical instruments—self-playing pianos, music boxes, and related items. Shown are representative pieces from the several hundred varieties known today. Most were produced during the late 19th and early 20th centuries.

The Atlantic Garden token offers a "grand concert" of music performed on a huge orchestrion or automatic self-playing orchestra. Made in Germany, this impressive instrument entertained several decades of visitors to the Atlantic Garden, a huge New York City beer hall. Another token reads "Good for 10¢ trade —drop in orchestrian" (*sic*) and was used around the turn of the century at the Cliff House in San Francisco. The huge orchestrion installed by Adolph Sutro was one of the many marvels in this famous seaside San Francisco resort. The Cliff House, built in the style of a French chateau, burned in 1907. Another token notes that "A fine orchestrion will perform every afternoon and evening" at the Territorial House located at 468 Pennsylvania Avenue, Washington, D.C. The Territorial House no longer stands, and the author has been unable thus far to learn any more about this intriguing instrument. The fact that many tokens keep their secrets well adds to their fascination and appeal! Also shown are several tokens of the type used in coin-operated pianos popular in saloons during the early 20th century.

William Kramer's Sons' Atlantic Garden, Bowery, N. Y. City
Largest Orchestrion ever built, taking the grand prize at the Chicago World's Fair

Craig-y-nos Castle.

I have much pleasure in saying how greatly I appreciate the marvelous Orchestrion you made for me, which has been the admiration of all the royal personages and celebrities who have listened to this perfection of mechanism and melody under my roof.

Adelina Patti-Nicolini.

H. M. THE SULTAN OF TURQUEY
Constantinople.
H. H. SULTAN OF DELI
Sumatra.
DAVID SALOMONS, BARONET
Broomhill, England,
BARON DE L'ESPEE
Paris.
Exc. TITO HEKEKYAN PASHA
Alexandria, Egypt.
ATLANTIC-GARDEN
New York
etc.

No. 9
Concert-Orchestrion

contains all the striking devices, Castanet, Carillon, two small drums.

Height 13 ft. 1 inches.
Width 11 ft. 1 inches.
Depth 5 ft. 3 inches.
Price, including 12 music rolls . . $ **7000.**—
Extra music rolls, each . . $ **20.**—

common variety, was issued by the Atlantic Garden, a hotel and restaurant located at 50–54 Bowery near Canal Street in New York. Although dated 1863, these tokens were issued over a long period of time, possibly until the turn of the century.

The "grand concert every night" was provided by an immense orchestrion featuring hundreds of pipes, drums, bells, and other effects. Built in Freiburg, Germany, by the firm of M. Welte & Sons, it was sold to the Atlantic Garden in the 1860's. The instrument played concerts automatically by means of tunes programmed on large pinned cylinders, much as a Swiss music box of gigantic proportions. For many years the Atlantic Garden advertised the instrument as "the world's largest orchestrion." Thousands of patrons came to see and hear it, and to consume what probably amounted to millions of gallons of beer, for existing photographs reveal the establishment as a gigantic beer hall or pleasure garden draped with flags, patriotic bunting, and other decorations.

In 1893, the firm of M. Welte & Sons exhibited an improved model of their orchestrion at the World's Columbian Exposition in Chicago. Following its appearance there, this huge instrument was sold to the Atlantic Garden to replace the earlier Welte instrument which had been in service for several decades.

An 1897 advertisement noted that the Atlantic Garden was owned by William Kramer's sons and was "the grandest and most select family resort." Every day from ten in the morning until seven in the evening the "Mammoth Pneumatic Orchestrion" played a varied program typically consisting of marches, overtures, a waltz or two, and popular tunes. The later orchestrion (the one from the Columbian Exposition) featured music programmed on perforated paper rolls—much like a player piano but more sophisticated in concept.

Unquestionably the Atlantic Garden contributed to the happiness of untold thousands of people during the late 19th century, many of whom came to the Atlantic Garden with one of the little 1863-dated tokens in their hand. What happened to this glorious orchestrion? Around 1907 the Atlantic Garden, orchestrion and all, burned to the ground.

Still another favorite token in my collection, this one the size of a dime, recalls the elegance of San Francisco's old Cliff House. From shortly before the turn of the century until it was destroyed in a spectacular blaze in 1907, San Francisco's famous French-chateau-style Cliff House, located above Seal Rocks near the entrance to that city's harbor, was one of the area's foremost attractions. Built by Adolph Sutro, who earned his fortune in Nevada's Comstock Lode, the Cliff House and the adjacent Sutro Museum exhibited all sorts of interesting things, including a large orchestrion played by paper rolls. When a dime or a dime-size token was put in the slot of this marvelous device a symphony concert filled the air. The Cliff House in its heyday was one of the world's most famous resorts. Adolph Sutro was one of the West's most colorful individuals. What a romantic story my little dime-size Cliff House token could tell!

And yet not all tokens give up their stories so easily nor can much be learned about them. Perhaps because it is presently an enigma, a recently acquired token in my collection is quite fascinating. Some day the key to it will be found. Perhaps a photograph will turn up showing the establishment mentioned on the token or, better yet, a view of the interior showing what must have been a really magnificent automatic musical instrument.

The inscription on the token reads H. SCHWARZENBERG'S TERRITORIAL HOUSE/468 PENN. AVE. WASHINGTON D.C. On the other side of the token is the inscription A FINE ORCHESTRION WILL PERFORM EVERY AFTERNOON AND EVENING. When was the Territorial House built? Who was Mr. Schwarzenberg? What design and style of orchestrion was used? Was the place a hotel, a beer garden, or a sporting house? What happened to the building? What happened to the orchestrion? What happened to Mr. Schwarzenberg? Such are the questions which often lead to a fascinating story!

One specialty among tokens is the field of so-called "dollars." These are very large tokens, often the size of a silver dollar, but varying somewhat from variety to variety. The aforementioned Erie Canal medal is a rare example. Most issues are commoner. Particularly popular with collectors are issues produced by various expositions, and literally dozens of varieties can be collected from the World's Columbian Exposition of 1893, the Panama Pacific International Exposition of 1915, and other such events.

During the presidential campaigns of 1896 and 1900, many varieties of "Bryan money" were issued by proponents and opponents of perennial presidential candidate William Jennings Bryan. A key issue was that a Mint silver dollar of that era contained less than a full dollar's worth of metal. Accordingly, numerous specimens of Bryan money were made in very large form, containing, for example, 823 grains of coin silver in value the equivalent of a gold dollar rather than just 412.5 grains of coin silver as per the current Federal standards of silver dollars. These impressive silver pieces were struck by Tiffany, Gorham, Spaulding, and other well-known jewelry firms. Today specimens, while not extremely rare, are fairly elusive. Attractive examples of certain varieties can be obtained in the $100 range.

"BRYAN MONEY." During the presidential campaigns of 1896 and 1900 many variations of "Bryan money" were issued by proponents and opponents of William Jennings Bryan. A key issue of the day was that a Government silver dollar of that era contained less than a full dollar's worth of metal. Accordingly, numerous specimens of Bryan money were made in very large form, to show what a silver dollar would be like if it did contain full value. Many of these pieces also had a smaller circle as part of the design to indicate the size of the actual dollar. Varieties from 1896 and 1900 are shown.

Medals

Medals have always been eagerly sought by collectors. While there is no precise definition of a medal, generally such pieces are circular in form, have designs or inscriptions on the obverse and reverse, and were issued, not to serve as currency for purposes of exchange, nor for issuance in quantity to advertise to the public, but, rather, for purposes of specifically observing or commemorating a person or event. Larger than a silver dollar, medals commemorating the opening of the Erie Canal were struck in pewter and silver. The interesting story of the Erie Canal medal is told by researchers Harold E. Hibler and Charles V. Kappen in their book *So-Called Dollars.*

The Erie Canal medal is dated 1826 (not 1825) and was issued by the Common Council of the City of New York. The piece was designed by Archibald Robinson and was engraved by Charles Cushing Wright, one of America's most prominent die-sinkers and engravers of bank notes. The striking was performed by Maltby Pedetreau.

Ground for the Erie Canal was broken on July 4, 1817, at Rome, New York. More than eight years and $7,000,000 later, the Erie Canal stretched 364 miles from the Hudson River to Lake Erie. The canal was formally opened on Oct. 26, 1825, by the vessel "Seneca Chief" carrying Gov. DeWitt Clinton together with other notables and luminaries, includ-

ERIE CANAL MEDAL. The Erie Canal, completed in 1825, linked Lake Erie with the Atlantic Ocean. In the following year, 1826, a special medal commemorating this event was produced. Specimens were struck in pewter and silver, the latter only in limited quantities.

ing our Lansingburgh "plough penny" friend, Alexander Walsh. The boat arrived in New York City on Nov. 4. Early in 1826 there was a huge celebration in New York City. "Several hundred" pewter medals and perhaps only a dozen or two silver ones were reported to have been presented to guests and officials. In the Bowers and Ruddy Galleries sale of the Stanislaw Herstal Collection in February, 1974, a pewter Erie Canal medal housed in its original presentation box fetched $500. Specimens in silver, the metal of which Mr. Walsh's example was struck, are valued at even more.

In recent years medals have been issued in large quantities and have been sold to the public by such firms as the Franklin Mint and the Medallic Art Company, some of which have billed these as "collectors' items of the future." Often modern medals depict a common theme and are issued in a long series on a subscription basis. Popular subjects include United States Presidents, historical events, prominent physicians, different states in the Union, and so on.

Medals have always been a very important part of numismatics. Indeed when the United States Mint Collection was formed in the 1850's and 1860's emphasis was placed upon medals rather than coins. Particularly in demand were medallic portraits of George Washington. Over the years the United States Mint has issued an illustrious series of medals, ranging from early issues commemorating peace treaties with various Indian tribes to modern issues observing presidential inaugurations and other events of importance. Many different medals, including restrikes of earlier issues, are available today from the Mint.

World's fairs and expositions usually provide the occasion for many medallic issues. During the late 19th and early 20th centuries, it was a common practice for various manufacturers of liquor, foodstuffs, musical instruments, printing presses, and just about everything else to exhibit their wares at expositions. A fee was charged for doing this, and thus a good income was derived by the exposition sponsors. Often all entrants, regardless of the merits of their products, were guaranteed a prize of one sort of another. Even today one can look at certain types of liquors, cocktail sauces, and so on and see representations of exposition awards from this era.

The practice got out of hand in certain instances. For example, the Louisiana Purchase Exposition desired to confer "gold medals" upon many entrants. After all, it would make a fine advertisement for a firm to say that it had received a "gold medal at the 1904 World's Fair" (the Louisiana Purchase Exposition held in St. Louis in that year). However, medals struck of gold were costly and profits would be diminished if *gold* medals actually had to be delivered. The fertile minds of the planners of that event came up with a novel solution: They issued *copper* medals with the words "gold medal" prominently lettered on them! Still even more enterprising (if this is the right word!) expositions didn't even bother to issue any kind of medal—they simply issued certificates with "gold medal award" or something similar on it. Today such medals and awards are eagerly sought by collectors.

Cataloging the medals, tokens, and other numismatic products of an exhibition may involve many years of work. Henry G. Spangenberger has spent countless thousands of hours enumerating the medallic products of the 1876 Centennial Exhibition. Nathan Eglit has done the same with the products of the World's Columbian Exposition. There are other examples as well.

Counterstamped Coins

Somewhat related to the field of tokens and medals are counterstamped coins. Such pieces consist of coins or tokens which have been stamped by additional dies at a later date to circulate an advertisement, spread a political thought, or even to create a new denomination or value of money.

For example, during the 1840's, the Free Soil party counterstamped United States large cents with the inscription VOTE THE LAND FREE. Similarly, the names of various patent medicines and nostrums were often stamped on coins as a method of advertising when the pieces passed from hand to hand. In England during the 1790's the portrait of King George III, prepared in a cameo-like oval die, was stamped on the center of Spanish eight-real pieces to signify that such pieces could pass as a medium of exchange within England. At the time, England's own money was being hoarded by the citizenry, and there was a severe shortage of coins in circulation. As noted in the earlier discussion of trade dollars, Oriental merchants often counterstamped these large American silver pieces to signify their acceptance when they circulated in China. It is not at all unusual for a trade dollar of this era (1873–1878) to have dozens of counterstamps or "chopmarks" on the obverse and reverse surfaces.

10

United States Paper Money

Collecting United States paper money can be a fascinating pursuit. Thousands of numismatists, many of whom are members of the Society of Paper Money Collectors, have followed this path.

Paper money takes many forms. We are all familiar with the $1, $5, $10, $20, and other bills in circulation today—but how many of us know that the United States once issued $7, $8, $35, $65, and other odd denominations? Today United States currency is carefully produced by the Bureau of Engraving and Printing. The power of issuing such bills belongs solely to the Federal Government. And yet at one time private individuals, businesses, and banks could and did issue their own paper money.

In his *Early Paper Money of America*, Eric P. Newman relates that the early paper issues of America have the unique distinction of being the first paper money issued by any government in the Western world. No country, state, or colony in Europe has made a prior issue of government-sponsored paper money.

On Dec. 10, 1690, the General Court of the Massachusetts Bay Colony issued under the British value system 7,000 pounds sterling worth of bills. Divided into issues bearing denominations of five shillings, ten shillings, twenty shillings, and five pounds, these notes were produced to pay the expenses for the military campaign against Canada during King William's War (1689–1697).

Over the next several decades, notes were issued by many other American colonies. Most bore denominations expressed in the British system (pounds, shillings, and pence) but others were expressed in Spanish dollars. An example of the latter is the five-dollar note issued by North Carolina in 1775. The legend reads CAROLINA CURRENCY. FIVE DOLLARS. THIS BILL ENTITLES THE BEARER TO RECEIVE FIVE SPANISH MILLED DOLLARS OR THE VALUE THEREOF IN GOLD OR SILVER ACCORDING TO THE RESOLUTION OF THE PROVINCIAL CONGRESS HELD AT HILLSBOROUGH AUGUST 21, 1775. Generally, the issues of a given state were accepted in channels of commerce only within that state, but there was some crossing of borders. For example, for a time the states of New Jersey, Pennsylvania, and Delaware each circulated currency of the other two.

Paper money issues have no intrinsic or metallic value and are based solely upon the conversion rate into coin specified by the governments of the various colonies and issuing agents. Thus such notes in effect are promises to pay, not actual intrinsic payment themselves. The depreciation of paper money, a popular subject today, began early. Eric P. Newman relates that by 1713 the value of Massachusetts paper money had depreciated more than 10 percent in relation to metallic money (British coins then in circulation). By 1746, in South Carolina 700 pounds face value of South Carolina paper money was the equivalent of 100 pounds face value of silver British coins. In some instances the currency systems later collapsed completely.

As values of each state's currency varied, often over a short span of time, periodic exchange tables were published in newspapers and in guides.

From early times in the colonies counterfeiting of various paper money issues was a great problem. As a warning against this practice certain notes bore inscriptions such as DEATH TO COUNTERFEIT and COUNTERFEIT IS DEATH, for example. Kenneth Scott, in a series of monographs for the American Numismatic Society, has outlined on a case-by-case basis the stories of many early American counterfeiters. The reports, taken from contemporary newspaper accounts, make fascinating reading. For example, the *Boston News-Letter* of June 9, 1718, printed a dispatch from Piscataqua bearing the date of June 6:

> Yesterday two young men were impillored here, and had their ears cut off, for forging and altering a Connecticut 40 shilling bill and a 15 shilling bill of this Province . . . their names we forbear inserting, hoping they'll repent of their wickedness and relate the facts as a warning to all others both in this and in the neighboring provinces to prevent others from committing the like crime; who if should, being fairly warned, are not to expect the like indulgence.

In other words, the treatment accorded to these two young counterfeiters was considered to be extremely lenient.

The first money issued under Federal auspices was the Continental Currency approved in June and July, 1775, by the Continental Congress in Philadelphia. Printed under contract by Hall & Sellers of Philadelphia, the notes were issued for a total of $3,000,000 in denominations ranging from $1 through $30. Although the United States was later to adopt a system of dollars of its own standard, the Continental Currency issues specifically note that the currency is valued in *Spanish* milled dollars.

From 1775 to 1785, many different Continental Currency issues were produced. Denominations included all values from $1 through $8, $20, $30, $35, $40, $45, $50, $55, $60, $65, $70, and $80. In addition there were the fractional denominations of $1/6, $1/3, $1/2, and $2/3.

Designs varied from issue to issue as did the inscriptions. Most contained a proverb or admonition, samples being the one-dollar note showing a crushed acanthus plant and the motto (in Latin as are illustrations to follow) THOUGH CRUSHED IT RISES AGAIN; the two-dollar note showing grain being threshed and the inscription AFFLICTION ENRICHES; the six-dollar note showing a beaver assiduously gnawing on a tree and the inscription BY PERSEVERANCE; the seven-dollar note showing a storm-tossed sea and the legend IT WILL BECOME TRANQUIL; and the thirty-five-dollar note with a plow and the inscription HENCE COMES OUR POWER.

Notes were hand-signed in ink, as evidence of official authorization, as a protection against counterfeiting, and as a general control of the quantity. Also, nearly all issues were serially numbered in ink by hand.

Many famous persons signed Continental Currency issues. Most notes were signed personally, but often a secretary was employed to do the job. Thus signatures often vary. Signers of the Declaration of Independence, the Articles of Confederation, the United States Constitution, and other important historical documents also signed these early currency issues in some instances.

In subsequent years Continental Currency was demonetized by the United States Government, and issues have no redemption value. As collectors' items, their prices vary from note to note depending upon the state of issue (for example, early Vermont notes are very rare), or among later issues, the particular issue, denomination, and signer. Many fine examples of commoner issues can be obtained for $5 to $15.

During the late 18th and early 19th centuries, thousands of bank notes, usually expressed in values of American dollars (the dollar system having been adopted by then), were issued by banks, merchants, and others. Banking laws were inconsistent, and often such issues had little actual worth. It was common, particularly in the 1830's and 1840's, for a small bank to issue millions of dollars worth of currency, with the hope that not all notes would be redeemed, at least not at one time. As might be expected, notes of such banks and of merchants were usually redeemable only by the issuers or cooperating banks and businesses within a restricted area. Generally, a note issued by a small bank in Connecticut would have little value in South Carolina, for example.

The term "broken bank notes" is derived from the fact that most of these early banks and businesses went broke, especially during the Panic of 1837. *North American Currency*, by Grover C. Criswell, Jr., is the standard reference in the field. Broken bank notes are listed in order by the states in which the various banks and businesses were located. Also enumerated and described are later private bank and merchants' issues, some of which were produced well into the late 19th century.

Denominations among such issues are quite interesting. For example, in Coshocton, Ohio, private notes of the value of 6¼¢, 12½¢, 25¢, and 50¢ were issued. The Citizens' Bank, a prolific issuer of notes in New Orleans, Louisiana, produced issues of the more standard values $1, $2, $3, $5, $10, $50, and $100.

Today we sometimes hear the expression "queer as a three-dollar bill." Actually among American currency issues there are many three-dollar bills. As noted earlier, this was a denomination issued in the Continental

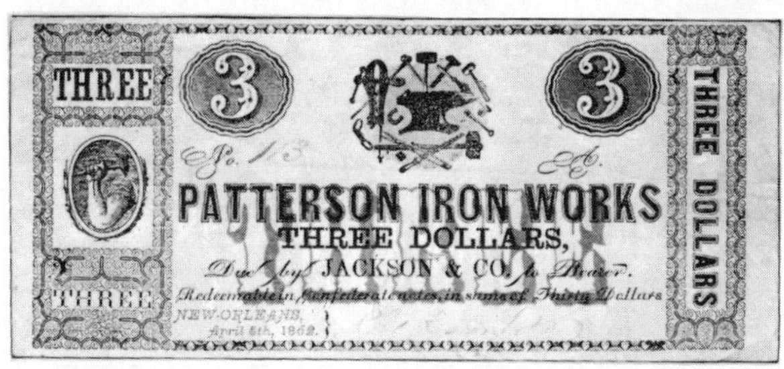

REAL $3 BILLS! "Queer as a three-dollar bill" is part of the American language. However, it is a fact that $3 bills actually did circulate in large quantities. During the early 19th century, many banks, merchants, and others produced pieces of this value. The notes illustrated are from the collection of Nancy Ruddy. Over the years she has collected nearly 500 varieties of $3 bills!

Currency series. Later the $3 value became quite popular with private banks. Nancy Ruddy, wife of James F. Ruddy, has made a specialty of collecting authentic early three-dollar bills. At last count she had nearly 500 varieties!

Designs among broken bank issues are wonderfully varied. Such well-known bank note engraving firms as the American Bank Note Company; Rawdon, Wright, Hatch, & Edson; Danforth, Wright, & Company, and others issued large posters depicting hundreds of suggested bank-note designs. Most depicted allegorical figures (such as goddesses representing Liberty, Justice, and so on), items of commerce (ships, trains, and so on), agricultural scenes, portraits of historical figures (Washington, Jackson, etc.), and so on. The perspective issuer of notes could then make up his own designs.

There are too many bank-note varieties for one person to collect them all. Accordingly, most numismatists make a specialty. Nancy Ruddy has assembled a fine collection of three-dollar bills. My close friend Murray Clark, a native of New Hampshire, has endeavored to assemble as many varieties and designs as possible from his native state. More than 90 varieties of New Hampshire notes are described in Criswell's *North American Currency*, and additional varieties come to light from time to time.

The amounts of notes vary from state to state. A lifetime specialty could be made collecting the prolific issues of New York, for example. On the other hand, virtually no notes are known from the State of Nevada, except some issued late in the 19th century by the Manhattan Silver Mining Company.

Another way to collect broken bank notes is by design topics expressed in the portraits and motifs, called "vignettes." Specialized collections can be made of broken bank notes showing sailing ships, railroad trains, buildings, or other subjects.

Notes of the Confederate States of America form yet another collecting specialty. From 1861 through 1864 many hundreds of different varieties were listed. These are enumerated and described in Grover C. Criswell, Jr.'s *Confederate and Southern States Currency*. Denominations issued range from 50¢ through $1,000, the high $500 and $1,000 values issued at Montgomery, Alabama, in 1861 being quite rare today. Confederate states including Arkansas, Georgia, Mississippi, and others issued currency in various denominations. All these issues—Confederate and Southern states notes alike—have no redemption value today. They are, however, quite popular with collectors. Once considered absolutely worthless, Confederate notes all have value—although it is modest in some instances.

Fine notes of certain varieties can be obtained for just a few dollars each.

Toward the end of the Civil War, emergency conditions faced many areas of the South, and this is reflected in certain currency varieties. Some notes are printed on paper the quality of newsprint.

About 15 years ago during a visit to the venerable firm of Spink & Son, Ltd., London coin dealers, I was asked if I wanted to purchase a large quantity of Confederate notes of 1864. I acquired many original bundles, mostly of $5 and $10 denominations, which had been kept intact since the Civil War. A British banking house had received them in payment from a Southern firm (England did extensive business with the Confederacy during the war) and, following the demise of the C.S.A., was left with a huge quantity of worthless paper money. This was saved by the bank for nearly a hundred years. Then space was needed, so the huge accumulation went to the trash bin, with the exception of the bundles of notes which some thoughtful person rescued and sold to Spink & Son.

Over the years many reprints and facsimiles have been made of Confederate currency. Some time ago a lady wrote to me and said that her uncle had saved from Civil War days more than $100,000 in Confederate paper money. Would I be interested? I would, I replied, for I knew that a large quantity must be involved. Most C.S.A. issues encountered are of the $5, $10, and other lower values, and quite a pile would be needed to make up more than $100,000 in face value. You can imagine my surprise when by return mail came a thin envelope containing a Confederate "$100,000 bill" plus one or two other pieces—items made up just a few years earlier as a novelty by a cereal company which issued them as premiums in its product! The denomination was a fantasy, of course, for the highest true denomination ever originally produced was $1,000.

Regular United States paper money as we know it today began in 1861 when the United States Government issued the first Demand Notes. These issues are so called because they bear the notation "The United States promise to pay to the bearer———dollars on demand." From that time onward many types of notes were issued. Often specific legislation resulted in a specific type of note being issued. Silver Certificates and Gold Certificates were backed by the respective metals indicated; this backing has since been repudiated by the United States Government, however. Compound Interest Treasury Notes, Interest Bearing Notes, Refunding Certificates, Treasury or Coin Notes, and others were all produced in a wide variety of designs and denominations.

From 1863 to 1929, many national banks issued distinctive notes: regular United States currency designs, and of legal tender value anywhere in the country, but with the name of the issuing bank imprinted. Today these are avidly collected, and many varieties have great value, especially in crisp New condition, "New" being the currency equivalent of "Uncirculated."

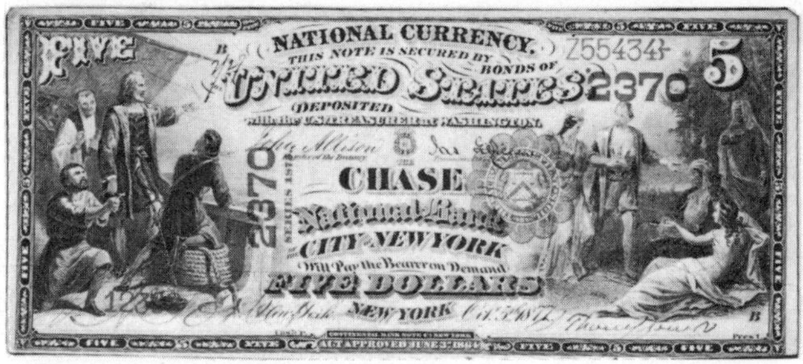

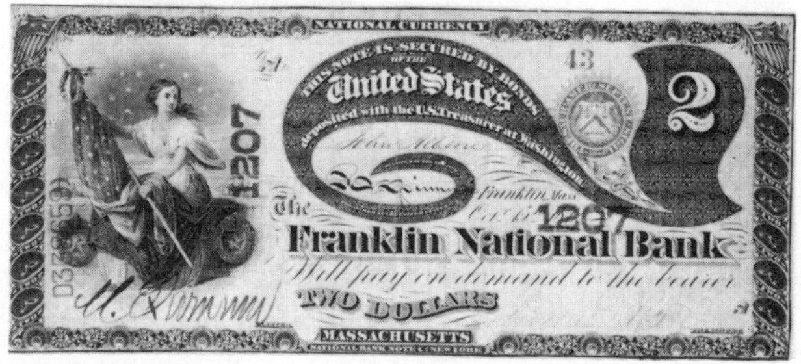

LARGE-SIZE U.S. CURRENCY. From 1861 until smaller notes were issued in 1928, United States currency was of much larger size than it is today—about the size of an IBM card, in fact. Throughout the years many beautiful designs, including those shown, made their appearance.

From 1861 through 1928, currency was considerably larger than that used today. The IBM data processing card, first made in the early 1920's, was made the size of the paper money of that era so people would find it easy to use. Now in the 1970's the IBM cards are still with us, but the large-size currency is long gone except for specimens carefully preserved by collectors. Beginning in 1928, the present-day small-size notes were introduced.

Just as during one period in the 19th century a person desiring a United States coin of the one-dollar denomination had several to choose from—the silver dollar, the trade dollar, and the gold dollar, the various types of notes—Coin Notes, Silver Certificates, and so on—often overlapped considerably. Many issues were produced concurrently, and a wide variety can be collected today. To aid the collector, several specialized references on the United States currency series are available: *Paper Money of the United States*, by Robert and Jack Friedberg, *United States Large Size Paper Money, 1861–1923*, by William T. Donlon, and the *Hewitt-Donlon Catalog of U.S. Small Size Paper Money* being among the most important. These and others are listed in the Bibliography.

Values of United States paper money have ranged from $1 to $10,000. In addition, a special series of fractional currency notes in denominations from 3¢ to 50¢ was produced. Today, denominations of $1, $5, $10, $50, and $100 circulate, the lower values being the most popular.

While paper money being made today is rather uniform in appearance, at one time the United States produced truly splendid designs, notes that were beautiful works of art. Many collectors consider the high point was reached with the Silver Certificates, Series of 1896. The $1 denomination portrays a scene of HISTORY INSTRUCTING YOUTH, the $2, a scene of SCIENCE PRESENTING STEAM AND ELECTRICITY TO COMMERCE AND MANUFACTURE, and the $5 (the largest in the 1896 series), an untitled scene showing the Goddess of Electricity as the dominant force in the world. Many other magnificent designs are found throughout the series of large-size notes from 1861 onward. Perhaps someday in the future the Treasury will think again in terms of artistry and will realize that currency can be beautiful as well as utilitarian.

While the motto IN GOD WE TRUST had been in use on United States coins since the 1860's, it found no place on paper money until the 1950's, and then through the efforts of Matt Rothert, distinguished past president of the American Numismatic Association, whose superb collection of United States currency was sold at auction by Bowers and Ruddy Galleries in 1973. In our catalog of this sale, I noted the many awards Mr. Rothert had received over the years, just about every outstanding honor

"IN GOD WE TRUST" ON U.S. CURRENCY. Shown is one of the first one hundred notes (bearing serial number A00000089A) issued in 1955 with the motto "IN GOD WE TRUST." Due to the efforts of Matt Rothert, past president of the American Numismatic Association, this motto was added to paper money in that year. The motto had been included on coins since the 1860's. Mr. Rothert, a deeply religious man, instituted Congressional action which resulted in its inclusion on paper money. The note shown was presented to James F. Ruddy and Q. David Bowers by Mr. Rothert.

available in the numismatic field, in fact. Then I went on to say:

> Matt Rothert's fame would be assured even if the many preceding awards and recognitions were not a reality. Even so he would enter the life of every American citizen, for it was Mr. Rothert who was directly responsible for having the motto IN GOD WE TRUST placed on United States currency. He first made the suggestion to the Secretary of the Treasury, George W. Humphrey, in November 1953. The idea came to him a few months earlier while attending church one Sunday morning. As the collection plate was being passed, it occurred to him that only the *coins* in the plate had this motto. He then thought that since our paper money has a much wider circulation abroad than our coins, a mention about this country's faith in God could be easily carried around the world if it was on United States currency. In March 1955, through Mr. Rothert's efforts, bills to this effect were introduced into the Senate by his friend, Senator Fulbright of Arkansas, and into the House of Representatives by Congressmen Bennett of Florida and Harris of Arkansas. The bill was approved by President Dwight D. Eisenhower on July 11, 1955, and IN GOD WE TRUST on currency became a reality.

As noted earlier, during the Civil War there was a great shortage of coins in circulation in the United States. The economic future was uncertain, and copper, silver, and gold issues were hoarded in quantity. Particularly painful was the lack of smaller denominations in circulation, coins used to make everyday purchases. Civil War tokens, issued by the millions, passed in circulation at the value of one cent each. To help fill the need for larger denominations, the Treasury issued fractional currency notes beginning in 1862. These were produced through 1876. Denominations include 3¢, 5¢, 10¢, 15¢, 25¢, and 50¢. In the fourteen years of issue, about $369,000,000 worth of fractional currency was printed. However, very little exists today. It is estimated that about $1,800,000 worth (speaking now of face value) was never redeemed. Of this amount many notes must have been lost and destroyed. The finest collection of United States fractional currency ever sold at auction, a collection replete with specimen and Proof notes and rarities, appeared at the sale featuring the Matt Rothert holdings.

For the collector of American paper money, the Fractional Currency Shield is a prize possession. In 1866 and 1867 the Treasury Department printed a special shield-shaped design on a large piece of stiff cardboard. To this shield, usually printed in gray, though green and pink shields exist as well, were affixed thirty-nine specimens of fractional currency. The Treasury covered each shield with glass and housed it in an attractive frame, usually with a gold inner molding. These were produced for sale to banks so that the financial institutions could have specimens of genuine fractional currency on hand for comparison should a suspected counterfeit be found. By comparing the suspected note with the note on the shield, authenticity could be confirmed or denied. It is estimated that several hundred fractional currency shields still survive. Nearly all show heavy water stains, for prior to shipment to the various banks they were stored in the basement of the Treasury Department which once was flooded to a depth of several inches.

11

Coins of the World

Coins of countries other than the United States—commonly called coins of the world by collectors—provide many fascinating numismatic opportunities.

The collecting and investing possibilities are vast. *The Standard Catalog of World Coins*, by Chester R. Krause and Clifford Mishler, covers *only* coins from the mid-1800's to the present, a span of slightly more than 100 years, and yet contains descriptions of more than 35,000 different coins from 273 countries! Add to this figure the multitudes of tokens, medals, and other numismatic items of the past century, plus coins dating back to ancient times, and it is probable that there are many hundreds of thousands of distinct varieties in the general field encompassed by world coins.

Of course no collector or museum can aspire to own one of each variety, or even come close to it for that matter. Rather, most have a specialty. Indeed, in the broadest sense of the word, collecting United States coins is a specialty of world coin collecting.

Canadian Coins

Canadian coins are an especially popular series with collectors. In many ways the history of Canadian coinage resembles our own. Prior to the first government decimal system issues in 1858, there were many private tokens and store cards which actually circulated, plus issues struck in France for use by the French regime in Canada.

Among privately issued tokens of the early 19th century, there are many fascinating varieties. One of the most curious is a crudely struck and amateurishly engraved (the work appears almost childlike) token of the 1830's. Bearing the inscription VEXATOR CANADIENSIS the tokens are thought to refer to the British Government as the "tormentor of Canada." The reverse inscription, written cryptically on the coin, means "don't you wish you could catch them?"—a reference to the secret coiners of these satirical pieces, whoever they may have been.

In its early years, Canada was divided into several sections. Upper Canada and Lower Canada, the present provinces of Quebec and Ontario, were united to form the province of Canada. During the late 1830's and early 1840's the Bank of Montreal, acting with official permission, produced a series of tokens which passed as currency. Most issues of the half-penny and penny denominations date from 1838 through 1844. In 1852, the Quebec Bank obtained permission to coin issues for circulation, and

COINAGE PRODUCTION AT THE ROYAL CANADIAN MINT, OTTAWA.

(1) At the Royal Canadian Mint in Ottawa this huge blanking press cuts planchets from long strips of metal. Coins are made from the planchets.

(2) This large coining press is capable of producing many thousands of one-cent pieces each day at the Royal Canadian Mint in Ottawa. The inspector is examining a freshly minted cent.

(3) Following coinage, pieces are examined for minting defects, counted, and put into bags for shipment.

240,000 pennies and 480,000 halfpennies were produced. Additional bank issues were produced later.

During the same period, a vast quantity of tokens appeared in circulation. Particularly ubiquitous were cent-size issues of 1837. Resembling United States Hard Times tokens in appearance and in some instances made in the United States by manufacturers of those tokens, the Canadian issues for the most part have a floral bouquet on the obverse, thus giving them the name "bouquet sous" among collectors. The pieces bear the French indication of value on the reverse: UN SOU. Varieties of bouquet sous are plentiful today, and choice examples can be obtained for just a few dollars each. To be sure, however, there are rare varieties which sell for more.

In 1858, Canada produced its first regular decimal coins. Issued in the values of 1¢, 5¢, 10¢, and 20¢, the pieces were struck in London at the Royal Mint. The first three denominations, a currency system patterned after that used in the United States, are still being used; twenty-cent pieces were made only in the year 1858. It was found that they were easily confused with United States quarters which circulated at that time to a limited extent in Canada.

Throughout the years there has been a close interconnection between United States and Canadian coins, not only numismatically but commercially as well. Although the exchange values have gone up and down in relation to each other over the years, usually Canadian and United States coins can be spent interchangeably in areas along the common border of the two countries.

In 1870, Canada produced twenty-five-cent pieces for the first time. During the same year, the first half dollars made their appearance.

The first Canadian decimal system issues, those struck in England at the Royal Mint, bear no mintmark. Supplementing Royal Mint production were many pieces produced over the year by the Heaton Mint, a private facility in Birmingham, England. The tiny H mintmark of these issues distinguishes them. Heaton was a prolific contract coiner for many countries all over the world, and coins from different areas of the globe carry this same tiny designation in many instances.

Since 1908, the Royal Canadian Mint in Ottawa has produced nearly all of Canada's coins. An interesting exception was provided in 1968 when, due to inadequate capacity at the Royal Canadian Mint, the United States Mint at Philadelphia helped out by producing 85,000,000 dimes. However, these dimes do not bear a distinguishing mintmark. Collectors, ever eager to spot any difference which could make a new variety, quickly learned that the issues produced in Philadelphia had a slightly different style of edge milling or reeding.

Generally, issues struck at the Royal Canadian Mint have no mintmark. Exceptions are the tiny C mintmark used on gold sovereigns made from 1908 through 1918 and certain coins produced on contract for Newfoundland.

In 1911, Canada considered a silver dollar coinage, and patterns were prepared. However, no coinage for circulation materialized until 1935 when the long-awaited silver dollar finally made its first official appearance. From then until the present day, Canada has issued on a nearly continuous basis (with only a few years being omitted) an illustrious series of silver dollars, many of which have commemorative designs and motifs. Among the Canadian silver dollars of commemorative designs are the 1935 issue celebrating King George V's 25th anniversary on the throne of England (it will be remembered that Canada is a member of the British Commonwealth and the monarchs of England appear on most of its coins), the 1939 silver dollar featuring the Canadian Parliament buildings, the 1949 issue honoring Newfoundland (which joined Canada in 1949, having been a separate British dependency earlier), the 1958 issue commemorating the hundredth anniversary of British Columbia, the 1964 issue observing the centennial of Charlottetown, Quebec, and the 1970 issue commemorating the centennial of Manitoba. While Canadian silver dollars were indeed originally made of silver, today they are made of nickel. The price of silver in recent years has risen to such an extent that a "silver dollar" of the large traditional size for this denomination, if made of silver, would be worth much more than face value. The United States abandoned the use of silver for most coinage in 1965 (although some special silver issues, including issues for collectors, were minted later) and within a short time most other countries of the world did likewise. Indeed, many countries of the world, Great Britain being an example, anticipated the United States in this regard.

The Royal Canadian Mint has always had a strong interest in numismatics. The commemorative issues are an indication of this, as are the special Proof sets struck each year for collectors. Hesitant to use the term Proof, the Royal Canadian Mint refers to its coins as "prooflike," although in most instances the pieces have the same type of finish as Proof coins produced by other nations. In addition other special issues for collectors have been produced from time to time, an outstanding example being a special 1967 twenty-dollar gold piece struck only in Proof grade, of which 337,688 were minted. Ironically, the United States laws governing the holding of gold coins by citizens restrict ownership of modern issues, although earlier gold coins can be collected in any quantity de-

COINS OF CANADA. Canada has issued coins under the decimal system since 1858. Prior to that a wide variety of privately issued tokens, coins of other countries, and other coins served as a medium of exchange.

Shown are a variety of Canadian pieces: (1) 1951 commemorative Canadian nickel depicts an ore smelter on the reverse. The mining and refining of nickel metal has always been an important part of Canada's economy. (2) 1870 twenty-five-cent piece or quarter dollar featuring Queen Victoria. (3) 1939 commemorative silver dollar illustrating the Canadian Parliament buildings. (4) The 1949 commemorative silver dollar issued to observe the entry of Newfoundland into the Dominion of Canada that year. (5) 1958 commemorative silver dollar observing the centennial of British Columbia. (6) 1964 commemorative silver dollar for the centennial of Charlottetown, Quebec. (7) 1973 Canadian dollar.

sired. Hence these beautiful 1967 Canadian commemoratives could not be sold or owned in the United States!

Other gold coins were issued by the Royal Canadian Mint earlier in the century. From 1908 through 1919, a series of sovereigns, identical in weight and design to British issues and bearing no mention of Canada, circulated as a bullion-type coin with changing face value depending upon the current value of gold. To distinguish these British-type sovereigns from similar pieces made in England, Australia, India, and other British Commonwealth nations around the world, the tiny distinguishing mintmark C was placed on the reverse of each.

Gold coins of the $5 and $10 denomination were produced from 1912 through 1914, inclusive. Several hundred thousand pieces were issued totally.

In addition to the coins of Canada, various issues of the separate provinces before they joined the Confederation are of interest to the numismatist. Newfoundland, which joined Canada in 1949, issued a long and illustrious series of coins in values of 1¢, 5¢, 10¢, 20¢, 25¢, 50¢, and $2, the last being struck in gold. Considering the relatively small size of this Atlantic island, coinages were often generous. For example, in 1913, 400,000 one-cent pieces were minted, and in the following year 702,000 cents were struck. More than a million one-cent pieces were made each year from 1942 through 1944.

To be sure, there are scarcities and rarities among Newfoundland coins. The 1946-C, the C being the mintmark of the Royal Canadian Mint, where the issue was struck, is rare. Only 2,041 were struck. All Newfoundland two-dollar gold pieces, minted intermittently from 1865 through 1888 inclusive, are elusive today. A complete set of this unusual denomination consists of eight different coins, one of which (the 1882-H) bears a mintmark. The others were struck at the Royal Mint in London and have no mintmark.

New Brunswick, which together with Nova Scotia joined Canada in 1867, issued its own coins from 1861 through 1864, inclusive. Denominations ranged from ½¢ to 20¢. Nova Scotia also issued coins in these denominations in some of the years between 1861 and 1864.

In 1871, Prince Edward Island joined Canada, but not before issuing its own coinage that year. The 1871 Prince Edward Island cent of which a million pieces were coined stands alone as the only issue of that province.

Coins of Canada have always been close to the hearts of United States collectors. Interest has sharpened in recent years due to the availability of excellent reference books in the field, J. E. Charlton being a pioneer author in this regard. Today hundreds of thousands if not millions of numismatists in the United States and in Canada eagerly seek Canadian issues.

Mexican Coins

Also very popular with collectors in the United States are coins of Mexico, our neighbor to the south. Mexico has a long and rich coinage history. The Mexico City Mint, opened in 1536, was the first mint located in the Western Hemisphere. Still operating, it is also the oldest.

In its early years, Mexican coins were based on the Spanish monetary system, the real and its parts and multiples. Especially important was the eight-real piece (the plural of real is reales), each real having the approximate United States equivalent value of 12½¢. A common slang term for the real was the "bit." Hence, a two-real piece, a denomination which once actively circulated in the southwestern part of the United States, was literally a "two bit" piece. The term still survives in the American language as a synonym for the quarter.

The real was basically a silver unit. Gold coins were expressed in escudos. Denominations range from the half escudo (equal in value to the "silver dollar" or eight-real piece) through the 1, 2, 4, and 8 escudos. The eight-escudo coin, worth approximately $16 in United States money, was the doubloon of pirate lore and legend.

Mexico is blessed with large quantities of native silver ore, so pieces struck in this metal, especially eight-real coins, were minted in tremendous quantities.

From 1636 until the early 19th century, the Mexico mint was one of the most important mints of the Spanish Empire. Mexico was the crown jewel in Spain's Western Hemisphere possessions. Accordingly, coins of Mexico were a monetary standard in many countries, including the United States. As noted earlier, various issues of Continental Currency issued in the United States during the late 18th century had their values expressed in Spanish milled dollars. As Mexico was under Spanish rule, dollars or eight-real pieces struck in Mexico were the "Spanish" coins usually circulated in the American colonies.

In 1810, an uprising against the Spanish rule occurred. In 1821, the Mexican Empire was founded, and in 1822, Augustín de Iturbide was crowned emperor. The Empire lasted but one year, and the Republic of Mexico came into being. After 1810 various branch mints were opened. These mints were necessary for commercial and economic reasons, for

COINS OF MEXICO. Mexico has a rich coinage history. At one time or another, 14 mints operated within the confines of that country! The mint at Mexico City was established in 1636, the first government-operated mint in the Western Hemisphere, and is still operating. Shown are several varieties of dollar-size coins.

the troubled conditions of the period prevented the free flow of coins and bullion to and from the central mint in Mexico City. During the 19th century the mints expanded in number until today collectors enumerate fourteen mints which once operated in Mexico. However, most of these mints were ephemeral and lasted only briefly. The fourteen mints were: Alamos, Catorce (formerly referred to as Real del Catorce), Chihuahua, Culiacan, Durango, Estado de Mexico, Guadalajara, Guadalupe y Calvo, Guanajuato, Hermosillo, Mexico City, Oaxaca, Potosí, and Zacatecas. Each mint had its own distinctive mintmark, which was often changed over a period of years. The main mint, listed in the preceding enumeration as "Mexico" (known as Mexico City to United States residents), utilized an MO mintmark most of the time.

The Republic of Mexico, to be in conformity with many other nations of the world, began converting to the decimal system in 1863. In time the old eight-real silver dollar-size coin became the new peso. Likewise, one-centavo, two-centavo, five-centavo, and other compatible coins were produced. Gold denominations were likewise expressed in pesos, the beautifully styled fifty-peso piece being the highest denomination. This coin, minted in large quantities, is slightly larger in weight and diameter than a United States double eagle. Fifty-peso pieces were struck bearing the dates 1921 through 1947. Realizing their popularity as an international medium of monetary exchange, and more recently as an investment medium for those interested in gold coins of high intrinsic value, the Mexico City Mint has restruck additional pieces bearing the 1947 date.

Following much internal strife, plus foreign dissatisfaction with Mexico's fiscal policy, French forces captured Mexico City in 1863 and established 32-year-old Archduke Maximilian of Austria as Emperor in 1864. In 1867, Maximilian's tenure and the short-lived empire he symbolized ended. Maximilian was executed.

During his reign a number of distinctive coins bearing his portrait were produced. However, dies and other materials were insufficient for complete distribution throughout the large system of branch mints, so certain mints in distant sections of Mexico continued producing coins of the older design styles.

In the late 19th century, Mexican coins were severely devalued. Mexico, one of the world's largest producers of silver, had long depended upon world markets to absorb her vast production. However, the world market became glutted, and Mexico then produced countless tons of silver pesos and other coins from the unwanted metal. (In the United States a similar situation occurred, and Morgan-design silver dollars were coined in huge quantities to absorb this glut.) As intrinsic value fell far below face value, the status of the peso on the world currency market fell sharply, and the pieces were valued only at what they could be melted down for. The result was a severe devaluation of the country's coinage. Gold coins, in the meantime, were eagerly hoarded as a hedge against the depreciation of silver. According to Prof. T. V. Buttrey, writing in his *Guide Book of Mexican Coins*, by 1905 a Mexican twenty-peso gold coin was actually worth 39.48 pesos in terms of silver. In other words, silver had depreciated nearly 50 percent.

The Mexican monetary system was reformed in 1905. The branch mints were closed, and the Mexico City Mint from that time onward has remained the only mint in the country. The metallic content of the various denominations was changed, and the intrinsic-value concept was abandoned. Numismatists often collect coinage produced since 1905, the era of Mexican modern coinage, as a separate specialty.

Fortunately, toward the end of 1905 the worldwide price of silver revived, and exports of Mexican silver were once again welcome on the world market. In the early 20th century, the international value of the Mexican peso was related to the rise and fall of the silver market due to the importance of this metal in Mexico's economy.

Today Mexican coins are collected avidly, particularly in Mexico and in the Southwestern United States. Some collectors make a specialty of large eight-real and one-peso coins. The multiplicity of mints which struck these coins plus the fact that, in addition to having distinctive mintmarks, issues have different assayers' initials on them as well (thus making even more varieties), has made assembling a representative collection quite a challenge. Modern issues, the pieces since 1905, are conveniently collected by date sequence. Sprinkled throughout various series are interesting commemorative issues.

British Coins

The coins of Great Britain form a fascinating part of world numismatics. During the late 18th century and 19th century, Great Britain and the British Empire flourished, and coin collecting, a pastime of affluent nations, secured a strong foundation there at an early date. By the 1780's and 1790's—when the United States was becoming adjusted to its new independence, American frontiers were still largely unexplored, and North America was considered a primitive country—coin collecting was well established in Britain. By 1795, thousands of armchair collectors kept busy assembling sets of coins and collecting varieties. Particularly in demand were copper tokens the size of a British halfpenny, which matched in size the contemporary American large cent, called "conder tokens." *The Virtuoso's Companion and Coin Collector's Guide*, published in 1795, became quite popular and subsequently went through several printings. This massive volume of engravings showed the proper English gentleman of his day everything he needed to know to identify his tokens. Many articles appeared in the popular press as well. The value of certain pieces multiplied in value almost overnight. This resulted in even more demand. Somewhere along the line an enterprising diecutter took time out to produce an interesting piece which typified the situation at the time. The legend read ASSES CHASING AFTER HALFPENCE. Taking the long, long view of several lifetimes, the values of these little tokens—as high as they might have been in the 1790's—are even higher today. In fact, the thousands of varieties within the conder token series form one of Britain's most popular numismatic specialties.

I am particularly fond of British coins and, for that matter, of Britain itself. When I first visited England around 1960 I was surprised to notice the great differences between the English method of collecting coins and the American way. British collectors, usually more studious than their American counterparts, gravitated toward older issues of Great Britain, classic coins of Greece and Rome, and other sophisticated specialties. Largely ignored were coins from the Victorian era (1837–1901) to the present time. I found it incredible, for example, that a rare 1919 English penny from the curiously named King's Norton Mint, a private mint located in Birmingham which issued coins bearing a KN mintmark, could be purchased in Uncirculated grade for the American equivalent of $2 or $3. At the time I made a study of British coins of the past 150 years and learned that the 1919-KN penny was indeed rare in high condition. It would be nice to be able to say that I purchased several hundred pieces for a few dollars each and then made windfall profits by selling them at several hundred dollars each, today's value. Alas, that was not the case. Such pieces are rare, and I was able to find only two or three Uncirculated examples.

At this time, there were only four major coin dealers in England: the respected and historic firm of Spink & Son, Ltd., the large house of B. A. Seaby, Ltd., and the venerable establishment of A. H. Baldwin Ltd., all in London, and a half day's drive away in Melksham in the province of Wiltshire, Fred J. Jeffrey. It was Mr. Jeffrey, incidentally, who shared my thoughts that modern British coins would be avidly collected someday. It was also Mr. Jeffrey who suggested that the special commemorative

British crown issued to observe the coronation of Queen Elizabeth II in 1953 be modeled after the design used 400 years earlier depicting the monarch on horseback.

During the 1960's, James F. Ruddy and I studied British coins intensively. We discovered a number of new varieties, including previously unlisted overdates, all of which are now described in literature on the subject. During the early years of my visits to England, there were no popularly circulated numismatic magazines in the country (apart from dealer catalogs) and there was no such thing as a commercial coin convention. Today that is all changed. There are many large dealers in Great Britain plus hundreds of smaller ones. Modern British coins are avidly collected by date and mintmark varieties by tens of thousands of enthusiasts. There are several fine numismatic magazines. Coin conventions, called "coin fairs," are held regularly.

The history of British coins is a fascinating one, and even to treat it lightly would require a volume several times the size of this one.

In 1971 Britain adopted the decimal system. Coinage values are still expressed in a familiar pounds, shillings, and pence terminology, but unit values have changed. For example, it took twelve pennies (the plural is properly expressed as "pence" in Britain) to make one shilling, and twenty shillings, or 240 pence, to make one pound. A pound today is 100 new pence.

The pre-decimal coinage itself was divided into many denominations. The farthing—about the size of an American nickel five-cent piece—was the lowest value to commonly circulate. Equal in value to ¼ penny, the farthing had little purchasing power. Next up the ladder came the halfpenny. In practice, during the 18th and early 19th centuries, halfpennies were the basic copper coin in circulation. Pieces are approximately the size of an American large cent of the time.

Next up the scale for commonly used denominations was the threepence. Next came the sixpence. Valued at the equivalent of six one-penny pieces, the sixpence was also equivalent to a half shilling. Next came the florin, a coin valued at two shillings; then the half crown worth 2½ shillings. The crown or "silver dollar" of Britain had a face value of 5 shillings.

Struck in gold were still larger denominations. One-pound (speaking of the denomination, not the weight) gold pieces of 20 shillings' value were known as sovereigns. These were struck in vast quantities over the years and were important in large international monetary transactions. Made in lesser quantities were gold half sovereigns.

The guinea is an interesting denomination. This gold coin had a value of 21 shillings, making it worth slightly more than a pound or sovereign, which had a value of 20 shillings. At one time, guineas and multiples of guineas were struck. However, these were not made later than the early 19th century. Largest of all British gold coins was the massive five-guinea piece. Although guinea coins have not been made in recent times, the value itself remained in commerce, particularly to price "fashionable" goods. Thus, a Rolls Royce automobile would nearly always be priced in guineas rather than the more "ordinary" pounds! So also would be jewelry, certain fashion items, and so on.

Coins have been used in England for more than 2,000 years. During the second century B.C., issues produced in Gaul found circulation within what we know as England today. Carasius (287–293 A.D.), who ruled in Britain, produced Roman-style coinage there.

Beginning around 650 A.D., thick, small coins, almost lumplike in some instances and known as "sceats" by collectors today, were first minted. The British monetary system evolved from Roman currency. The term shilling or fractional part of a pound was devised from an Anglo-Saxon word *scilling*, meaning "to divide."

By the 16th and 17th centuries, Britain had an advanced coinage system. Mints were operated at a number of locations, and many varieties of coins were produced. It is interesting to observe that early mintmarks, rather than being letters, were often of a pictorial nature—a tiny castle, a rose, a sun, and so on. Later coinage was standardized at the Royal Mint in London, and the branch mints were discontinued. Occasionally coins were produced on a contractual basis by private mints, certain pieces made in Birmingham by Heaton and bearing H mintmarks and by the King's Norton Mint bearing KN mintmarks being examples. However, the majority of the pieces have emanated from the Royal Mint and in recent years the government's use of the aforementioned private mints has been discontinued.

With relatively few exceptions, British coins of recent centuries have featured the portrait of the reigning monarch on the obverse. A list of monarchs and their regnal dates follows:

James I (1603–1625), Charles I (1625–1649), Charles II (1649; 1660–1685), Commonwealth (some issues of which portray Oliver Cromwell) (1649–1659), James II (1685–1688), William III and Mary II (1689–1694), William III alone (1694–1702), Anne (1702–1714), George I (1714–1727), George II (1727–1760), George III (1760–1820), George IV (1820–1830), William IV (1830–1837), Victoria (1837–1901), Ed-

CROWNS OF GREAT BRITAIN. During the past several centuries many different "crowns" or five-shilling pieces have been issued. Representative examples are shown:

(1) 1552 crown portraying Edward VI on horseback. During his reign the first dated British crowns were struck, the earliest date being 1551. (2) Crown of Queen Elizabeth I issued during the Shakespearean era. (3) 1656 crown issued by the Commonwealth of England. Unlike monarchial issues, the Commonwealth crown depicts no ruler. When the monarchy was restored kings and queens again appeared on British coins. (4) 1736 crown of King George II. (5) 1790 eight-real piece featuring King Charles IV of Spain. On the neck is counterstamped within a small oval the portrait of England's King George III. Such pieces served during the turn of the 19th century when English-minted silver coins had all but disappeared from circulation. (6) 1804 dollar issued by the Bank of England. The obverse portrays King George III. (7) 1818 crown of King George III featuring the reverse design of St. George slaying the dragon. (8) 1839 crown portraying Queen Victoria as a young woman. Although Victoria ascended to the throne in 1837, it was not until 1839 that crowns were first issued during her reign. (9) "Gothic crown" of Queen Victoria, 1853. (10) 1893 crown depicting Queen Victoria as an older woman. (11) One of the rarest of all 20th-century world coins is the 1934 crown of King George V. Only 932 pieces were minted!

VICTORIA DEI GRATIA
1839
8
BRITANNIARUM REGINA FID: DEF:
9
VICTORIA DEI GRA BRITT REGINA FID DEF IND IMP
10
1893
GEORGIVS V DEI GRA: BRITT: OMN: REX
11
DEF IND
1934
FID IMP
CRO WN

ward VII (1901–1910), George V (1910–1936), Edward VIII (1936), George VI (1936–1952), and Elizabeth II (1952 to the present).

Silver-dollar-size crown or five-shilling pieces have been a popular specialty with many collectors. Many interesting varieties occur throughout the series.

One of the most famous of all British crowns is the 1663 "Petition Crown" by Thomas Simon. For a number of years, Simon engraved many dies for English coinage. His dies for the 1658-dated Commonwealth crown of Oliver Cromwell were superb. Although Simon worked under relatively crude conditions, his artistry compares favorably with the finest coinage and medallic work of the present century.

In 1661, Jan Roettier of Antwerp was brought to England to serve as co-worker with Simon. Soon the two engravers disagreed on certain details of the coinage, so Roettier and Simon each prepared separate crown-size patterns. Disregarding Simon's earlier accomplishments such as the 1658 Oliver Cromwell crown, Simon's pattern was rejected by the government and Roettier's accepted. Simon, seeking the recognition rightfully his, produced the famous Petition Crown. This piece was engraved with remarkable attention to even microscopic details, producing an incomparable work of art from an engraving viewpoint. On the edge of the Petition Crown was lettered in perfect form the following inscription: THOMAS SIMON MOST HUMBLY PRAYS YOUR MAJESTY TO COMPARE HIS TRYALL PIECE WITH THE DUTCH AND IF TRULY DRAWN & EMBOSS'D MORE GRACEFULLY ORDER'D AND MORE ACCURATELY ENGRAVEN TO RELIEVE HIM. Simon's Petition Crown came to naught, and the dies for larger English coins continued to be engraved by the Dutchman Roettier.

Another fascinating coin in the British crown series is the 1703 issue with the word VIGO prominently lettered on the obverse below the portrait of Queen Anne. The British Navy in October, 1702, trapped a fleet of Spanish vessels, each heavily laden with gold and silver treasure, in the closed harbor of Vigo, Spain. The ships were bringing home bullion from the Spanish empire in America. Aware of the hopelessness of their position in Vigo harbor, the Spanish captains scuttled most of their ships. This vast treasure of silver and gold remains essentially intact on the floor of the harbor, covered with deep mud and shifting sands, guarded by treacherously changing currents. The total value is estimated to be in the hundreds of millions of dollars, if not far more.

The British did succeed in capturing a number of ships, however. To commemorate this naval victory the silver coins of Queen Anne in 1703 bore the VIGO notation. In addition, a limited number of gold pieces were produced with the same inscription. Here indeed is a fantastic coin—

Spanish treasure you can hold in your own hands! What a story such a coin has to tell! As I have noted numerous times throughout this book, therein lies much of the fascination of numismatics.

In 1723, crowns were prepared with the lettering SSC on the reverse. Such pieces were struck from silver bullion obtained from the South Sea Company as part of the damages paid after the "South Sea Bubble" speculation burst.

Crowns were struck in 1746 with the word LIMA under the portrait of King George II on the obverse. In his *Crown Pieces of Great Britain*, Howard W. A. Linecar observes that these coins were struck from bullion captured by Admiral Anson from a Spanish ship in the Philippine Islands during his voyage around the world. Mr. Linecar also notes that another theory is that the word only commemorates the use of bullion seized from various Spanish ships over a period of years, all of which bullion went to the Royal Mint for coinage. Anson never attacked Lima or captured any bullion there. He further notes that research into the subject is still continuing. It is interesting that such a prominent feature of English coinage (LIMA was used on other British denominations as well, and the coins were made in tremendous quantities) has lost its meaning over the years, and what was once a fact is now a series of theories. This is another fascination of numismatics: Not everything is known, and there is ample room for the scholar to discover interesting things.

During the late 18th and early 19th centuries, coins were very scarce in circulation in Britain. The Bank of England, concerned that commerce might grind to a halt, proposed an interesting interim solution whereby crown-size coins could be readily and rapidly obtained: The bank took Spanish milled dollars, many of which were minted in Mexico City, and counterstamped them on the obverse with the tiny portrait of King George III within an oval. The Spanish coins in question mainly featured the portrait of King Charles III or King Charles IV. The dollars were disliked by the public for several reasons: Spain was not a popular country and was an enemy of England in earlier times, the value of Spanish empire silver coins fluctuated, and in addition there were many counterfeits to further confuse the situation. Referring to the newly-counterstamped coins featuring the head of King George III stamped at the center of the portrait of Charles III or IV, a "naughty" rhyme of the period related: "The Bank to make its Spanish dollars pass, stamped the head of a fool on the neck of an ass."

Throughout the 19th and 20th centuries, there were many interesting crown varieties. Generally crowns were issued only at intermittent intervals. For example, crowns of King George IV (1820–1830) were issued for circulation only in 1821 and 1822. In addition, certain rare Proofs and patterns, specifically of the date 1826, are occasionally seen, but these are elusive.

The reign of William IV (1830–1837) produced only one major crown issue: the piece included as part of specimen Proof sets of 1831. No William IV crowns were ever struck for circulation. Today these Proof pieces are very rare, and a choice example fetches several thousand dollars.

Crowns of Queen Victoria (1837–1901) were made in several styles. Those produced in 1839, 1844, 1845, and the first part of 1847 portray the Queen as a lovely young girl. Following an 1846 pattern coinage, approximately 8,000 of a new Victorian crown design were released in 1847. Called the Gothic Crown, the piece has Gothic-style letters and ornamentation and is classic in its appearance. In 1853 an additional 500 pieces which bore the 1853 date were made for use in Proof sets. The Gothic Crown is considered to be one of the world's most beautiful issues.

In 1887, Queen Victoria celebrated her jubilee—fifty years on the throne of England. The crown was redesigned so that the obverse featured an older portrait of Queen Victoria with a small crown and veil. Specimens were minted from 1887 through 1892, inclusive. The reverse of this type, called the Jubilee Crown, featured a motif of St. George slaying the dragon, a style used several times throughout British coinage during the 19th and 20th centuries.

From 1893 through 1900, the "Old Head" Victoria crowns appeared. Queen Victoria, then in the final years of her life, is depicted as an older woman. Unlike earlier issues, coinage throughout this span was continuous and examples were struck each year.

The only crown of the reign of King Edward VII (1901–1910) was issued in 1902. Pieces were made for inclusion in Proof sets plus slightly over a quarter million specimens for circulation. A graphic example of the difference in coin collecting interest between the United States and England at this time is illustrated by the fact that 15,123 King Edward VII crowns were struck for use in Proof sets in 1902. During the same year, just 777 American counterparts—the Morgan silver dollar—were struck in Proof condition at the Philadelphia Mint for distribution to collectors. The balance has tipped the other way since then, and today collectors in the United States vastly outnumber those in England.

Crowns of King George V (1910–1936) were produced from 1927 through 1936, inclusive. The 1935 issue is a commemorative design celebrating the 25th year of his reign. The reverse of the 1935 crown has the

COINS OF KING EDWARD VIII. In 1937, in anticipation of the impending coronation of the Duke of Windsor as King Edward VIII (actually he served all functions of king following the death of King George V in 1936), a series of coins bearing the portrait of King Edward VIII were prepared at the Royal Mint in London. When the Duke of Windsor then abdicated the throne to marry Wallis Warfield Simpson, in one of the greatest love stories of all time, Edward VIII coin designs were held in abeyance. Here are illustrated the farthing (quarter penny), penny, sixpence, shilling, half crown, and crown of King Edward VIII—the only specimens ever to appear on the numismatic market. These coins, acquired by Bowers and Ruddy Galleries in 1973, are said to have been the property of Mr. T. H. Paget, who designed the obverse of each issue. These pieces are among the most valuable coins of the world. A king's ransom could not secure duplicate specimens!

earlier-used St. George and the dragon motif, but done in starkly modernistic style, which offended the traditional sense of many British citizens and caused great criticism at the time. Crown issues of 1927–1934 and 1936 are remarkable for their low mintages. Fewer than 10,000 were struck of every year except 1927, when 15,000 were struck. The figures touched bottom in 1934 when only 932 pieces were made—truly a rarity in our own time!

In 1937 in anticipation of the impending coronation of the Duke of Windsor as King Edward VIII (actually he had performed all functions of king following the death of George V in 1936), a series of coins bearing the portrait of King Edward VIII were prepared. These pieces included the denominations of farthing, halfpenny, penny, brass threepence, sixpence, shilling, florin, half crown, and crown. The only denominations actually released into the hands of the public were some of the brass threepence pieces. These were given to manufacturers of coin-operated machines for testing purposes, for the brass threepence was a new type of coin that year (previously threepence pieces had been made only in silver). It is not known how many of these brass threepence pieces were actually circulated this way, but guesses range from one dozen to two dozen specimens. In 1963, James F. Ruddy and I purchased one of these rare 1937 King Edward VIII threepence pieces and sold it into the magnificent collection of Carl Nickel of Canada, who then considered it to be the centerpiece of his exhibit. It is interesting to note that the Duke of Windsor, whose abdication from the throne of England was part of what is probably the greatest love story of all time, searched for many years for a specimen of a coin bearing his portrait as King. Finally he was able to obtain one of the brass threepence pieces through a coin dealer in America.

As I related in my *High Profits from Rare Coin Investment*, one of the most outstanding finds of my numismatic career occurred when Bowers and Ruddy Galleries in 1973 purchased six different official British coins bearing the portrait and inscription of King Edward VIII. These coins, of various denominations from the farthing through the large crown, were said to have been the property of T. H. Paget, who designed the obverse of the coin for the Royal Mint in London. I personally consider the 1937 King Edward VIII silver-dollar-size crown to be one of the world's most valuable, romantic, and rare issues. A king's ransom could not buy another!

Other crowns have been issued intermittently. In 1937 and 1951, pieces bearing the portrait of King George VI were produced in quantity. In 1953, the Queen Elizabeth coronation crown whose design was suggested by British coin dealer Fred Jeffrey was struck to the extent of 6,000,000 pieces. Popular also was the 1965 commemorative featuring the portrait of Elizabeth II on the obverse and Winston Churchill on the reverse.

Until the 19th and 20th centuries, when designs for various denominations began to differ, often a half crown resembled nothing else so much as a miniature crown, and the silver sixpence and shilling were also similar in design. Thus, in 1746, not only were crowns struck with LIMA on them, but other silver denominations as well were produced. Likewise, the various copper denominations often followed each other in design.

The number of interesting stories among British coins is nearly endless. I will close with one about the famous farthing (¼ penny) of Queen Anne. This was produced, in limited quantities, bearing the dates 1713 and 1714. Today a choice specimen can be purchased in the $100 to $200 range. Twenty years ago a choice example could be secured for £5 to £10 (approximately $20 to $40 at the time). Several hundred pieces are known to exist.

An interesting legend is attached to the Queen Anne farthing. The late C. Wilson Peck, in his classic *English Copper, Tin and Bronze Coins in the British Museum 1558–1958*, noted that the origin of this popular belief has been lost in history, but for a long time it was considered that the possessor of such a piece had a fortune in his hands. He quotes an earlier account:

> Amongst the many infatuations which have possessed the people of this country, the popular error connected with the farthings of Queen Anne is one of the most curious and remarkable. The common belief was, and is even yet with many persons, that only three were ever struck and that these are of immense value. The origin of this idle story is unknown.
>
> One account has it that a lady from Yorkshire many years since, having lost a Queen Anne farthing, which probably had from some circumstance or other great value *for her*, offered a large reward for its restoration. Another account is that a possessor of one of these farthings offered it for sale in a newspaper for 500 pounds sterling. Yet another tale is that an auctioneer to advertise himself once offered one of these coins for sale and nominally sold it to a bidder for 500 pounds which, of course getting very much talked about, served his purpose.
>
> Although nothing is clearly known from whence this error sprung, the fact remains that for a long period it has been in existence. In *Esperella's Letters from England*, 1808, it is stated that "a man was brought before the magistrates charged by a soldier with having assaulted him on the highway and robbed him of eight pounds, some silver, and a Queen Anne farthing. The man protested his innocence and brought sufficient proof of it. Upon further investigation it was discovered that some pettifogging lawyer, as ignorant as he was villainous, had suborned the soldier to bring this accusation against an

innocent man in the hopes of hanging him and getting possession of the farthing.

At Dublin, 1814, an extraordinary trial took place in connection with one of these coins, an account of which appeared in *The British Press* newspaper, on the 14th of February in that year, by which it appears that a man named George Hone received 12 months' imprisonment for stealing a Queen Anne farthing. And so impressed were the parties of its great value that it was estimated that 700 pounds was only half the price that would be realized by its sale! The counsel for the Crown further informed the jury that only three specimens were known, that the die broke upon striking the third farthing, and that one farthing was in the King's Museum, the second in the British Museum, and the third was missing—and was presumed to be the one in question.

Peck further notes that over the years many people have traveled to London from all parts of the country with Queen Anne farthings, hoping to make a fortune by selling them. It is Peck's estimation that several hundred or more Queen Anne farthings actually exist. The coin is scarce today and was less scarce years ago.

QUEEN ANNE FARTHING. Farthings bearing the portrait of Queen Anne were struck in 1713 and 1714. While these are scarce, they are not extremely rare and several hundred specimens are known to numismatists today. Over the years a number of legends have arisen concerning this piece. Once in a court trial the British Government stated that only three specimens were known, and the possessor of one of these was given 12 months imprisonment for allegedly stealing one of these rarities! Other examples are given in the text.

The sun never sets on the British Empire, so it has been said. Likewise, coins minted under the authority of Britain were struck by countries in all parts of the globe. While many such countries have since become independent, others are members of the British Commonwealth. Many British Commonwealth nations issue coins today bearing the portrait of Queen Elizabeth II. Considering history as well as the present, many dozens of countries, islands, territories, and settlements have been under British rule. In fact, the United States is included in this category. During the popularity of coin collecting in Great Britain during the 1780's and 1790's the coins of America were much sought after, the colonies comprising the United States having recently been British possessions. It will be recalled that during the 18th century coins were specifically struck in England for use in America: the 1773 Virginia halfpenny, the Rosa Americana issues, and the coins prepared under the auspices of Cecil Calvert, being examples.

Numismatic issues of Ireland and Scotland are closely intertwined with those of England. A partial list of geographical areas once or presently under British control or rule or affiliated with Britain follows: Aden, Antigua, Australia, Bahama Islands, Bandarmassin, Barbados, Bermuda, British Caribbean Territories, British Guinea, British Honduras, British West Africa (Nigeria), Brunei, Burma, Canada, Cape of Good Hope, Celebes Island, Ceylon, Cyprus, Dominica, East Africa (Mombasa), Fuji, Ghana, Gibraltar, Gold Coast, Grenada, Griquatown, Guadeloupe, Guernsey, Hong Kong, India, Ionian Islands, Isle of Man, Jamaica, Java, Jersey, Kuwait, Lundy, Malacca, Malaya, Maldive Islands, Malta, Martinique, Mauritius, Montserrat—and that is just the first half of the alphabet! Jerome Remick, to mention just one author actively engaged in research in British Commonwealth issues, has spent many years enumerating coin varieties of British Commonwealth countries, and each year he continues to make new discoveries.

German Coins

Select any major country of the world and chances are it will have a rich numismatic history. The coins of Germany, for example, far outnum-

COINS OF GERMANY. Collecting coins of a given country is a popular pursuit with numismatists and investors. Certain countries—England, France, Germany, and Mexico are examples—have long and rich coinage histories. (1) 1765 "city view taler" depicting the cityscape of Nuremburg. (2) 1843 double taler depicting Frankfurt. (3) 1913 pattern crown by Goetz depicting Kaiser Wilhelm II in a war helmet. On the reverse a defiant eagle protects the crown. (4) 1927 commemorative three-mark piece observing the centennial of Bremerhaven. (5) 1927 commemorative three-mark piece issued for the 450th anniversary of Tübingen University. (6) 1928 commemorative three-mark piece depicting artist Albrecht Dürer. (7) 1929 commemorative five-mark piece celebrating the round-the-world flight of the Graf Zeppelin.

ber those of the United States and rival the extensive issues of Great Britain. Until its unification in 1871, Germany was partitioned into many states. Prior to the 18th century there were actually several hundred separate entities, each with its own government. Many of these issued coins. Dr. John Davenport, noted authority on the field of world crowns, has compiled several books just on German issues! A complete reference covering all German coins from tiny copper coins to large gold issues would fill a large bookshelf should it ever be written.

Particularly interesting are large crowns, called talers in Germany, from several hundred years ago. A popular practice was to depict on one side the panorama of a city. Such coins are called "city view talers" by collectors today. By assembling a set of such pieces one can graphically see how Nuremberg, Frankfurt, and many other German cities appeared in former times. Likewise fascinating are the many German commemorative issues of the 19th and 20th centuries. These latter coins were produced in some instances in fairly large quantities, for at the time many collectors desired them.

SWISS SHOOTING TALERS. Popular with collectors today are commemorative dollar-size coins of Switzerland, particularly those called "shooting talers" issued during the 19th and 20th centuries to commemorate sportsmen's festivals in various Swiss towns and cities.

ZÜRICH
5 FRANKEN
1859
1836 · 1876
5 F
5 FR.
1861
ARNOLD
5 FRANKEN

Swiss Coins

The commemorative crowns of Switzerland, particularly the "shooting talers" issued during the 19th and 20th centuries, celebrate the sportsmen's festivals in various Swiss towns and cities. Thus we find, for example, that 6,000 shooting talers were issued in 1859 to commemorate that year's get-together in Zurich. In 1874, 15,000 examples were struck for the event in St. Gallen, and 30,000 in 1881 for Fribourg. There are many, many other examples.

French Coins

France has produced thousands of coin issues over the years. Like Germany, Mexico, and certain other large countries, France has had many mints, each with its own distinctive mintmark. Now the Paris Mint produces the country's coinage. The list of French mints and mintmarks from the past is an extensive one. A sample follows: Paris, mintmark A, Metz, AA, Rouen, E, Strasbourg, BB, Caen, C, Lyon, D, and so on. Over the years there have been more than two dozen official mints, making even Mexico's total of fourteen seem small! At one time during the "glory of France" that nation was the world's cultural center. Accordingly, many fine numismatic issues—some with superb artistry—can be collected from the 18th and 19th centuries, in particular.

Collecting Coins of the World

In the United States, the collecting of coins of the world, that is, from countries other than the United States, is very popular. Specialties are divided into several groups. Some collectors aspire to build specialized series of one country only. Often within that country a further specialty is made—the eight-real pieces of Mexico or the pennies of Great Britain, for example. Still other collectors assemble a wide spectrum of issues—one crown or silver-dollar-size coins from as many countries as possible, as another example. Still other numismatists may aspire to own one gold coin from as many countries as possible. Another way is to assemble a collection of pieces from a particular era of interest: coins from World War I or World War II, for example. In the field of stamp collecting (philately), collecting by design topics—ships, birds, and so on—is popular. Strangely enough, this way of collecting, something which could be easily done with world coins, has never caught on with collectors. To be sure, there are some exceptions: The lovely collection of coins featuring ship motifs sold to us by noted collector P. B. Trotter a few years ago is an illustration.

Tokens and store cards of the world, paper money, and medals form still additional numismatic specialties.

One advantage of the field of world coins is that many issues remain undiscovered so far as values are concerned. Great rarities can often be obtained for fairly nominal sums. Adding to this advantage is the possibility of making an important discovery. While the coins of the United States have been carefully studied by date, mintmark, and die varieties (although more varieties remain to be discovered), the same is not true of many other world countries. Therein lie many possibilities for research.

Investment-wise, coins of the world have done well over the years. As coin collecting becomes more and more popular throughout the world, citizens of individual nations will desire their own countries' coins as well as coins from other parts of the globe. There is vast potential in this regard, for there are many heavily populated areas of the globe which have only a nominal number of coin collectors today.

12

Coin Grading

In 1970, my long-time business associate James F. Ruddy published *Photograde*, a guide to the grading of coins. This useful book has been adopted as a standard grading guide by the American Numismatic Association. In addition it has received much praise from other organizations, the numismatic press, and collectors and dealers in general. Much of the information in the present chapter is drawn from Jim Ruddy's writings in this field.

The condition or grading of a coin is extremely important. The frequent question "What is it worth?" has its answer dependent to a large degree upon how much wear a particular coin has received. When it leaves the coining press, it is in "new" condition, a grade which collectors designate as "Uncirculated." Such a coin has never seen circulation. An Uncirculated coin at the time of mintage is brilliant and frosty and shows no sign of wear or use. After such a piece has been used in the channels of commerce for many years, possibly for half a century or more, it becomes extremely worn. Often coins are encountered which are almost illegible due to the amount of wear they have received. These coins would be at the opposite end of the scale and would grade what collectors call "About Good." Between these two extremes there are many other grades. In order from the lowest to the highest, the standard conditions are: About Good, Good, Very Good, Fine, Very Fine, Extremely Fine, About Uncirculated, and Uncirculated. And then there is a special condition, a condition which describes a coin with a mirrorlike surface struck especially for collectors, Proof.

It is common practice to capitalize the grade of a coin. Thus such a description as "Here is an 1848 cent in Good condition" means, not that the coin is "good" in the sense of being desirable or worthwhile but, rather it is "Good" by the strict grading standards defining that term. Thus capitalization serves to prevent confusion. Likewise, if you are offered a coin described as being Fine or Very Fine grade, these are specific coin grades—not meaning that the coin is in "nice" or "very nice" grade but that the coin will grade to meet established standards.

To an investor or collector, coin grading is extremely important. Next to the information on the coin such as the date, mintmark, and denomination, the grade is the single most important factor you must know to determine a coin's true market value. Any catalog or pricing guide will give you a range of current values, but for any given coin these values will depend upon condition.

Let me take as an example a 1926-S quarter, a Liberty standing quarter struck at the San Francisco Mint that year. In the 1974 edition of *A Guide Book of United States Coins* the 1926-S was priced as follows: Good, $1.25; Very Good, $2.50; Fine, $4.50; Very Fine, $18.50; Extremely Fine, $45, and Uncirculated, $160. Note that the difference between Good and Uncirculated is a factor of over 100!

While no collector is apt to mistake a Good coin for an Uncirculated one, because of obvious differences in the coin's appearance, there is ample room for error in grades which are near each other. For instance, if you are offered a coin described as Very Fine, but in reality it is just Fine, then you would be paying in this example $18.50 for a coin worth just $4.50! This is a very important thing to remember—grading is vital. Typically someone seeking to misrepresent a coin—a practice called overgrading—will take, in our example, a Fine coin worth $4.50 and will call it Very Fine. However, he will not advertise it at $18.50 but, rather, will seek to give the buyer a real "bargain." The price might be advertised as only $9. The would-be buyer thinks he has made the purchase of the century and rushes in with his check. In reality, he is paying twice what he should for a $4.50 coin. However, at the same time he thinks he is getting an $18.50 coin for half price, so he is pleased. Of course, if he knows about grading, this is not a problem. In my examples, by the way, I am assuming that each grade sells for strictly catalog value. In practice sale prices do vary from catalog, but the principle remains the same.

Another illustration is the 1936 Washington quarter. In the pricing guide this coin catalogs as follows: Good, $.40; Very Good, $.45; Fine, $.75; Extremely Fine, $1.50; Uncirculated, $7, and Proof, $335. Several years ago some unscrupulous persons decided to polish Uncirculated coins to make them artificially appear as Proofs. Of course, the deception would not fool the knowledgeable collector, but it was not knowledgeable collectors to whom such pieces were offered. Rather, they were distributed through antique shows and other places where collectors gathered and where buyers are not necessarily knowledgeable numismatists. Typically such a coin might be offered with a sales talk such as this: "Here is a really good value on a 1936 Proof quarter. I don't know much about coins myself, but I purchased this in an estate (or some other place) and bought it cheaply. I see that it catalogs $335, but I don't have much in it so you can have it for just $150."

The buyer, entranced with the thought of buying a Proof coin at half catalog value, jumps at the opportunity. If the deception should be discovered at a later date, then there are several possibilities: The collector might seek to find the antique dealer only to find that he has long since disappeared, or the dealer might be found and will then say that the coin was sold "as is" with some comment such as "You had a chance to look at it before you bought it." Or, in the most favorable circumstances so far as the collector is concerned, the dealer might be located and a refund might be forthcoming. Then the unscrupulous vendor might take the coin to another show and sell it to someone else with the same story.

The preceding illustration makes several points. It is best to buy coins from a knowledgeable dealer who guarantees the authenticity of his coins. Any leading dealer will be happy to guarantee in writing that the coins offered are authentic. No one is perfect, and being human, leading dealers occasionally make errors. However, when such a dealer makes an error it is rectified—and a refund is forthcoming. Indeed, members of the Professional Numismatists Guild and the International Association of Professional Numismatists, the two leading dealers' organizations, pledge themselves to a rigid code of ethics that includes customer service, guaranteed authenticity, and high standards of professional conduct. There are also many fine dealers who are not members of these or other organizations for financial reasons or because of the size of their businesses or the length of time they have been in business. Generally, membership in the two organizations mentioned is limited to larger dealers who have been in business a long time and who have large amounts of capital. However, an association member or not, any dealer should be willing to guarantee the authenticity of what he sells.

Never buy a coin in "as is" condition. If you buy 100 coins "as is" chances are you will get one true bargain and 99 pieces which are relatively worthless. This warning was succinctly put by Lee Hewitt: "There is no Santa Claus in numismatics." In other words, you get what you pay for. The margin on truly choice and rare coins is nominal, and, for example, coins that are really worth $200 simply cannot be bought at half price. Mr. Hewitt, one of the country's most distinguished numismatists, founded the *Numismatic Scrapbook Magazine.* For many years he had an overview of the coin business as he watched transactions between collectors all over the world and the thousands of dealers and vendors who advertised in his magazine.

As a coin buyer you should no more accept a coin in Fine Grade while paying a Very Fine price than you would accept a coin with a date or mintmark different from the one you ordered. The value of each individual coin is specifically determined by its grade. It is not at all uncommon to find a difference of many dollars or even many hundreds of dollars in value from one grade to another. Thus, coin grading is too important to be dependent on instinct or guesswork. It is important to use a standard authority such as *Photograde.*

It is not my intention to tout *Photograde*; the book sells wonderfully without my help—more than 100,000 copies are in print. I do, however, consider it basic, and the importance of grading is such that it cannot be overemphasized. As James F. Ruddy has written, the basic rules should be such that every dealer and collector abides by them. A coin is designated by a specific grade in accordance with the amount of wear it has received. The condition should not change because of transfer from one owner to another. Unfortunately, when buying a coin some might grade a particular specimen as being in Fine condition—but after owning it and then deciding to sell it, it might magically (or perhaps hopefully would be a better word) become Very Fine! Such practices can be eliminated, of course, by widespread knowledge of grading.

In numismatic research grading is equally useful. Common grading terminology permits the interchange of information in a concise manner. A scholar doing research on a rare variety of 1795 half dollar will know he has made an extremely important discovery if he locates a particular variety in Extremely Fine grade, if the best other specimen of this variety grades just Very Good. By using common grading terminology our researcher knows he has made an important find without even seeing the next best coin. Extremely Fine fits certain grading standards and Very Good fits other standards, thus permitting an interchange of information.

COIN GRADING USING THE PHOTOGRADE SYSTEM. The value of a coin is dependent upon its condition—how much wear it has received. These illustrations are ones used in *Photograde*, the standard photographic guide to coin grading that is available at most coin shops. The piece in these examples is the Liberty nickel, a design used from 1883 through 1913, but all coin designs from 1793 to date are covered in *Photograde.* Also shown are four grades of the Buffalo nickel. Grading coins is both an art and a science. Often a small difference in grade means a large difference in value.

LIBERTY HEAD NICKELS 1883–1913

About Good

Obverse: The rim will be worn down into the stars and/or the date.

Reverse: The figure "V" and the wreath will be visible.

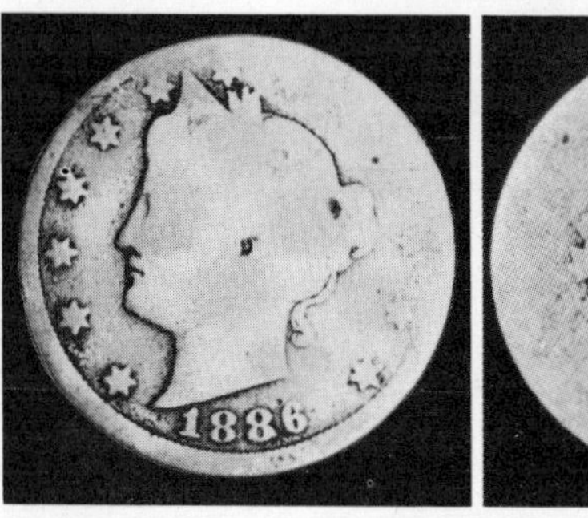

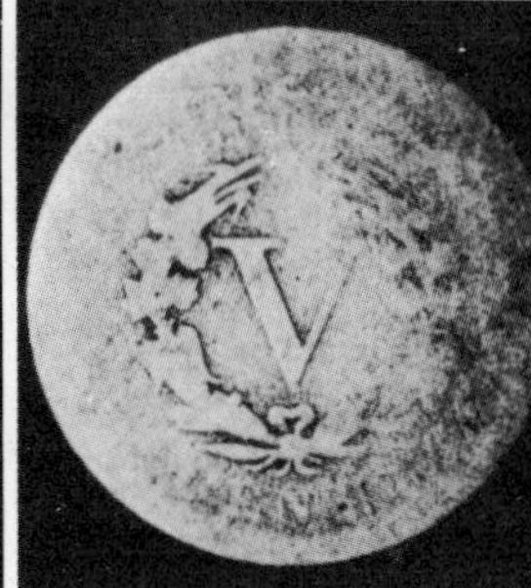

Good

Obverse: Liberty will be outlined but the legend LIBERTY will not show on her headband.

Reverse: The rim may be worn down to the tops of the letters. E PLURIBUS UNUM will be barely visible.

Very Good

Obverse: A total of any three letters of LIBERTY must show. This could be a combination of two full letters plus two half letters as not all dates of Liberty nickels wore uniformly.

Reverse: The wreath will be sharply outlined. E PLURIBUS UNUM will show weakly.

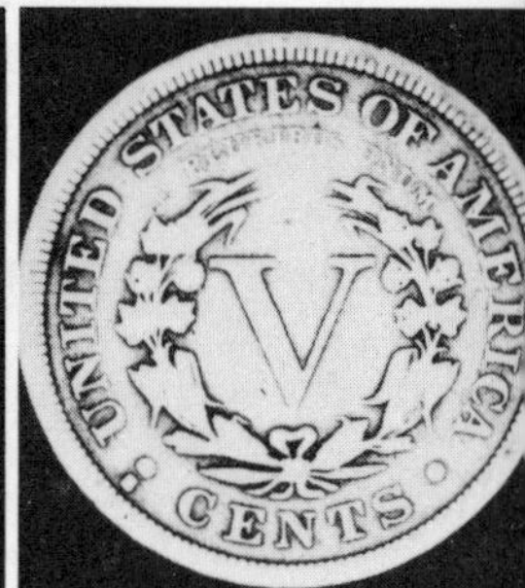

Fine

Obverse: A full LIBERTY must be readable, including the letter "I." About half of the hair detail will be visible.

Reverse: Detail will begin to appear in the wreath. E PLURIBUS UNUM will be strong.

Very Fine

Obverse: LIBERTY will be complete and bold. The hair will show about 75% detail.

Reverse: Partial detail will show on the leaves of the wreath and the ear of corn.

Extremely Fine

Obverse: LIBERTY will be very bold. All of the details will be visible but may be weak on the high points above the ear and forehead.

Reverse: There will be wear on the high points of the wreath and ear of corn.

About Uncirculated

Obverse: There will be only the slightest trace of wear on the highest portion of the hair above the ear and forehead.

Reverse: There will be only a trace of wear on the highest portions of the wreath.

BUFFALO NICKELS 1913–1938

About Good

Obverse: The rim will be worn down well into the letters. Only a partial date will show, but date must be recognizable.

Reverse: The rim will be worn down into the letters.

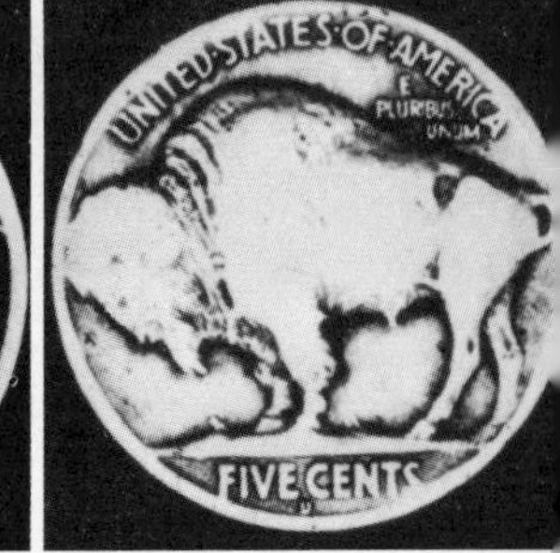

Good

Obverse: The rim will be worn down into the tops of the letters of LIBERTY. The date will be readable but some of the numbers will be well worn.

Reverse: The rim may be worn down into the tops of the letters. The horn need not show.

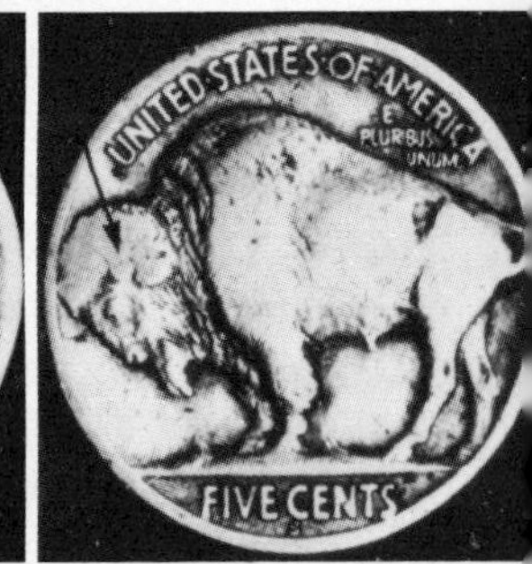

Very Good

Obverse: The rim may touch the tops of the letters of LIBERTY. The date will be distinct.

Reverse: There will be a full rim. Half of the horn will show. The buffalo's back will be almost smooth.

Fine

Obverse: LIBERTY will be separated from the rim. The date will be very bold.

Reverse: ⅔ of the horn will show. The major detail on the buffalo's back will show.

Coin grading, extremely important today, has not always been so. People have been collecting coins for more than 2,000 years, making numismatics one of the oldest hobbies. Before the 20th century, most collectors classified their coins as either new or used. Sometimes grading was used, but the grade differences were minimal—perhaps just three grades were used such as Good, Very Fine, and Uncirculated, plus the addition of Proofs when this grade appeared from time to time. Rarely did the price of a coin dictate that a finer distinction in grading be made. Most United States coins, including some great scarcities and rarities, could be purchased for a small premium over their face value.

The situation today is much different. In recent decades there has been an ever-increasing demand for rare coins. The supply of such pieces remains constant since the mintage of a given year can never be changed. The natural result following economic laws has been a dramatic appreciation in value. It has thus become increasingly more important to grade coins carefully. Whereas a difference between Fine and Very Fine might have meant just a dollar or two twenty years ago, and perhaps $50 to $100 in the 1960's, now it may mean $100 to $200. In the future the differences will probably be even more significant.

Actual grading information on a coin-by-coin basis can be found in *Photograde.* As you become an experienced collector, you will learn to recognize coin grades almost subconsciously when you see them. In the basic grading descriptions that follow, all comments are general in nature and apply to United States coinage. Individual coins and series may frequently vary.

The basic lowest condition used by knowledgeable collectors is the About Good classification. This represents a well-worn coin which can still be identified as to date and mint. The date will be visible in its entirety, or at least the significant digits, such as the last one or two numerals, will be present to permit identification without equivocation. The mintmark, even though it might be worn so as to only be a blob or an indication, will still be identifiable. Lower grades, descriptions such as Fair and Poor, are sometimes used to describe coins which only have a tiny portion of the design visible. For instance, you might be able to tell that a given coin in Poor condition is indeed a United States Indian cent, but you might not have the foggiest notion of its date. So, About Good represents the minimum that a collector will usually accept for his collection, for the coin can then be identified as to the place and time in which it was minted.

Next up the grading ladder is Good. This usually indicates an overall clean-appearing coin which has all or nearly all lettering visible and basic features outlined, except for certain coins dated in the 1700's and early 1800's.

Very Good is the next popular intermediate grade. It is also one of the easiest grades to classify. Although the description of Very Good varies from one coin design to another, for the majority of United States coins the word LIBERTY on the headband or in the shield can be used to determine this grade. For many coin designs, a total of any three letters of the word LIBERTY serve to identify a coin as being in Very Good grade. This is a useful tool particularly in reference to issues of the late 19th and early 20th centuries; on earlier issues the word LIBERTY often appears separately on the coin and is not used as a grading landmark. The total of three letters can consist of three separate letters, or perhaps two full letters and two half letters, or even one full letter and an equivalent number of partial letters. Of course it is important that all other features of both the obverse and reverse verify this grade as well. If just the distinctive letters of the word LIBERTY show but the date and mintmark are not visible, then the coin of course grades lower.

Fine condition is probably the most widely collected circulated grade. The major design features are usually visible. The word LIBERTY, except on twenty-cent pieces and on certain silver dollar varieties, is complete. Fine condition often represents an attractive compromise between the cost of a coin and the availability of all the design features. Thus, it is a very popular condition and many numismatists collect by this grade.

One more rung up the grading ladder is Very Fine. More of the intricate design feature will be noticeable than on a coin in Fine condition. We are now getting into a technical realm, and it is difficult to give here the distinguishing differences. The comparison of actual coins or coin photographs in *Photograde* will define the grade.

Next comes Extremely Fine or, as some sometimes say, "Extra Fine" (although extra is really not an appropriate term, for extra means superfluous). Nearly all the design details will be visible on an Extremely Fine coin. This is a coin which has seen limited circulation, possibly for just a few years.

About Uncirculated describes a coin which is nearly Uncirculated, a piece which has only been circulated for a short period of time. Often some mint luster will show in the field and in protected spaces such as areas between letters.

Uncirculated coins are those which have not seen actual circulation in hand-to-hand use in commerce. Collectors and dealers recognize several variations of the Uncirculated grade. Brilliant Uncirculated describes a piece which has full mint color. The coin which has acquired toning over the years is described as being Toned Uncirculated or, in the case of copper coins, as Brown Uncirculated, Red and Brown Uncirculated, or other adjectives are used to describe the coloration. Toning on some coins is quite beautiful, and occasionally picturesque descriptions such as "a beautiful 1896 quarter with superb iridescent toning" will be used to describe such pieces in a sale catalog.

Certain early coins are extremely difficult to find in Uncirculated condition without any bagmarks or handling marks. Such flawless pieces are sometimes designated as Choice Uncirculated or Gem Uncirculated. Choice describes an above-average Uncirculated specimen, usually well struck and with a minimum of minor bagmarks or minting defects. Gem Uncirculated is the finest available, a sharply struck coin free of the usual minor bagmarks and minting defects.

Another description often used is Brilliant Uncirculated with light rubbing. This is a coin with full mint luster which may show some rubbing, particularly on the very highest parts, due to rubbing from an album slide in a coin collection or by rubbing against other coins in a mint bag.

It must be remembered that coins are produced for commercial purposes—to provide a medium of exchange in commerce and trade. Mints of the past and present, faced with working long hours to satisfy an ever-increasing demand for such pieces, cannot afford to mint coins carefully so far as collectors are concerned. James F. Ruddy uses as an example a typical coin, a twenty-dollar gold piece minted at Carson City, Nevada, in 1883. This coin, when first minted, was ejected from the coining press and dropped into a hopper. Immediately the surface acquired several nicks and other marks from having contacted other coins. Our new coin was then dumped from the hopper, possibly inspected for any major minting defects (such as a faulty planchet), and then put with other coins mixed loosely in a bag. During these handling processes no care whatsoever was taken to handle the coin by its edges or otherwise give it the care that a collector would have. To have done so would have tremendously increased the mintage expense.

Once bagged, our new coin would have been transferred, possibly over a long distance and not necessarily using gentle means of transportation, to a storage area in a bank. It then might have been moved from bank to bank several times during the next few decades. For purposes of illustration, we will assume that the coin was never released into the official channels of commerce but was, say, obtained from a bank for use as a Christmas gift many years ago. Even though our 1883-CC double eagle is technically Uncirculated, it is evident from the handling it has received that it will show some marks. In fact, as you may suspect from the preceding description, to find an 1883-CC double eagle (or any other early double eagle from this Far West mint) in Gem Uncirculated condition would be virtually impossible. And this is precisely the case.

On the other hand, a small coin such as a modern dime is of much less weight and can more easily survive the rigors of bank-to-bank or intra-mint handling. So, finding a modern coin in Choice Uncirculated condition or Gem Uncirculated grade is usually not difficult.

Proof represents another coin grade. Proof is not a grade *superior* to Uncirculated but, rather, is a *different* grade. Proof coins are those struck especially for collectors. Special dies polished to a high, mirrorlike finish are used. Special planchets, blank metal pieces, are likewise carefully treated before the designs are impressed on them. The result is a specially created coin with a mirrorlike or Proof surface. When a Proof coin becomes worn (as it might if someone inadvertently "spends" it!) it does not then become Uncirculated or Almost Uncirculated, as the coin was never Uncirculated in the first place. This distinction is often overlooked by collectors. Rather, a Proof which has seen wear is best described as being an "impaired Proof." Of course if the wear is such that all the Proof surface is gone, then it can be graded by normal lower grades such as Fine, Very Fine, and so on.

Proofs have been made in a number of varieties. During the early 20th century, the Philadelphia Mint, following the lead taken by the Paris Mint, experimented with several different types of Proof finishes including Satin Proof, Sandblast Proof, and Matte Proof. Although the manufacturing processes differ from one another, these terms are sometimes used interchangeably today. These types of Proofs have a grainy surface that serves to highlight the higher parts of the coin in an almost medallic relief. Recognizing a Matte Proof and being able to distinguish it from an Uncirculated coin is very important. Sometimes there does not appear to be a great difference to the untrained eye. However, Matte Proofs invariably have sharp, squared-off rims which serve to differentiate them. The best guide in this regard is experience.

The standard type of Proof is that with a "brilliant" surface. These are the Proofs minted with mirrorlike dies. Although specimens with prooflike characteristics occur from earlier years, equipment for the production of Brilliant Proof coins was first installed in the Philadelphia Mint in 1817 when new equipment was brought in to replace that lost or damaged in a fire the previous year. From 1817 through the early 1850's, Proofs were produced only on infrequent occasions, mainly for presentation to government officials, visiting foreign dignitaries, and so on. Collectors could obtain them upon special request, but there weren't many collectors at that time so the numbers produced were small.

Today many countries, the United States, Canada, Panama, and Great Britain among them, issue Proof sets. Some countries issue Proof sets on a continuing basis, but most issue them intermittently, Great Britain being an example of the latter practice. Nowadays United States Proof sets can be ordered from the Treasury Department each year. During the early 1970's, approximately 3,000,000 sets were produced each year at the San Francisco Mint. Before 1968, Proofs for collectors were struck at the Philadelphia Mint and bore no mintmark, with the solitary exception of a certain variety of 1942 nickel which has a P mintmark. Since 1968, the San Francisco Mint has issued these sets, each coin with an S mintmark.

Proof coins are now offered in sets. At one time the United States Mint sold Proof coins on an individual basis. While precise ordering instructions varied from time to time, generally one could order minor coins, one cent through five cents in nickel, as a separate group. Thus, in 1878, for example, a set of minor Proof coins would contain the cent, nickel three-cent piece, and shield five cent in nickel. Silver coins could be purchased as a separate set as well. Thus, in the same year, a set of silver Proof coins would consist of all denominations from the dime through the trade dollar. Gold coins could be ordered individually on a coin-by-coin basis. There were variations in mintage from time to time when special quantity orders were received by the Mint for certain Proof issues. For example, 1,987 Proof silver trade dollars were made in 1880, whereas just 1,355 specimens were produced of each of the other silver denominations.

Proof gold coins, extremely desirable today, were not always popular. To purchase a Proof double eagle 100 years ago represented a great outlay of capital for the average collector due to the coin's high face value. Thus, in the year 1875, just twenty specimens of the Proof twenty-dollar gold piece of that year were ordered from the Mint. On the other hand, many hundreds of minor and silver Proof coins of each denomination were ordered.

Proof coins were first generally sold to collectors in 1858. During that year eighty sets were distributed. From 1858 through 1916, Proofs were sold of most Philadelphia Mint issues. Then Proof coinage lapsed and was not resumed until 1936. From then until 1942 sets were again made. Then coinage was suspended due to World War II. Coinage was again resumed in 1950 and continued through 1964. In 1965 a critical nationwide coin shortage forced the Mint to turn its full attention to producing coins for circulation, and Proof sets were again suspended. In 1968 Proofs were again issued, this time by the San Francisco Mint.

Many beautiful Proof sets can be collected from countries around the world. For example, Great Britain issued specimen Proof sets for presentation purposes and for sale to collectors in 1826, 1831, 1839, 1853, 1887, 1893, 1902, 1911, and 1927—to mention just issues of earlier years. In addition, occasional Proofs were struck in limited quantities for other years, but such sets generally are not available today. Canada issued presentation Proof sets in 1858, 1870, 1911, and a few other early years, but these are very rare today. On the other hand, the United States produced an almost continuous flow of sets, and anyone with the capital can assemble over a period of time a date run of Proof sets such as 1858, 1859, 1860, 1861, 1862, and so on, even a complete set from 1858 through 1916 if he can afford it.

For conciseness, abbreviations are often used to designate coin grades. About Good is often abbreviated as "Abt. G" or "AG." Good is abbreviated simply as "G" and Very Good as "VG." Fine is abbreviated as "F," Very Fine as "VF," and Extremely Fine as "EF" (or sometimes as "XF"). About Uncirculated is conveniently shortened to "AU." Uncirculated is often seen as "Unc." Brilliant Uncirculated is commonly abbreviated as "BU." Proof is shortened to "Pr" occasionally.

Strange as it may seem, one coin can often be correctly described as being in two different grades! The obverse or front side of a coin might be in Extremely Fine condition, for example, while the reverse is in just Fine condition. The explanation is simple: Many coins, particularly ones from the 18th and 19th centuries, were struck with different degrees of die detail and relief. Take, for instance, a certain variety of 1794 United States large cent. The obverse of the coin is struck with a high relief, almost like a sculpture or medal. Less attention was given to the reverse side of the coin, and all of the reverse design details were cut very shallowly. The rim around the reverse, while present, was very low. After the coin had been in circulation for twenty or thirty years, the reverse was worn considerably as the features were not very distinct to begin with. On the other hand, the obverse features, being protected from wear by the high rim and having a higher relief to begin with, wore to a much lesser extent. The result is that the coin today might be accurately described as having an Extremely Fine obverse and a Fine reverse. This particular coin would be described in abbreviated form as being EF/Fine condition. The obverse grading, always listed first, is Extremely Fine. The diagonal mark then separates the obverse grade from the reverse grade, which is Fine.

When you take into consideration that early coins were made from hand-crafted dies, it is apparent that some features used in grading will vary from issue to issue. On a certain variety of 1795 half cent, the date was cut into the die so lightly that even specimens in AU grade have the date scarcely visible. On the other hand, 1807 one-cent pieces had the date cut into the die so heavily that specimens in About Good condition have the date showing extremely boldly.

Colonial coins are even a better case in point. Take as an example the colonial coins of Connecticut. From 1785 through 1788, the State of Connecticut produced its own copper coinage, not at an official state mint, but through private contractors. The coins of 1785 were struck carefully for the most part and show the details in sharp relief. The planchets were fairly round, heavy, and contained a goodly amount of metal, and the dies were carefully cut. It was soon realized that more profit could be obtained if the dies were made more quickly and if less attention was paid to the correct metal content. So, the inevitable happened: The dies were made more and more quickly and with less and less detail as the years went by. The planchets were carelessly prepared and often were not completely round! Specimens of the last year of Connecticut coinage, 1788, often were very weakly struck and sometimes had large parts of the design or lettering missing when first issued. It is such history that makes collecting of Connecticut coins (and other colonial issues) interesting to numismatists. To many, such pieces have a fantastic degree of "romance" attached to them. However, from a grading viewpoint it is very important to note that one cannot grade a Connecticut cent of 1785 by the same standards of one of 1788.

When grading any coin it is important to consider the coin "on the average." As shown by the preceding example, variations in the particular die variety or striking of that variety must be taken into consideration, especially with earlier issues. The collector must average out the plus and minus factors in grading a coin. If an early one-cent piece, for example, shows weak letters on the left side of the coin and very strong letters on the right side of the coin, it must be assumed that the coin could not have been worn on only a portion of its surface over the years. Rather, the entire coin must be averaged to arrive at a grade. When you grade a particular coin, take into consideration *all* features on each side, not just an isolated weak spot which may have been the result of striking and not of wear.

The subject of cleaning coins interests many collectors and dealers. At the outset I might mention that more coins have been damaged by cleaning than have been improved, so be careful! Cleaning any coin that grades less than About Uncirculated in condition will generally produce an unnatural appearance that is not acceptable to most collectors. The cleaning of *copper* coins in any grade should be avoided unless it is absolutely necessary to remove an unsightly fingerprint or large carbon or corrosion spot.

To clean coins use only a clear liquid "dip," not a paste, powder, or polish. It is important to think independently in this regard, for many manufacturers of pastes and polishes advertise heavily to sell their products, without regard to the tremendous amount of damage that many such products can inflict upon coins. Pour some dip into a plastic dish. For copper coins use a diluted mixture of half dip and half cold water; for other coins use full strength. Completely immerse the coin in the liquid. Holding the coin in your fingers and using a cotton swab to apply the dip may result in uneven cleaning. Do not leave the coin in the liquid longer than a few seconds. Immediately rinse the coin thoroughly under running cold water. Pat—(do *not* rub)—the coin dry with a soft absorbent cloth; a terrycloth towel is ideal. Always make sure your coins are thoroughly dry and at room temperature before storing. Practice cleaning with low value coins: if you do something wrong, you will not suffer a monetary loss.

It is sometimes desirable to remove the light film of oxidation that sometimes forms on circulated copper coins. A gentle rubbing with a soft cloth lightly treated with a commercial liquid product called Care (available at coin shops) will usually accomplish this task. Tape, glue, flecks of paint, and other substances found on coin surfaces usually will come off with the application of acetone, a solvent which is available at drugstores. Care must be taken to use acetone, coin dip, and other such solutions in a well-ventilated area to prevent inhalation of harmful vapors.

Repeated cleaning of any coin will dull its surface over a period of time. For this reason many advanced collectors prefer to have their coins with a light degree of toning, such as is normally acquired by the surface of a coin over a period of many years. The newcomer to the hobby, however, invariably thinks that "brilliant" equals "better," and wants his coins as bright as possible. No discussion of cleaning would be complete without mentioning what is referred to as "treating" and "processing." This is something that no ethical coin dealer will do. Certain unscrupulous persons will take a lower-grade coin—an Extremely Fine or an AU piece, for example—and attempt, sometimes very convincingly, to make it appear to be in Uncirculated or Proof condition. By brushing an AU coin against a wire wheel or other abrasive substance a pseudo-luster can sometimes be obtained. This will not fool the advanced collector, and you can be sure that it will not fool a dealer when you sell your coins, but it will fool many beginners. A common trick is to take, for example, an Extremely Fine coin that is worth $10 and try to make it into an Uncirculated coin that would normally be worth $30. The trap is set when the newly created "Uncirculated" is offered at the "bargain" price of just $20. A collector thinks he is making the buy of a lifetime. Of course, the coin is worth only $10, perhaps not even that considering that the surface has been treated.

The best defense in this regard is to know your dealer. If in doubt, check with other numismatists for references. Remember also that the most successful dealers are not necessarily those with the largest advertising budgets, and a big advertisement does not automatically imply that the dealer is either large or successful. Indeed, some of the most successful of all dealers operate quietly, successfully, and efficiently by selling coins privately or by means of catalogs with limited circulation to a highly selective list of advanced collectors and dealers.

Don't let grading scare you. Approach the subject carefully and deliberately and with a degree of study, and you should have no problems at all. The *Photograde* book will be a valuable, continuing aid. Also important is to purchase rare coins from a rare coin dealer who guarantees the authenticity of what he sells. The use of common sense and these precautions will assure you of success.

13

Building a Coin Collection

Some people collect coins for their historical value, others for their investment value, and many for a combination of both. As the investment value of any coin is predicated upon the ultimate demand for that coin by a *collector*, it is important that investor and collector alike understand the various rules by which the field of coin collecting is conducted: how to grade coins, the best ways of buying and selling, different ways to collect, and so on. The more that the investor knows about collecting coins, the better. Of course the collector will want to know as much as possible to further his aims and satisfy his curiosity. However, some investors overlook the collecting field, and in doing so ignore the very reason for the potential success of what they are buying for the future.

Kinds of Collections

There are many ways to collect coins. The two ways most popular so far as United States coins are concerned are collecting by date and mintmark, and collecting by design types.

A date and mintmark collector aspires to have one of each and every variety of a certain coin design produced. Thus the assembly of a complete set of Indian cents is a popular goal with numismatists. Such a set would begin with 1859, the first year of issue, and end with 1909. Included would be one of every date within that span, plus additional varieties such as the 1869/8 overdate and the 1908-S and 1909-S branch mint varieties struck in San Francisco. There have been several other interesting Indian cent varieties throughout the years.

The collector of Barber design quarter dollars from 1892 through 1916 desires one of each date and mintmark variety within that span. Challenging are several rarities: 1896-S, 1901-S, and 1913-S, all of which have low mintages, are elusive, and are expensive when they are found. Completing a set of Barber quarters, especially a set in Uncirculated grade, can well take several years if the buyer is particular about quality. Lesser-grade sets can be made up more quickly. For example, in circulated condition most date and mintmark varieties are readily available and all that is needed is to visit or write to a half dozen or so dealers.

Many other specialized fields exist within American numismatics. A complete set of individual die varieties of Connecticut copper coins would comprise more than 300 varieties. Likewise, hundreds of die varieties of early United States large cents can be collected. As Dr. William H. Sheldon, a prominent physician and author of *Penny Whimsy*, has observed, part of the fascination of collecting early coins lies in the fact that it is impossible to build a truly complete collection and many specimens simply do not exist in higher grades. He likens the challenge to a game of golf: No serious golfer aspires to complete the course with just 18 strokes, but working toward that goal can be very rewarding over a period of years.

Collecting coins by design types has become increasingly popular in recent years. Called "type sets," such collections can take several forms—from a representative grouping of 20th-century coins to a complete set which includes one of each and every major design regularly issued from 1793 to the present. The popularity of type collecting has been accelerated by the growing number of collectors. Years ago when I visited a collector to purchase his collection or list it for auction I would usually be confronted by many albums: complete and nearly complete sets of Liberty nickels, buffalo nickels, Jefferson nickels, Barber quarters, Liberty standing quarters, Washington quarters, Barber half dollars, and so on down the list. Today it is virtually impossible for a collector to aspire to such heights, especially if he wants the finest in condition. Not only would such an undertaking involve hundreds of thousands of dollars, the coins themselves are so widely dispersed that many years would be needed to assemble them. To be sure, some collectors are doing this, but from a financial viewpoint the type set is an attractive alternative.

A complete set of United States coins by design types is of immense historical interest. At the same time, such a set can be an excellent investment. For many years James F. Ruddy and I have recommended a type set of United States coins as the best way to begin a combination collection and investment. We consider a type set to be an ideal introduction, for in this way many designs of coins can be obtained for relatively low cost. Such a set can also lead to specialization later. Fascinated with some of the unusual denominations in a type set—two-cent pieces and three-cent pieces, for example—a collector might later decide to build a specialized collection of those particular series.

The future of type set collecting seems assured. Hence, type sets should continue to be superb investments.

As the type collector desires to have but one specimen of each major design, it is sensible to seek out the lower-priced issues within a given series. Thus, among Mercury dimes (issued 1916–1945) the type set collector would seek out, not the 1916-D, a coin which in Uncirculated condition costs above $1,000, but rather a common issue from the 1940's, perhaps a specimen in the $2 range. Even with this precaution, the type collector would have to acquire a number of costly rarities among United States coins from 1793 to date. A prime example is the 1796 quarter, a low mintage issue which is the only year of the design with draped-bust obverse and small eagle reverse. Likewise, half dollars of the same style were minted only in small quantities in 1796 and 1797 and are rare and expensive today. A type set of 20th-century coins, issues minted since the year 1900, contains about 30 designs. In choice Uncirculated condition, such a collection is now valued at close to $2,000. In worn grades, the collection is available for far less than $100. Thus, there is something for every budget.

Acquiring Coins

There are several ways to acquire coins. Current issues can be obtained from banks and from the United States Treasury Department. From the latter source come special mint sets and Proof sets packaged especially for collectors. However, earlier-dated coins are not available.

Years ago it was possible to find scarcities and rarities in circulation. However, today finding even a single silver coin, however common it might be in numismatic terms, in circulation and bearing a date before 1965 would be unusual. So, the chances of finding a rare 1916-D dime or a 1932-D quarter would be minimal. And, if such were to be found, chances are it would be in a low grade. The alternative is the numismatic marketplace.

There are several thousand coin dealers in the United States, one 1974 estimate being from 6,000 to 8,000 small coin shops plus several hundred large coin firms. In addition, thousands of vendors are found in other parts of the world. If you live in a large city, your needs can often be filled locally, especially if there are a number of coin dealers with large inventories. Even a small coin shop can be a valuable source for supplies and rare coins. Often a dealer with a modest inventory can work with your want list and find additional pieces for you by contacting other dealers on your behalf, by using the nationwide Teletype system which links many dealers, and so on.

So far as major scarcities and rarities are concerned, most business is done by mail. If you become an advanced collector, you will quickly learn that it is desirable to compare the selections, prices, and service of leading dealers. Fortunately, ordering through the mail is one of the safest and easiest ways ever devised to do business. Coins can be shipped from one part of the country to another at low cost. Insurance is available for reasonable rates through the Post Office. The safety of this method is perhaps no better demonstrated than by mentioning that, when the Hope Diamond was sent from New York City to the Smithsonian Institution, several ways were considered: sending it by armored vehicle, dispatching it in a car or plane by personal messenger, or sending it by mail. After careful thought, it was decided to send it by registered mail with appropriate insurance. Shortly thereafter the diamond arrived in Washington safely.

Offerings of dealers can often be found in the pages of *Coin World* and *Numismatic News*, the nation's two leading weekly newspapers in the field. *The Numismatist* (official journal of the American Numismatic Association), *CoinAge*, and *Coins Magazine* are published monthly and furnish additional sources. Several dozen other numismatic magazines and periodicals—some of a general nature and others pertaining to a specific numismatic specialty—are available. Often the emphasis in periodical publications is on price rather than quality. To attract attention low prices are given, often with a sacrifice in grading. This is why it is extremely important to compare price as well as quality, for a comparison of one without the other is absolutely meaningless. Remember, a $4.50 Fine coin is not a bargain if it is advertised as Very Fine (and supposedly worth $18.50) for a super-low $9 tag. In fact, you are paying twice what the coin is worth. Most seasoned collectors and investors do some comparison shopping. Do this and you will soon find where you get the best value for your money. Believe me, there are vast differentials in the marketplace.

Most larger dealers issue periodic catalogs which are available on a subscription basis. Many large dealers are members of the Professional Numismatists Guild and/or the International Association of Professional Numismatists.

Buying at auction is another important way to acquire prize pieces. Indeed, most large collections are sold this way. Auction provides the ideal way for the advanced collector to sell large holdings. In my own business it is always a pleasure to describe a spectacular collection and offer it at auction. Auctions that featured the Terrell Collection, Robert Marks Collection, Matt Rothert Collection, Armand Champa Collection, Stanislaw Herstal Collection, and Austin Collection, for example, are numismatic landmarks. In fact, our firm has found that auction catalogs themselves have become collectors' items and often sell for more than the original issue price!

To buy outright from a dealer or to bid at auction, it is desirable to be acquainted with current values. The *Guide Book of United States Coins* is issued yearly and is a good comprehensive guide as to what is available and the price. This reference is usually most accurate in the lower grades, for often the higher grades change in value more rapidly. As the *Guide Book* only *reports* coin prices and does not *create* them, the prices listed are often a year or so behind the values on the marketplace. For example, the 1975 edition of the *Guide Book* was actually compiled from statistics gathered in 1973 and early 1974. However, this popular reference is the most handy guide to United States coins in print, and owning a copy is a "must."

Supplementing the *Guide Book* are lists of current values published in various numismatic periodicals. These are often compiled by averaging the listed prices posted by different dealers, ones who grade conservatively as well as ones who do not. Thus, when using these guides you will probably find that a dealer who grades strictly and conservatively will charge higher prices and one who is less careful about his grading practice will charge lower prices. It is important here to remember Lee Hewitt's admonition: "There is no Santa Claus in numismatics"—and you get what you pay for.

Lists of prices realized at major auctions are also a useful guide, particularly with respect to rarities. Also useful are individual dealers' price lists.

Attending coin clubs and conventions is yet another way to acquire information and also to purchase coins. There are many regional and local numismatic organizations. In addition you may wish to join the American Numismatic Association (ANA), the leading nonprofit numismatic organization in the United States. Membership information can be obtained by writing to: American Numismatic Association, P.O. Box 2366, Colorado Springs, Colorado 80901. James F. Ruddy and I, both of whom are Life Members (Nos. 336 and 337, respectively), would be happy to sponsor your membership. Each year the association holds a large annual convention. Usually more than 10,000 collectors and dealers attend from all parts of the world.

Handling and Storage

It is important to handle coins properly and to store them safely. The coins should always be carefully held by the edges, and the surfaces should never be touched. Also remember to hold the coin over a soft surface so that it will not be harmed if accidentally dropped.

Coins can be stored in several ways. Perhaps most convenient are small paper envelopes which measure 2 inches square. Within the envelope, a protective polyethylene sleeve will keep the coin free from harmful substances. Main enemies of coins are dampness and toxic fumes, both of which can cause corrosion. It is important to store your coins in a dry place and away from industrial fumes, salt spray, or other unfavorable atmospheric conditions.

On the market are several varieties of coin albums made of stiff cardboard. Coins are housed in circular openings protected on both sides by acetate slides. When pushing these slides in and out, it is important not to rub the slide against the coin's surface lest a "slide mark" be created on it. Such albums are inexpensive and are ideal for housing a collection during its formation. Coins can be put in and taken out of the albums easily as you add coins to your collection or upgrade existing pieces.

Once your set is completed, a plastic holder makes an ideal combined display and storage unit. Holders are available for most popular United States series. In addition, plastic display cases can be made up at relatively low cost on a custom basis. Plastic is an inert substance, and coins stored this way are very secure.

Most collectors and investors consider the bank safe deposit box to be the ideal home for coins over a long period of time. Insurance rates are much lower for coins kept this way, lower than for coins kept at home or in other locations. A policy can be purchased through the American Numismatic Association if you are a member, or through another source, to cover coins in transit and while they are at your home or office for enjoyment, evaluation, or study. Such insurance is available for a nominal cost.

Selling Your Coins

When the time comes to sell your coins, there are several possibilities. One is to offer your collection intact to one or more dealers. If you have evaluated the collection carefully and know what price is "right" for it, then such a transaction can be effected simply and quickly. In my more than twenty years as a rare coin dealer, I have never seen an instance in which choice and rare coins were not in strong demand. Indeed, the main problem of our firm has always been *buying* coins, not selling them! So it is with other coin dealers as well.

Auction is a popular way to sell, especially if your holdings consist of choice and rare pieces. By selling at auction the transaction places the seller (you) and the dealer on the same side: Both have the incentive to get the best price possible. Auction sales are handled on a commission basis, the charge being made based upon the prices realized. Auction rates vary from firm to firm. As in other aspects of the coin business and in life itself, you get what you pay for. The firms that can do the best job for you and that produce the best catalogs are not the cheapest. On the other hand, these same auction houses frequently can do the best job with your coins.

You will find that in coin collecting one idea will lead to another—and the reading of this book will undoubtedly furnish many inspirations and possibilities for different directions in collecting. Coin collecting offers many advantages—history, art, romance, investment potential, to mention just a few. Buy carefully and from responsible dealers and you should do very well over the years.

14

Investing in Coins

Coins have been a wonderful investment for many years. In fact, given the performance statistics of rare coin investment over the years many people cannot believe them. During the past quarter century or so, gains of 1,000 percent have been *common*, and gains of several thousand percent aren't unusual!

With the permission of Kenneth Bressett of the Western Publishing Company, Inc., the figures used in this chapter are from various issues of *A Guide Book of United States Coins*, published yearly from 1946 to the present. Most issues bear a cover date one year in advance of the date of publication, so the statistics we give for 1974, for example, are from the *Guide Book* with a cover date of 1975. (The issue was actually published in July, 1974.)

In any study it is easy to use hindsight. On Monday morning it is easy to pick Saturday afternoon football winners, and in 1974 it is easy to look through some issues of *The Wall Street Journal* and "select" IBM and Xerox as winners—and to overlook the losers. I have avoided doing this. The examples cited are average coins of the kind available to an average coin buyer in 1946, 1949, and other years I cite. As a starting point I begin with the first issue of *A Guide Book of United States Coins*, published in 1946, and from that point go to 1949. From 1949 onward, the prices are in five-year intervals up to and including 1974.

Concerning my own experience in this field, I have been recommending coins as an investment for many years. I can read today my price lists of twenty years ago and see that spectacular performances did indeed occur. Recently I was looking through a copy of the February–March, 1959, issue of a catalog prepared by James F. Ruddy and me, in which I said:

> Our outlook on the coin market for 1959? With the possible exception [of very modern issues] most United States coins should continue their steady appreciation in value. This will be particularly true of early material in choice condition. . . .

In that issue of fifteen years ago our customers were offered many choice early coins. *Without exception* each and every choice (Uncirculated or Proof) coin has *multiplied* in value. I don't mean to imply that every coin I have ever sold over the years or have recommended for investment automatically has made its owner a fortune, but I can say that going back over the years I certainly proudly invite comparison of my recommendations across the board with recommendations made in any other investment area, whether it be real estate, securities, or whatever.

In *High Profits from Rare Coin Investment*, I noted that much has been and is written in the name of "coin investment." Some of this is thoughtful and meaningful. Other information is not worth the paper it is printed on. During many years of writing articles and features on rare coins for such publications as *Coin World, Numismatic News, Numismatic Scrapbook Magazine, The Encyclopedia Americana*, and *Reader's Digest*, I have endeavored to be objective and honest and to present all sides of the story. So it was with pleasure that I read the introduction to Harry J. Forman's book, *How You Can Make Big Profits Investing in Coins*. Mr. Forman said:

> Anyone can make predictions, and if he does so in a field in which he is already well known they are sure to be widely read. Moreover, by waiting until people's memories have become somewhat blurred, and then republishing only his successes, he can often build up a rather good reputation for himself.
>
> In the numismatic field we have three kinds of forecasters. The first and commonest is the person who makes predictions simply as a promotional device to help sell whatever he has on hand. I don't say that in all, or even most cases, this involves a deliberate deception. On the contrary, the very fact that a person has invested his own money to purchase one or another item would indicate a certain amount of faith in its market potential. But such predictions necessarily lack true discrimination and depend for their success, if not on luck, then on the progress of the market as a whole.
>
> A second type of forecaster is the non-professional numismatist who dabbles in speculation and writes books or articles on market trends. Such an individual is more serious in his selections and understands that there are always

widespread differences in the potential of various issues and series. But for all that, his livelihood is not dependent on his predictions, and even should they fail he is still reimbursed by his royalties.

The third and rarest type is the successful full-time dealer who forecasts not for promotional purposes, but simply to share his insights with the general investing public. My good friend Q. David Bowers is one such forecaster, having given much excellent investment advice through the *Empire Review* and more recently the *Rare Coin Review* (Bowers and Ruddy Galleries, Inc.).

At this point I must also mention that, while the past can provide many lessons for the future, the future is always unknown. While I personally believe coin investment has a bright future ahead of it, there can be no guarantee in this regard, any more than there can be a guarantee that any other type of investment will be a success.

The investment aspect of coins has always been one of their most popular appeals. Indeed, the theme of investment appears, though tentatively at first, in advertisements dating back to the past century. In 1912, when Wayte Raymond, a leading New York coin dealer of the time, specifically cited the investment appeal of coins in a full-page advertisement this was a bold step, a departure from tradition. Raymond said:

> COINS AS AN INVESTMENT. Many harsh words are said about collectors who interest themselves in a natural speculation as to whether or not the coins they are buying today will have appreciated in value ten years from now. Numismatists of the old school tell us that a true collector is not interested in any such appreciation in the value of his collection but derives his entire profit and pleasure from the coins while in his hands. We feel, however, that the average American collector while he greatly enjoys his coins also feels very pleased if on disposing of his collection he realizes a profit. . . .

Beginning in the 1930's, interest in coin investment mushroomed. This was the decade of many commemorative half-dollar releases. A prime selling point for these coins was their investment and speculative appeal. Indeed, many made large profits. Commemoratives served as a catalyst, and before long thousands of new collectors and investors were looking to the left and right discovering Lincoln cents, twenty-dollar gold pieces, British crowns, and other items.

Interest continued to grow during the 1940's. The Depression had been left behind, and more money was available for the pleasures of life, including coin collecting. At the same time, coins continued their steady increase in value. The supply of older coins remained constant, and economic laws dictated that prices should rise—as they did.

The growth of interest accelerated during the 1950's and 1960's. During the previous century, most coin investment had been limited to numismatists. Collectors *knew* coins were a good investment—it was taken for granted. The interest of the outside world, the investment community as a whole, did not extend to coins. After all, coins were not familiar as a collectible item to most people. But gradually investment came to be cited as a major appeal for buying art, real estate, and many other things. Coins, hitherto largely overlooked as an investment, were discovered. It was found that coins had many unique advantages. Of course, collectors had known this all along as had coin dealers, but few had taken the time to sit down and actually put it in print.

Gradually more information on coins became available. During the 1960's and early 1970's, *A Guide Book of United States Coins* had gone through many editions, so pricing statistics were readily available for those caring to seek them out. Rapid interchange of coin information became a reality with the advent of *Numismatic News*, founded in 1952, and *Coin World*, founded in 1960. Around 1962–1963, Teletype systems linking dealers became popular, especially for modern coins traded in quantities. The number of dealers increased. The number of collectors increased. Today there are perhaps 6,000 to 8,000 dealers in the United States and 8,000,000 to 10,000,000 collectors. When I first developed my interest in coins in 1953, I believe the number of dealers was in the low hundreds; the number of collectors was in the hundreds of thousands.

Coins have become big business. This has been good in some ways and not so good in others. A *not-so-good* aspect is that many companies, eager to participate in numismatics but lacking serious knowledge of the subject, have entered the field and often use large display advertisements in magazines and publications oriented toward people other than coin collectors. It is hard to fool coin collectors, for they know about grading and know about prices. Apparently it is not so hard to fool the general public, so in recent years there have been many firms that called themselves "one of America's largest dealers," yet have never been recognized as serious coin dealers by the trade. The firms with the largest advertising budgets are not necessarily the largest or most knowledgeable coin dealers. This is an important point to consider. If you want to buy coins, buy them from a coin dealer—*not* from a coin merchandising firm. When buying coins from any source you always have the question of will they go up in value or won't they. Why add to it the risks of overpaying in the first place and of overgraded coins? By doing business with a leading professional coin firm these risks are minimized or eliminated.

There are many advantages to coin investment. A number of these have been touched on earlier. I will repeat some of the most salient here:

- Coins can be easily stored. You can take possession of rare coins and store a large value in a small space, in a bank safe deposit box, for example. Indeed, many of the largest collections our firm has handled in recent years have been stored in toto in safe deposit boxes. Coins are not fragile. They require a minimum of care and no unusual treatment. Insurance is available at low rates.

- Coins are easy to buy and sell. There are large numbers of buyers and sellers, making the market a truly viable one. You don't have to wait for "the right buyer" to come along as you might in real estate. Rather, a dealer's main problem is in buying, not selling. When you offer your collection for sale, you will have many people competing for it. Never during my years as a professional numismatist have I ever seen a choice group of coins come on the market without great interest being shown by purchasers.
- Nomenclature is standard. Grading systems are standard and coin descriptions can be stated in a concise manner. Thus, a New York owner can write to a dealer in London or Los Angeles and in one sentence describe any coin. No long explanations are necessary.
- Coins are usually taxable at low capital gains rates, provided they have been held for a minimum length of time. In most areas no property tax is levied on rare coins. Thus, coin profits are taxable only when the coins are sold, and then the taxes are at favorable rates.
- Coin information is readily available. There are a number of excellent periodical publications which can be obtained on a subscription basis. In addition, dealers' price lists and auction catalogs provide valuable data. Many fine reference books are available with which to build a numismatic library. The Bibliography contains a selection of titles.
- The coin market as a whole moves steadily. Changes tend to be on a month-to-month or a year-to-year basis. Over the past years the trends have been upward, sharply upward.
- In addition to being a good investment over the years, coins have been an interesting and fascinating hobby. With coins you can literally have your cake and eat it, too. Few other fields of life, investment, or hobby activity offer such a two-in-one situation!

The tables in Appendix A show accurately how excellent coins have been as an investment since 1946. I did not select exceptional performers in compiling these statistics. Had I done so super-spectacular profits would be indicated. As they are, the profits are indeed spectacular. Even a cursory examination will show that coins have sharply outpaced popular stock indexes, money in savings banks, and so on. For example, at the end of 1946, the Dow Jones Industrial Average closed at 177. As of August,

1974, the averages were in the mid-700 range, an increase of about 350 percent. Added to this, of course, must be dividends received over the years, but still the rate of return is small compared to even poor performers among coins. When compared to good performers among coins, there really isn't any comparison at all. If $1,000 had been put into a savings account at 5% interest in 1946 (which would have been hard to do for interest rates were not as high then as now), it would have yielded on a compounded basis $3,920 in 1974. This is an increase of nearly 300 percent.

On the other hand consider coins. To select my examples I took representative grades (often picking several different grades for the same coin to illustrate how prices have moved within various grades) of issues used to build a type set of United States coins, one of each major design variety. It is this type of collection which I have recommended more than any other over the years, so the examples are good ones. In addition, within each design type I selected representative or average coins—not exceptional performers. Still, the overall performances are indeed exceptional compared to most other investment mediums.

For example, take small cents, one of the most popular series. A relatively common 1857 Uncirculated flying eagle cent was a $5 coin in 1946 and a $400 coin in 1974—making a gain of 7,900 percent during the past 28 years. On a year-to-year basis, its prices were: 1946, $5; 1949, $6, 1954, $10; 1959, $25; 1964, $80; 1969; $115; 1974, $400—for an overall gain of 7,900 percent. An 1857 flying eagle cent in Proof condition was a $35 coin in 1946 and a $2,300 coin in 1974, posting a gain of 6,471 percent. On the other hand, a worn example of the same coin—a coin in Fine grade—increased in value "only" 1,000 percent during that time. In 1946 it was a $1 coin; in 1974, an $11 coin.

The 1859 Indian cent in Fine grade posted an 800 percent gain during the same period; in Uncirculated condition, a 7,678 percent gain, and in Proof grade, a 7,400 percent gain. An 1863 Indian cent, one of the commonest issues of its era, posted gains of 1,088 percent in Fine Grade, of 5,400 percent in Uncirculated grade, and of 3,150 percent in Proof grade.

These gains, impressive as they are, pale when compared to some others on the list. The 1858 silver three-cent piece, a coin of which I have bought and sold many over the years, was a $2.50 item in 1946 and a $410 coin in 1974, registering a gain of 16,300 percent! Even more spectacular is the performance of the 1835 dime, another relatively common issue of its type and another coin of which I have handled many over the years. In 1946, it was a $2.75 coin. In 1974, it was a $700 coin, thus registering a gain of 25,355 percent!

Are there any negatives, you might ask. In the entire survey not a single coin dropped in value over the period! This does not mean, however, that there were not some year-to-year fluctuations, for often speculative activity within a certain series or just a tendency of various series to sometimes move ahead of other series and then slow down and then move ahead again have resulted in different rates of increase. But on the whole all have increased handsomely. Allowing for individual differences in coin selection, the typical collector who built a type set using higher grade (Uncirculated and Proof) coins in 1946 would have seen his coins go up in value on a coin-by-coin basis an average of 2,000 percent to 3,000 percent or more!

One of the pleasures of having been a professional numismatist for more than twenty years is having seen this happen. It is a really great feeling to make money for others; it is like doing a favor for a fine friend. Many of my clients who spent $25,000 to $75,000 on coins years ago will be extremely wealthy when they sell their holdings. Indeed, in the course of buying large collections over the years from my former clients I have yet to meet a man who, upon selling his coins, has not realized a substantial profit if he purchased a choice coin collection to begin with and if he has held it for five to ten years or more. And this statement covers the purchase of literally thousands of different collections!

15

Rare Coin Investment—Questions and Answers

During the past twenty years James F. Ruddy and I have been asked countless questions on the subject of rare coins and rare coin investment. These queries have covered a wide variety of topics. Many of the questions asked of us have already been covered in this book. Others of interest and importance follow.

Is Quantity Important?

QUESTION: Is it better to have just a few very expensive coins or many inexpensive ones? For example, is it better to have a single $10,000 coin, ten $1,000 coins, or 1,000 coins valued at $10 each?

ANSWER: There is no definite right or wrong reply to this. A charting of values over a long period of years reveals that great rarities which cost thousands of dollars twenty-five years ago have soared in value since that time, as have many pieces which just cost a few dollars at the time. My own personal preference is that the quantity of coins and their average value depend upon the amount of money you wish to invest. If, for example, you want to invest $100 each month in a collection or investment group of coins, then it would be foolish to save up your money for two years to own just a single coin, a rarity costing $2,400. Rather, you would undoubtedly experience much more satisfaction of ownership if you were to have a nice portfolio of coins in the $10 to $100 range per item. The inclusion of a few items priced at several hundred dollars each would not be out of line.

On the other hand, if you wanted to spend $1,000 a month on your coin investment, then a $2,400 coin might be a logical thing to own—assuming, of course, that it met your other requirements as well.

Coin Price and Marketability

QUESTION: Does the price of a coin affect its marketability?

ANSWER: This is a question which is often asked. Some buyers are worried that expensive coins might not find ready sale when they are put on the market. This fear is unfounded, and here is why. The price of a coin is usually based upon the rarity of a coin and the demand for it. As the coin market is an active one, prices have equated themselves with supply and demand. Thus, a rare 1838-O half dollar, to cite one example, is an extremely salable item, for there are few specimens known to exist. In fact, only twenty of these half dollars were originally coined!

Of course, the number of people desiring 1838-O half dollars is also small. But the number of collectors desiring them, even taking the price into consideration, has always been more than the available supply. Despite the ups and downs of certain segments of the coin market, the 1838-O has always been a "blue chip." Over the years, James F. Ruddy and I have owned several beautiful 1838-O half dollars. One example will illustrate the price movement of this famous rarity. In 1962, James F. Ruddy and I purchased at auction for $9,500 the specimen from the collection of Mr. R. E. Cox, Jr., a Fort Worth, Texas, business executive who earlier had been one of our clients. We subsequently resold this 1838-O to a prominent Eastern industrialist. In 1973, our firm had the pleasure of putting this coin, a splendid Proof example, on the market again. The price tag? $75,000—a figure which represented a very attractive profit for the collector who sold it. The coin was subsequently sold again and now reposes in a beautiful Midwestern collection.

The 1838-O half dollar has always been a famous coin, and an expensive one in relation to other coins. However, there has never been a period in American numismatic history in which it was not in demand, in good economic conditions and in bad. An 1838-O half dollar was worth more in 1970 than it was in 1960. It was worth more in 1960 than it was in 1950. In 1950 it was worth considerably more than it was in 1940, and so on back through numismatic history. Undoubtedly, in 1980 and in 1990, it will be worth far more than it is today.

Another example is the Uncirculated 1876-CC twenty-cent piece, a coin formerly in the collection of noted composer Jerome Kern, offered in *Rare Coin Review*, No. 20, published by Bowers and Ruddy Galleries in 1974. In 1972, two years earlier, the same piece was sold by us at auction at the Armand Champa Collection sale. In strong competition it sold for $24,000, by far a new record price at the time. The sale record caused much comment and was widely reported in the numismatic press. Then, in 1974, we were offered the coin by the purchaser at the Champa sale and again had the opportunity of handling it. With a price tag of $59,000, it was listed in our *Rare Coin Review*. The piece was sold immediately, and within a week or two of the time the catalog came out we had three or four additional orders for it! Of course, we only had one coin, so three or four prospective purchasers were disappointed. Probably the $59,000 price will also seem cheap a few years from now.

Prime American rarities—the 1838-O half dollar, 1876-CC twenty-cent piece, 1894-S dime, 1804 silver dollar, and other examples—can perhaps be likened to Rembrandt paintings. They are quite expensive to be sure, but when a choice one comes on the market it creates a lot of excitement and usually a new price record is set!

How High Can Coin Prices Go?

QUESTION: How high can coin prices go? Are coin prices too high already?

ANSWER: The future is unknown, of course, and no one can predict it with accuracy. However, on a comparative basis it can be said with certainty that coin prices have a long, long way to go in relation to prices of rarities in certain other fields. In 1973 and 1974, a number of important American rarities appeared in auctions or in dealers' advertisements. A specimen of the rare 1804 silver dollar, a piece designated as "The King of American Coins," appeared at $165,000. The sale of a 1907 MCMVII extremely high-relief pattern twenty-dollar gold piece was reported at $200,000. A rare 1913 nickel was valued at over $200,000 by its owner. Several other coins were valued in the $100,000 to $200,000 range.

When one considers that rare stamps have broken the $100,000 mark on several occasions (one was actually sold for $380,000) and that for a painting to realize a million dollars or more is scarcely news these days, then famous American coin rarities priced in the $100,000 to $200,000 range seem cheap by comparison! Early in 1974 it was announced that a Ming vase was sold for more than $1,000,000 at auction. The collecting of vases is much more specialized than the collecting of coins, and yet a rarity in this field has sold for many multiples of the highest price ever realized for a rare coin.

Perhaps for a comparison to end all comparisons I should mention the Velásquez painting "Portrait of Juan de Pareja" which now hangs in New York City's Metropolitan Museum. At an auction sale held by Christie's of London $5,544,000 was paid for this painting. For the same money one could spend a lifetime collecting United States coins from colonials through territorial gold pieces, collect them in the finest available condition, and still have money left over! Are coin rarities overpriced? You be the judge!

Should One Buy Rare Coins or Common Coins?

QUESTION: The average investor will not have the opportunity to own such great rarities as the 1876-CC twenty-cent piece and the 1838-O half dollar. If one cannot own great rarities, then should a collector or investor concentrate on owning just common coins of low value? Or is there an ideal point of compromise between these two extremes?

ANSWER: In answer to this I repeat one of my favorite aphorisms: A common coin that is common today will be common in the foreseeable future. A common coin by very definition is common and is not rare! To buy common coins in the hope that they magically will become rare is a futile effort. This simple admonition is overlooked by many people who buy coins as an investment. In *High Profits From Rare Coin Investment*, I used this same example and said: "This is so important that I suggest you underline it in your copy of this book!"

Many millions of dollars have been expended by people who prefer quantity to quality. For some people there is a false security in amassing quantity. This situation is not unique to coins; it exists in stamps as well. In our sister field of philately, countless misguided souls religiously "invest" in new sheets of postage stamps as they are issued. The sad truth of the matter is that one can purchase from any stamp dealer sheets of stamps that are ten to twenty years old—and pay only face value for them! The investment potential, or lack of it, needs no further explanation. So it goes with buying large quantities of common modern coins.

In my opinion, the best path is to purchase coins which have a present

RARE 1838–O HALF DOLLAR. One of the rarest of all American silver coins is the 1838–O half dollar. Only twenty specimens were coined in 1838, the year that the United States branch mint at New Orleans opened. The specimen shown above was offered by Bowers and Ruddy Galleries for $75,000 in 1974 and was sold into a midwestern collection. It is in Proof condition and is one of the finest known examples of this classic piece. Note the identifying "O" mintmark on the obverse above the 1838 date.

scarcity and value—either realized or unrealized—in the marketplace.

To be desirable for investment a coin does not have to be rare or even extremely scarce. It can be moderately scarce and still do quite well. Scarceness and rarity are relative. As an example, take the 1917 Type I Liberty standing quarter issued at the Philadelphia Mint. This particular coin is in great demand for type sets to illustrate a design made in only two years, 1916 and 1917. The mintage for the 1917 Type I is fairly large: 8,792,000 total. However, 1917 Type I quarters were issued during an era when coin collecting was in its infancy. Few people bothered to save these quarters. Although no figures are known, probably all but a few thousand at most went into circulation and became worn as they passed from hand to hand. If we assume that just a few thousand are known today, then the pieces are fairly scarce when you consider that there are perhaps several hundred thousand collectors desiring to assemble a type set of 20th-century United States coins and that each will need a Liberty standing quarter of the 1916–1917 issue. Even when one considers that many collectors will be satisfied with a coin in a worn grade, the investment possibilities of a 1917 Type I quarter remain obvious. In 1963, I wrote that "the 1917 issue sells well for $22.50 to $25.00 (in Uncirculated grade). I believe that this price is a strongly based one and that it will continue to advance." Advance it did, and by 1974 several sales had taken place in the $200 to $300 range.

Let me repeat: To buy common coins in the hope that they will magically become rare is a futile effort. And yet common coins provide the basis for many careless "investment recommendations," simply because common coins are very easy to buy and don't require much effort to locate. On the other hand, scarce and rare coins sell themselves.

Expansion of the Coin Market

QUESTION: What will make the price of coins rise above today's levels?

ANSWER: Of course this is basic economics, but if the number of collectors increases then the demand for rare coins will also increase. Now the question becomes: Will the number of collectors increase?

This seems quite likely. The average citizen is working an ever-shorter week. More and more time is being directed toward leisure activities. Coin collecting is an ideal leisure activity. It can be conducted in private and does not require a large amount of space (a fine collection can be assembled by an apartment dweller, for instance). A coin collection can be conveniently and cheaply stored, and so on. As leisure time activities increase, coin collecting will surely increase also. More collectors will bring an even greater demand.

Then there is the international expansion of the market to consider as well. Other countries are also developing large numbers of collectors. As the "affluent society" spreads throughout the world, more and more attention will be paid to leisure pursuits such as coin collecting. This is already happening in several countries. Japanese collectors and dealers are becoming an important factor in the market. England, which had only four major dealers and just a few thousand collectors in the early 1960's, now has dozens of dealers and tens of thousands of collectors. Germany, Italy, France, and Switzerland have been strong numismatic markets in recent years. Danish, Swedish, and Norwegian collectors have been bidding ever-increasing prices for their own coins as well as for coins of other countries. It makes sense for buyers around the world to desire American coins, just as American collectors for years have avidly assembled sets of crowns, gold coins, patterns, and other desirable issues of foreign states. Coin collecting, long an international hobby from the viewpoint of the variety of coins collected, is now becoming an international hobby from the viewpoint of collectors collecting them!

There is also the important consideration of monetary inflation. If the purchasing power of the American dollar continues to depreciate, then the thought of paying $100, $200, or whatever for a coin won't seem to be so important. It wasn't long ago that $200, for instance, would have been a "big price" for an Uncirculated 1796 quarter. I mention this particular coin for I remember that Aubrey Bebee, the Omaha dealer, showed me a 1796 quarter with a prooflike surface at the American Numismatic Association convention in 1955. He stated that he had paid $200 for it. A "staggering price" at the time, today it seems absurdly cheap. A comparable coin would sell for well over $10,000 on today's market (I sold one at auction for $17,000 in 1973). I don't mean to suggest that the average coin purchased for $200 today will be worth $17,000 in twenty years, for I don't think it will be. On the other hand, it certainly is reasonable to expect many of today's $200 coins to multiply in value several times.

What Grades of Coins Should I Buy?

QUESTION: What grades of coins should I buy? Is it better to buy, for instance, ten coins in Good condition or one coin in Uncirculated grade for the same total price?

ANSWER: From an investment viewpoint all grades of coins have done well. Scarce coins in lower grades such as Good and Very Good have been excellent investments over the years, as have been Uncirculated and Proof pieces. However, Uncirculated and Proof coins and other higher-grade issues such as Fine to Very Fine or better for certain 19th-century and earlier examples have been in stronger demand and are scarcer than lower-grade pieces, so the dealer's margin of profit is smaller.

Take as a random example an Uncirculated coin which sells for $50. A dealer might well pay $40 to buy the coin for stock, giving him a profit of 20 percent. It is the higher-grade pieces that turn over the fastest in a dealer's stock, so he is willing to take a smaller margin of profit for them. On some closely traded high-grade items, the margin between buying and selling may be only 5 percent to 10 percent.

On the other hand, if a dealer were to have ten coins in stock, all of the same variety, and priced at $5 each, he may only want to pay $2 or $3 per coin, for a total of $20 to $30 for the lot, to buy such pieces for stock, as more handling per item is involved. I am assuming that the latter coins are in worn grades. From an investment viewpoint, I personally would rather have one Uncirculated $50 coin than ten well-worn $5 coins. There is no strict right or wrong answer to this—it is more a matter of personal preference. It has been said that collectors and investors should "buy the best grade they can afford." Generally I agree with this advice.

Accurate Grading Is Important

QUESTION: I read a lot about coin grading. Is this an important factor? Do all dealers grade the same?

ANSWER: Grading is very important. Accurate grading is essential. When you purchase coins for investment you are faced with the uncertainty of what they will do in the future. Will they go up in value or won't they? Of course, we hope that they will. Why add to this the uncertainty of whether or not your coins are in the correct condition? Instead, be very sure you are buying the grade you expect, the grade you are paying for.

In recent years, many coins have been "treated" and "processed." Lower-grade coins have been given the false appearance of "Uncirculated" or "Proof." A lot of money can be made by selling processed and treated coins. Such operators prey on the bargain seeker.

An Extremely Fine large cent of 1853, a coin worth, say, in the $20 range, if "processed" and wrongly sold as "Uncirculated" for $40 (just a tiny fraction of the going price for true Uncirculated) is no bargain at $40. In fact, you are overpaying by a factor of two or three times! And yet it is continually amazing to see how many collectors, particularly new ones, fall into such a trap. While dealers are sometimes reluctant to discuss "processed" coins, if you want a discussion on this subject you can talk with the representatives of leading numismatic publications. Grading is a big problem. Ethical dealers do not "process" coins. Your best protection is to buy from an ethical dealer.

Bear in mind also that a large advertising budget has little to do with a dealer's experience or the quality of the coins he sells. Indeed, some of the most successful dealers enjoy a fantastically large business by modestly circulating price lists and auction catalogs to a selected number of proven clients who have been with them over the years. They do not need a continuing stream of new faces! Even worse is the so-called "investment adviser" who sells overgraded coins at full retail prices to potential investors, hoping that these collectors will never gain access to other established collectors who might tell them the true condition of their coins. Knowledge of the American Numismatic Association and other organizations is "hidden" from their investors! My reaction to this situation you can easily guess, and there is no sense wasting print on it here.

Do not overlook the grading problem. A copy of *Photograde*, written by my associate James F. Ruddy, will pay for itself many times over. This book has been accepted and acclaimed by numismatic publications everywhere as a standard authority in the field of coin grading.

It costs no more, in fact it is infinitely cheaper in the long run (when the time comes to sell your coins), to buy properly graded coins. Otherwise, you are just kidding yourself and are impairing the chances for the success of your investment. I do not mean to be negative in a book which perhaps should be 100 percent positive, but I do want to clarify this situation and make you aware of it. In many years of buying collections I have seen large sums of money lost by collectors who were hoodwinked in this regard. I repeat one of my favorite quotations: "There is no Santa Claus in numismatics." You get what you pay for.

If you are uncertain about coin grading, do some comparison shopping. The same coin advertised as "Uncirculated" at $10 and $15 can be a better buy at $15 than $10 if, for instance, the $15 is really Uncirculated and the $10 is really Extremely Fine.

The Importance of Authenticity

QUESTION: How concerned should I be with the genuineness of coins offered to me?

ANSWER: Authenticity is important. If you don't know the technical aspects of coin authenticity (and few amateur collectors or investors are expected to know this), then by all means do business with one of the many dealers who guarantee the authenticity of what they sell. Members of the International Association of Professional Numismatists and the Professional Numismatists Guild—two very important dealers' organizations which are internationally recognized and which have very, very strict admission standards—pledge that their members will guarantee the authenticity of coins sold. A refund in full awaits the purchaser of any coin which is later proven to be not genuine. This is a *tremendously important* protection, for a fake coin is absolutely worthless. Moreover, it is illegal to own one.

Never buy a coin "as is." The collector who buys from an established professional dealer is at a great advantage, for only rarely will a professional make an error, and when he does the error will be corrected.

However, there are many fake coins for sale in the coin marketplace, though the number of forgeries in the coin field is less than those in certain other collecting fields. However, unlike the situation in other fields (modern art is an example), publications in the field of coin collecting give great publicity to counterfeiting and the problems it causes.

Should counterfeiting be publicized or shouldn't it? James F. Ruddy and I are sure which side we are on! Our stand on the subject of fakes is well known: We are against them. We have spent countless hours working with numismatic associations, government authorities, publications, and others to combat counterfeiting. We are happy to say that many arrests and convictions have been made as the result of our efforts. Concerning publicity, however, one camp advocates that fakes should be widely publicized and played up so that everyone takes notice. This undoubtedly scares off many would-be collectors who are afraid to enter the hobby. This emphasis on fakery is *not* a featured part of publications on art, antiques, and so on, although the problem exists there to an equal or greater extent than it does in coins. The other camp advocates that fakes be privately handled without fanfare. This second idea would be feasible if all dealers would guarantee their merchandise and collectors could be persuaded to buy only from those dealers. But as no license or even experience is needed to hang up a "Rare Coins for Sale" or "Coin Investment Center" sign, perhaps it is best that fakes be nipped in the bud by publicizing them. This is a controversial point.

I have presented both sides to the authenticity/publicity situation—so, rightly or wrongly, you know that this can be a problem. You know also that the problem is a simple one, and that you can do your part. You have no risk whatsoever of a financial loss in this regard if you buy from a dealer member of the International Association of Professional Numismatists or Professional Numismatists Guild, or if the dealer otherwise guarantees *in writing* that the coins are absolutely and positively genuine.

Aspects of Investment Timing

QUESTION: How long should I hold my coins?

ANSWER: The answer to this depends on your investment objectives. Generally speaking, I recommend a minimum of three to five years. Really spectacular profits have been shown by clients who have held their coins from ten to fifteen years, as is often possible with a retirement program or employee benefit fund, for example.

In my personal opinion rare coins should be considered as a long-term investment. While short-term profits are possible, by far the largest and most consistent profits have accrued to the long-term investor—and I speak from much experience in this regard!

I have seen fabulous profits made by many collectors and investors who assembled fine groupings of coins over a period of years and then sold them upon their retirement. It is not at all unusual for my firm to pay $10,000, $25,000, $100,000, or even more for coins which originally cost the customer a fifth or a tenth of that sum. I might further add that this is a very, very gratifying aspect of my business. Whenever I look through the many catalogs that James F. Ruddy and I prepared in the 1950's, I know that the people who bid in our auctions and ordered from our catalogs then can be nothing less than delighted if they still have the coins today. The coin market has done wonderfully well for our clients. This, in turn, has contributed to our own success, for there is no better client than one for whom you've made a lot of money!

Learning About Coins

QUESTION: How can I learn about coins?

ANSWER: When building your coin portfolio—for collecting, for investment, or for a combination of both—it will pay you to learn as much about coins as possible. If you plan to spend a few hundred dollars or more on rare coins, then I recommend that you subscribe to several different magazines, join the American Numismatic Association, start a numismatic library, and learn all you can about coins.

There is no substitute for knowledge. Any success I have personally had in the rare coin field I can attribute directly to studying and learning about the coins I have sold. The coin investors who have done the best over the years have been the ones with the most knowledge, the ones who took the time to learn about what they were buying. This point isn't even debatable. In my opinion it is basic.

When you buy coins, compare the prices and quality of several dealers. Don't compare price alone, for such a comparison is meaningless. Absolutely meaningless. Compare grading and you will see why one "Uncirculated" coin advertised at $100 can be a poor buy and another really Uncirculated piece at $150 can be a great value.

Once you've determined where your best values are from, then take advantage of your new-found knowledge by concentrating your purchases with those dealers who give you the best quality and value for your money. By doing so you will greatly enhance the chances for your investment's success.

16

Building an Investment "Portfolio" of Rare Coins

The sum of $1,000 invested 28 years ago in a 5 percent savings account would have yielded on a compounded basis $3,920 by 1974. The same amount invested in stocks comprising the Dow Jones Average would have yielded approximately $4500 plus dividends. What about rare coins? The price performance tables in Appendix A of this book show average coins of the kind I have recommended in the past have done better, quite a bit better. The prices given were all published in *A Guide Book of United States Coins* from 1946 to the present time. An equal amount of money invested in each one of the 237 coins charted from 1946 to date would have multiplied in value nearly 40 times. To be more specific, $1,000 invested this way would have yielded the princely sum of $38,485! An investment "portfolio" costing $30,000 in 1946 would have made you a millionaire.

The gains made in the past are indeed real, and it is pleasant for me to think back upon the fortunes I have made for clients. And though there is no guarantee that future performance will match that of the past, I am confident that the future for coin collecting and investment is bright. Many positive indicators point in this direction. The advice given in this book can be your passport. Follow my suggestions and you will reap the benefit of the experience of thousands of clients who have gone before you, the benefit of my having sold tens of millions of dollars' worth of coins over a period spanning more than two decades.

So, now the question is "How do I begin?"

At this point I will assume that you have a discretionary income, an income over and above what you need for normal day-to-day living expenses. I have never recommended that people borrow money to buy coins if such borrowing means pledging vital life assets to do so. Coin investment always entails a risk, and it should be viewed in this way. All investments, whether in securities, real estate, art, or in any other field are risks.

I will likewise assume that you will have several years to let your investment mature. In the past, the greatest gains have been the reward of those who have held their coins for the longest period of time. Buy a group of coins this month and sell it next month, and you make money just for the coin dealer. Over a period of years, the dealer's commission is minimized and your profits are maximized. I recommend holding your investment for a minimum of three to five years, and five to ten years would be ideal. Not one of my clients who purchased choice coins in the course of forming a fine collection has failed to make an attractive profit if he held his coins from five to ten years or more. At the same time I have heard many tales of people who wanted to get rich quick—and failed to do so. In this latter vein particularly vivid is a recent conversation I had with a prospective coin investor.

This gentleman wanted to invest $10,000 in coins. Accustomed to doing business on the commodities market, he wanted to make his $10,000 control a much higher value of coins. He asked if he could buy rare coins on margin or take an option on them. I respectfully suggested that he view rare coins as an investment, not as pure speculation. I suggested that he buy a few books on coins and take time to read some of our firm's catalogs. (He had never seen any of our firm's literature and learned of us through a friend. Also he had never seen any other numismatic publications.) My approach apparently was too conservative, and after a few further minutes of talk it was clear that the idea of purchasing selected rare coins in a studied manner and holding them for several years wasn't what he wanted.

Not more than a month or so later, this same man called me. It turned out that a "rare coin investment firm" had been very willing to sell him bulk coins on a margin basis. I don't know what the exact terms were, but I gathered that his $10,000 enabled him to control $50,000 or $60,000 worth of coins. Anyway, the price of bulk coins experienced a fluctuation downward, and our friend was left holding a worthless piece of paper (he never did take delivery of the coins). "In our last conversation you mentioned you put out catalogs about rare coins. Could I ask you to send me one now?" my telephone caller then said. He then went on to explain that he no longer had $10,000 to invest but would like to start over "the right way" and might spent $500 or $1,000. Hopefully, over a period of years this man will do well in coin investment—and I am sure he will if he takes the right path now. However, $10,000 was an expensive way to learn this. The moral is that there are always people who will take your money and promise you all sorts of things. Sometimes a dealer who urges caution and care isn't half as romantic as some "rare coin investment firm" which has flashy advertisements and high-pressure salesmen. However, in the long run there isn't much comparison between the results achieved by the two.

So, my recommendation is to think of yourself as a long-term investor —and buy to hold for several years or more.

A study of coin prices over the years shows that all grades have done well. Coins in Good grade, a relatively low condition, have increased in value sharply as have coins in the higher grades of Uncirculated and Proof. Generally, I recommend purchasing for investment purposes Uncirculated and Proof coins of the past 100 years or so. Earlier coins should be acquired in Fine or better condition. The reason for this is that higher grades have traditionally been in stronger demand, and dealers are willing to work on a lower profit margin when buying and selling them. Also, higher-condition coins are rarer than lower-condition ones, and this sharpens buyers' appetites for them.

Forming a Collection as an Investment

One of the most popular ways to invest in coins is by forming a collection. As mentioned earlier in this book, my friend Oscar G. Schilke had a rich and rewarding numismatic career by forming a series of high-grade collections over the years. When the collections were sold, attractive profits were realized. In the meantime, Oscar Schilke derived countless hours of enjoyment from the challenge of assembling the collections, not to mention the fellowship with collectors by mail and in person all over the United States.

Forming a collection requires some time and patience. It also involves an interest to enter coins as a hobby in addition to an investment. If the appeal of having a fascinating hobby in combination with a potentially excellent investment is interesting to you, then I strongly recommend forming a coin collection.

Traditionally James F. Ruddy and I have recommended building a type set as the ideal way to begin a coin collection. A type set contains one of each major design produced over the years. Within the field of United States coins a type set would contain one of each major design of half cent through silver dollar from 1793 to the present. Many collectors limit their type set to copper, nickel, and silver issues. Gold coins can be collected by type as well. Among American gold coins the date ranges are from 1795 through 1933 and the denominations go from the one-dollar gold piece through the twenty-dollar issues. Another way to collect a type set—and an interesting way to begin in a conservative manner—is to collect just 20th-century coins. At the present, less than $2,000 will form a complete collection of choice Uncirculated 20th-century copper, nickel, and silver coins from the cent through the silver dollar. This set will not become redundant later. If you decide to go back further in history and collect all United States coin designs since 1793, then your 20th-century collection will fit in nicely.

Coins of the world can likewise be collected by types: one silver-dollar-size coin or crown from as many countries as possible, different major design types of crowns from Great Britain, and so on. There are literally endless possibilities. Likewise colonial coins, paper money, and other series can be collected by types.

A type set has a great interest and educational value. Mounted in an attractive album or plastic holder, such a collection makes a fascinating exhibit.

Collecting by dates and mintmark varieties is the second major way to assemble a series. Throughout numismatic history many successful and prominent collectors have been specialists. Herbert Bergen, a past president of the American Numismatic Association, collects a wide variety of things but specializes in quarter dollars. Matt Rothert, also a past president of the American Numismatic Association (we sold Mr. Rothert's collection at auction in 1973), formed one of the finest specialized collections of United States paper money ever put together. When sold at auction, his paper money brought record prices, due both to the quality and to the completeness of the offering. In 1973, we also sold at auction the specialized collection of United States colonial coins formed by George A. Merriweather and the superb collection of half dimes by date and mintmark formed by Dr. W. E. Caldwell. I could cite hundreds of other examples. The challenge of completing a collection is perhaps like filling in a crossword puzzle. It is a combination of competition and completeness.

In forming a type set or specialized collection by dates, mintmarks, and varieties it is important to emphasize quality. I recommend you acquire

Uncirculated or Proof condition for pieces dated within the past 100 years. Earlier issues can be in Fine or better grades.

Many investors do not want to become collectors. Indeed, pension funds, profit-sharing programs, and other institutions by their very nature do not wish to collect. Also, there are many business executives, professional people, and others whose everyday duties simply do not permit enough time to study coins and become involved in the collecting aspects. For such investors we recommend an arrangement with a leading *numismatic* firm.

Investing Without Collecting

James F. Ruddy and I have long recommended investing in rare coins. Working closely with clients in the 1950's and 1960's we achieved many spectacular records of success. Word of the profits began to spread. Soon we received such inquiries as "How can I invest in rare coins?" and "I have heard about your customers' successes, how can I join them?"

We then began our Collection/Investment Program, a plan whereby the investor could buy from us choice rare coins, coins of proven scarcity and value and in higher grades. We delivered to our clients coins which we hoped would be of even greater value to collectors in the future, top-grade Uncirculated and Proof coins of the past century and selected Fine or better earlier issues. At the same time we permitted payments to be made at regular intervals. Coins were offered with a guarantee of quality and value. Any piece not pleasing a buyer for any reason could be returned within a stated time period.

No service charges, interest charges, or other "extras" were levied. We have never encouraged our customers to borrow money to buy coins from us, nor do we sell coins on margins, give options, or otherwise depart from our normal practice of selling coins of proven scarcity and rarity on a regular basis. Further, our customers were under no obligation whatsoever. If a customer was not pleased, the Collection/Investment Program could be discontinued at any time.

While this program might not sound "aggressive" compared to the "hard sell" position certain others might take, it has nevertheless been extremely successful. Certainly we have missed a few accounts here and there—our man with $10,000 who wanted to spend it in a hurry being a good example. However, we gained something worth far more to us: a large number of clients who became "friends" of our company as well as customers. We soon found that there were even longer-term benefits.

When these same people decided to sell, we were usually selected to handle their coins either by auction or outright purchase. Our main problem over the years has been buying coins, not selling them, but now we find that participants in our Collection/Investment Program are giving us a built-in source of coins for our needs in the future though our clients are under no obligation to sell coins back to us—they can sell them wherever they wish. However, we are competitive so far as outright purchase and auction are concerned, and most have selected us.

In contrast with the collector who assembles coins by date and mintmark sequence and without duplication, participants in our Collection/Investment Program receive coins selected not to complete a particular series, but rather pieces selected for their quality, rarity, and value. A collection of dates and mintmarks would have common coins as well as scarce ones whereas the typical "portfolio" of one of our Collection/Investment Program clients would consist only of pieces of proven scarcity and rarity.

We have always encouraged our clients to learn about coins. In our publications we have provided information concerning the American Numismatic Association, have encouraged clients to subscribe to numismatic magazines, and even to do comparison shopping with other dealers. We feel that what we sell can stand close scrutiny and comparison, and we have never been disappointed in this regard. Importantly, our customers have been just as pleased as we have been.

Bulk Coins as Investment

There are other forms of coin investment which interest many prospective purchasers. Recent variations in the price of gold and silver bullion have led many to buy bags of silver coins or common-date gold coins in quantities. I personally consider this type of investment to be a speculation. This is more in the realm of the commodities specialist than the numismatist. My study of rare coins since 1946 shows that an equal amount of money invested in each of 237 different randomly selected type coins would have yielded an investment which increased in value nearly 40 times. More specifically, I noted that $1,000 invested this way would have produced $38,485 by 1974. Equally important, within that time not one single coin in the study decreased in value. The commodities market is something else entirely. Characteristically there have been sharp profits as well as sharp losses. During the past several years, metal prices have risen sharply, so the profit side of this situation has been in the limelight.

Will this rate of profit last forever? I doubt it. However, that is beyond the ken of what I have to say here.

My recommendation in this regard is that if you are interested in commodity options and enjoy speculation (and it is important to be aware of the large downside risks plus the high cost of interest when buying things on margin), then by all means become involved in bulk coins. Otherwise, I think the safest route is numismatically rare coins, the main subject of this book. I am a rare coin dealer and I can look back with great satisfaction on the thousands of clients who have built collections with James F. Ruddy and me over the years. Equally pleasing to me is that not a single one of these clients, to my knowledge, has ever lost any money when he has held his collection of U.S. coins for five to ten years or more and has followed our recommendations concerning purchasing quality coins as part of a type set or as part of a specialized collection.

Common-Date Gold Coins

Related somewhat to bulk coins but in a slightly different category are so-called common-date gold coins. All gold coins are basically scarce by comparison to smaller denominations of a given country. However, there are some which are known as "common gold" issues, simply because the coins, while scarce in a relative sense, are common within their own series. For example, the 1911 twenty-dollar gold piece is a common date. The price movement of such a coin tends to be more influenced by the world market price of gold bullion than by numismatic consideration. The 1911 or any other United States twenty-dollar gold piece contains .967 ounce of gold. Thus, if the bullion price of gold is $40 per ounce, this gold piece contains $38.68 worth of this precious metal. If the gold price is $50 per ounce, the piece is worth $48.37 from a metallic value, and so on. As the coin has numismatic value as well, the price of a 1911 twenty-dollar gold piece is always over the bullion or melt-down value. As an example, in mid-1974 when gold was at about $170 per ounce, a 1911 Brilliant Uncirculated double eagle sold for about $325 to $350. Worn pieces sold for slightly less.

Popular with investors who desire a high metallic value are the following world gold coin issues: Austria four-ducats (.443 oz. gold) and one hundred-corona (.980 oz.); Belgium twenty-francs (.187 oz.); Colombia five-pesos (.235 oz.); France twenty-francs (.187 oz.); England one-pound or sovereign (.235 oz.); Hungary twenty-korona (.196 oz.); Mexico fifty-pesos (1.206 oz.), ten-pesos (.241 oz.), five-pesos (.121 oz.), two-

and-one-half-pesos (.060 oz.), and two-pesos (.048 oz.); Netherlands ten-guilders (.195 oz.); Peru one-libra (.235 oz.); Russia five-rubles (.124 oz.); Switzerland twenty-francs (.187 oz.); United States twenty-dollars (.967 oz.), ten-dollars (.484 oz.), and five-dollars (.242 oz.).

Prices of common-date world gold coins move in relation to international monetary and political crises as well as in relation to the price of gold bullion. Our previously mentioned common-date 1911 Uncirculated twenty-dollar gold piece has cataloged for the following amounts over the years: 1946, $75; 1949, $70; 1954, $65; 1959, $62.50; 1964, $85; 1969, $135; 1974, $375. The overall price appreciation during this period has been 400 percent. Taken on its own, this quintupling of value (expressed another way, the 1974 price is 500 percent of the 1946 price) has resulted in the coin having been a really fine investment. No one can quarrel that a 400 percent profit is not to be sneezed at! However, across the board *numismatically rare* gold coins have done far, far better.

In the past, investment in common-date gold coins appealed mainly to investors interested in hedging against the depreciation of the United States dollar and, at the same time, taking advantage of the price rise in gold bullion. It is abundantly evident that the price rises over the years are very modest in comparison to profits from numismatically rare pieces, but nevertheless the profits have been attractive.

Concerning common-date gold coins I have two recommendations:

- If you are mainly interested in hedging against the value of the dollar and if you are interested in the price fluctuation of gold bullion, then common-date gold coins provide an interesting way of participating in this. I think that the best profits are to be found with numismatically rare coins, but I also realize that it is natural for an investor to want to diversify. Bear in mind that the values of common-date gold coins have tended to fluctuate whereas the values of numismatically rare gold coins have a reasonably steady trend upward. If you want to invest in gold metal, then common-date gold coins are ideal for this.
- However, if you do invest, I recommend paying a small additional premium to buy Uncirculated coins. Most sales of common-date gold coins are by "sales organizations," not established rare coin dealers, and their customers for the most part don't know about coin grading. This is an advantage for you, for it means that Uncirculated pieces can be obtained for just a little more than it takes to buy worn coins. By buying Uncirculated coins you will then have two future markets: the common-date gold coin market and also the numismatic market. This gives you a double market for just a slightly added cost.

Afterword

So ends my discussion of rare coins and rare coin investment. Over the years coins have been wonderful to me. I have had the satisfaction of having a really great business and at the same time meeting many fine people from all over the world. James F. Ruddy and I have made fortunes for many clients. Profits for our investors have been the rule, not the exception.

It is my hope that the preceding pages have been of value. You are now in a position to take advantage of the knowledge which has made untold millions of dollars for the customers of Bowers and Ruddy Galleries, Inc., as well as of other reputable dealers. I have also put in some "don'ts" in addition to some "dos," to present both sides of the story. The story itself is one-sided in a sense, for the investment performance of choice coins has been one-sided—the trend has been sharply upward over the years. There would be no sense in finding fault with a good thing.

However, there are some common-sense precepts to follow. When I first began dealing in coins many years ago the business was a small and orderly one, and almost all leading dealers knew most other dealers in the profession. Likewise, personal relationships with clients were more possible then than they are today. Now coins are a big business. Many vendors are simply coin *sellers*, not *professional numismatists*—and there is a big difference. A professional numismatist has a reputation to protect. More often than not, his firm is built upon many years of responsible dealings with many buyers and sellers. On the other hand, many sales organizations are simply using the good name of coin investment to sell anything that is round and shiny. So, I cannot stress too highly the importance of doing business with an established firm with impeccable *professional* credentials.

It is a really wonderful feeling to make money for others, and in past years I have done this many times. It is my wish that this book will be your guide for making lots of money in the years to come. Follow the precepts I have outlined and this volume should literally be worth its weight in gold to you.

The gains of the past, as spectacular as they may be, belong to those who lived in the past. 1946 is not today, you might say—and this is true. However the principles which guided successful coin investment in 1946, 1953 (the year I began in coins), 1960, or any year and have resulted in fortunes for our customers since then are still in effect today. A "treasure for the future" is awaiting you. Let this book be your passport!

APPENDIX A

Selected Coin Prices, 1946-1974

The tables that follow give the price histories of selected United States coins in the copper, nickel, silver, and gold series from 1793 to date. I have selected one coin of each major design type and have given the price range of each piece in several grades (in many instances). No attempt has been made to select exceptional performance. Rather, in my opinion the prices represented give a realistic average of how different design types have performed over the years.

The prices given are from *A Guide Book of United States Coins* and are used with the permission of Western Publishing Company, Inc. As the "cover date" of each issue is one year in advance of the publication date, my 1974 figures, for example, are from the "1975 edition" (published in 1974). For consistency I have used the catalog figures; however, really choice examples of scarcities and rarities have nearly always sold for over *Guide Book* prices in the past, so, if anything, the prices listed may be conservative.

Taken as a whole, prices of choice rare coins have advanced steadily upward over the years. However, individual coin prices move upward at varying rates of advance. For this reason I have always recommended diversification across many different choice and rare coin issues. It is also important to remember that the future is always unknown, and while the past furnishes research material for thought and study, the figures given are not necessarily representative of future performance.

Selected Coin Prices, 1946–1974

	1793 ½¢	1793 ½¢	1797 ½¢ Plain Edge	1797 ½¢ Plain Edge	1806 ½¢ Large 6, Stems	1806 ½¢ Large 6, Stems
	Good	**Fine**	**Good**	**Fine**	**Good**	**Fine**
1946	17.50	45.00	8.00	17.50	.75	2.00
1949	20.00	50.00	8.00	17.50	1.00	2.50
1954	32.50	65.00	12.50	25.00	2.50	5.00
1959	65.00	115.00	18.50	42.50	3.00	6.00
1964	170.00	425.00	42.50	100.00	7.00	15.00
1969	250.00	650.00	60.00	150.00	9.50	19.00
1974	275.00	700.00	60.00	165.00	14.00	25.00
Increase in value from 1946 to 1974	1471%	1456%	650%	843%	1767%	1150%

	1832 ½¢	1832 ½¢	1851 ½¢	1851 ½¢	1793 Chain Cent "America"	1793 Chain Cent "America"
	Fine	**Unc.**	**Fine**	**Unc.**	**Good**	**Fine**
1946	2.00	6.00	1.25	4.00	35.00	125.00
1949	1.25	6.00	1.25	4.00	35.00	100.00
1954	2.50	8.50	2.50	5.50	45.00	110.00
1959	4.00	17.50	4.50	12.00	75.00	190.00
1964	9.00	35.00	10.00	32.50	195.00	525.00
1969	20.00	62.50	16.00	60.00	285.00	750.00
1974	19.00	200.00	22.00	115.00	350.00	1100.00
Increase in value from 1946 to 1974	850%	3233%	1660%	2775%	900%	780%

	1793 Wreath 1¢ Vine & Bars	1793 Wreath 1¢ Vine & Bars	1795—1¢ Plain Edge "One Cent" High	1795 1¢ P.E., "One Cent" High	1802 1¢	1802 1¢
	Good	**Fine**	**Good**	**Fine**	**Good**	**Fine**
1946	27.50	60.00	3.50	8.00	1.00	3.00
1949	27.50	60.00	3.75	10.00	1.00	3.00
1954	35.00	70.00	6.50	15.00	2.00	4.50
1959	65.00	125.00	9.00	19.00	3.75	8.00
1964	130.00	325.00	22.50	50.00	7.00	17.00
1969	220.00	600.00	30.00	87.50	9.00	24.00
1974	275.00	725.00	35.00	110.00	13.00	36.00
Increase in value from 1946 to 1974	900%	1108%	900%	1275%	1200%	1100%

Selected Coin Prices, 1946–1974

	1812 1¢ L. D.	1812 1¢ L. D.	1838 1¢	1838 1¢	1851 1¢	1851 1¢
	Good	**Fine**	**Fine**	**Unc.**	**Fine**	**Unc.**
1946	1.00	4.00	.75	6.00	.75	3.50
1949	1.25	4.00	.75	6.00	.75	4.00
1954	2.50	7.00	1.75	8.50	.75	4.50
1959	4.00	10.00	2.50	12.00	1.50	9.00
1964	9.00	22.50	6.00	35.00	3.50	22.50
1969	12.00	31.00	8.75	85.00	5.75	65.00
1974	13.50	36.00	11.00	175.00	6.50	125.00
Increase in value from 1946 to 1974	1250%	800%	1367%	2817%	767%	3471%

	1857 Flying Eagle 1¢	1857 Flying Eagle 1¢	1857 Flying Eagle 1¢	1859 1¢	1859 1¢	1859 1¢
	Fine	**Unc.**	**Proof**	**Fine**	**Unc.**	**Proof**
1946	1.00	5.00	35.00	1.00	4.50	10.00
1949	1.00	6.00	45.00	1.00	5.50	11.00
1954	2.50	10.00	70.00	1.50	8.50	12.50
1959	5.00	25.00	165.00	3.50	30.00	65.00
1964	9.75	80.00	1500.00	9.00	82.50	600.00
1969	8.50	115.00	2100.00	7.00	82.50	600.00
1974	11.00	400.00	2300.00	9.00	350.00	750.00
Increase in value from 1946 to 1974	1000%	7900%	6471%	800%	7678%	7400%

	1863 1¢	1863 1¢	1863 1¢	1907 1¢	1907 1¢	1909 V D B 1¢
	Fine	**Unc.**	**Proof**	**Unc.**	**Proof**	**Unc.**
1946	.40	1.00	10.00	2.00	3.75	.20
1949	.35	1.00	10.00	1.75	4.50	.25
1954	.75	2.00	14.00	1.75	5.00	.50
1959	1.50	5.50	39.00	3.75	15.00	1.50
1964	5.00	22.50	300.00	11.00	55.00	6.00
1969	3.75	25.00	300.00	9.25	52.00	5.25
1974	4.75	55.00	325.00	22.50	52.50	9.50
Increase in value from 1946 to 1974	1088%	5400%	3150%	1025%	1300%	4650%

Selected Coin Prices, 1946–1974

	1943 1¢	1944 1¢	1865 2¢	1865 2¢	1865 2¢	1881 3¢ Nickel
	Unc.	**Unc.**	**Fine**	**Unc.**	**Proof**	**Fine**
1946	.10	.05	.25	1.00	12.50	.50
1949	.10	.05	.25	1.00	11.50	.50
1954	.15	.10	.90	3.00	13.50	.90
1959	.50	.25	2.25	7.00	40.00	1.00
1964	1.00	.60	4.00	16.00	85.00	3.75
1969	.55	.35	4.75	27.50	130.00	4.25
1974	.60	.25	7.50	100.00	230.00	6.00
Increase in value from 1946 to 1974	500%	400%	2900%	9900%	1740%	1100%

	1881 3¢ Nickel	1881 3¢ Nickel	1852 3¢ Silver	1852 3¢ Silver	1858 3¢ Silver	1858 3¢ Silver
	Unc.	**Proof**	**Fine**	**Unc.**	**Fine**	**Unc.**
1946	1.65	4.00	.75	3.25	1.25	2.50
1949	1.65	4.50	.75	3.50	1.25	2.75
1954	3.00	5.50	1.50	5.00	2.50	6.00
1959	4.75	10.50	3.00	9.00	5.00	11.00
1964	12.00	30.00	7.25	21.00	11.00	40.00
1969	20.00	50.00	8.50	50.00	14.00	80.00
1974	52.50	72.00	11.50	115.00	17.50	410.00
Increase in value from 1946 to 1974	3082%	1700%	1433%	3438%	1300%	16,300%

	1858 3¢ Silver	1862 3¢ Silver	1862 3¢ Silver	1862 3¢ Silver	1866 Rays 5¢	1866 Rays 5¢
	Proof	**Fine**	**Unc.**	**Proof**	**Fine**	**Unc.**
1946	12.00	.75	1.50	7.00	5.00	12.50
1949	13.00	.75	1.75	10.00	3.00	10.00
1954	17.50	2.00	5.00	11.50	4.50	13.50
1959	110.00	4.50	9.50	22.50	6.50	27.50
1964	350.00	10.00	26.50	60.00	12.50	85.00
1969	525.00	15.00	52.00	135.00	15.00	120.00
1974	850.00	18.00	120.00	200.00	16.50	225.00
Increase in value from 1946 to 1974	6983%	2300%	7900%	2757%	230%	1700%

Selected Coin Prices, 1946–1974

	1866 Rays 5¢	1882 5¢	1882 5¢	1882 5¢	1883 No Cents 5¢	1883 No Cents 5¢
	Proof	**Fine**	**Unc.**	**Proof**	**Unc.**	**Proof**
1946	35.00	1.00	2.00	4.00	.50	2.50
1949	30.00	1.00	2.75	4.00	.50	3.25
1954	40.00	2.00	5.00	7.50	1.00	4.50
1959	200.00	3.00	9.00	15.00	3.00	11.50
1964	1000.00	4.00	17.50	40.00	6.00	28.50
1969	1250.00	4.50	30.00	70.00	11.50	46.00
1974	1200.00	8.00	75.00	100.00	40.00	125.00
Increase in value from 1946 to 1974	3329%	700%	3650%	2400%	7900%	4900%

	1910 5¢	1910 5¢	1910 5¢	1913 T-1 5¢	1913 T-1 5¢	1913 T-1 5¢
	Fine	**Unc.**	**Proof**	**Fine**	**Unc.**	**Proof**
1946	.50	2.00	3.50	.50	.75	6.00
1949	.50	2.75	3.75	.50	1.00	6.50
1954	1.00	4.50	6.00	.45	1.25	8.00
1959	1.75	9.00	14.00	.75	3.00	17.50
1964	2.25	15.00	32.50	2.00	7.00	145.00
1969	2.00	25.00	55.00	2.00	11.00	215.00
1974	2.00	55.00	77.50	2.00	22.50	240.00
Increase in value from 1946 to 1974	300%	2650%	2114%	300%	2900%	3900%

	1937 5¢	1937 5¢	1946 5¢	1942-P Wartime 5¢	1942-P Wartime 5¢	1795 ½ Dime
	Unc.	**Proof**	**Unc.**	**Unc.**	**Proof**	**Good**
1946	.35	5.00	.10	.25	1.75	6.00
1949	.35	5.50	.15	.25	1.75	6.50
1954	.40	9.00	.20	.25	2.50	11.00
1959	.75	50.00	.40	.65	5.00	30.00
1964	3.00	60.00	.80	12.50	25.00	30.00
1969	4.25	85.00	.45	8.00	30.00	115.00
1974	6.50	250.00	.30	10.00	75.00	170.00
Increase in value from 1946 to 1974	1757%	4900%	200%	3900%	4186%	2733%

Selected Coin Prices, 1946–1974

	1795 ½ Dime	1796 ½ Dime	1796 ½ Dime	1800 ½ Dime	1800 ½ Dime	1834 ½ Dime
	Fine	**Good**	**Fine**	**Good**	**Fine**	**Fine**
1946	10.00	12.50	30.00	7.00	12.50	.60
1949	12.50	15.00	35.00	8.00	15.00	.85
1954	22.50	25.00	50.00	12.00	20.00	2.00
1959	50.00	45.00	95.00	30.00	60.00	3.50
1964	230.00	120.00	250.00	80.00	180.00	6.50
1969	325.00	175.00	375.00	130.00	300.00	11.00
1974	350.00	200.00	400.00	140.00	325.00	55.00
Increase in value from 1946 to 1974	3400%	1500%	1233%	1900%	2500%	9067%

	1834 ½ Dime	1837 ½ Dime No Stars L.D.	1837 ½ Dime No Stars L.D.	1859 ½ Dime	1859 ½ Dime	1859 ½ Dime
	Unc.	**Fine**	**Unc.**	**Fine**	**Unc.**	**Proof**
1946	2.25	2.00	4.50	.50	1.75	10.00
1949	2.50	2.50	7.50	.50	1.75	8.50
1954	4.50	6.00	15.00	2.00	4.00	12.00
1959	9.00	21.00	52.50	3.50	8.00	27.50
1964	35.00	65.00	175.00	7.50	22.50	87.50
1969	77.50	80.00	285.00	8.00	45.00	150.00
1974	250.00	70.00	500.00	11.00	170.00	200.00
Increase in value from 1946 to 1974	11,011%	3400%	11,011%	2100%	9614%	1900%

	1862 ½ Dime	1862 ½ Dime	1862 ½ Dime	1796 10¢	1796 10¢	1807 10¢
	Fine	**Unc.**	**Proof**	**Good**	**Fine**	**Good**
1946	.50	1.50	5.00	17.50	35.00	4.00
1949	.50	1.25	4.00	20.00	40.00	5.00
1954	.85	3.00	10.00	27.50	52.50	8.50
1959	1.50	5.50	20.00	85.00	150.00	15.00
1964	4.00	15.00	50.00	235.00	600.00	50.00
1969	2.75	40.00	90.00	300.00	710.00	90.00
1974	6.00	130.00	145.00	325.00	750.00	100.00
Increase in value from 1946 to 1974	1100%	8567%	2800%	1757%	2043%	2400%

Selected Coin Prices, 1946–1974

	1807 10¢	1807 10¢	1827 10¢	1827 10¢	1835 10¢	1835 10¢
	Fine	**Unc.**	**Fine**	**Unc.**	**Fine**	**Unc.**
1946	12.00	25.00	1.50	7.50	1.00	2.75
1949	10.00	30.00	1.75	8.50	.75	2.75
1954	22.00	45.00	2.75	12.50	1.10	5.00
1959	32.50	75.00	6.50	21.00	1.75	9.00
1964	100.00	450.00	12.50	100.00	6.00	40.00
1969	135.00	600.00	19.00	160.00	9.50	120.00
1974	150.00	1450.00	27.50	1000.00	16.00	700.00
Increase in value from 1946 to 1974	1150%	5700%	1733%	13,233%	1500%	25,355%

	1837 L.S. 10¢ L.D.	1837 L.S. 10¢ L.D.	1853 Arrows 10¢	1853 Arrows 10¢	1859 10¢	1859 10¢
	Fine	**Unc.**	**Fine**	**Unc.**	**Fine**	**Unc.**
1946	3.00	12.50	.50	1.75	.65	2.50
1949	4.00	15.00	.50	2.50	1.50	5.00
1954	8.00	25.00	1.10	4.50	2.00	6.50
1959	30.00	65.00	1.85	7.50	2.25	9.00
1964	80.00	200.00	5.00	25.00	4.50	22.50
1969	95.00	350.00	5.00	55.00	7.50	45.00
1974	80.00	1000.00	8.00	300.00	6.50	185.00
Increase in value from 1946 to 1974	2567%	7900%	1500%	17,043%	900%	7300%

	1888 10¢	1888 10¢	1888 10¢	1892 10¢	1892 10¢	1942 10¢
	Fine	**Unc.**	**Proof**	**Unc.**	**Proof**	**Unc.**
1946	.50	1.50	2.75	2.50	4.50	.25
1949	.65	1.75	3.50	2.00	4.00	.20
1954	.85	2.75	5.50	3.75	7.50	.30
1959	1.00	5.00	16.00	6.50	25.00	.45
1964	3.00	9.50	32.00	12.00	40.00	.85
1969	3.00	35.00	75.00	25.00	77.50	1.50
1974	5.50	125.00	130.00	70.00	140.00	2.75
Increase in value from 1946 to 1974	1000%	8233%	4627%	2700%	3011%	1000%

Selected Coin Prices, 1946–1974

	1942 10¢	1946 10¢	1875-S 20¢	1875-S 20¢	1796 25¢	1796 25¢
	Proof	**Unc.**	**Fine**	**Unc.**	**Fine**	**Unc.**
1946	1.25	.20	1.75	4.00	65.00	100.00
1949	1.00	.15	2.00	6.00	70.00	135.00
1954	2.00	.25	7.50	15.00	125.00	275.00
1959	5.00	.65	10.00	30.00	625.00	1250.00
1964	10.00	.80	20.00	70.00	1750.00	3750.00
1969	22.50	.50	40.00	160.00	2150.00	5750.00
1974	60.00	1.00	45.00	475.00	2300.00	10000.00
Increase in value from 1946 to 1974	4700%	400%	2471%	11,775%	3438%	9900%

	1806 25¢	1806 25¢	1818 25¢	1818 25¢	1835 25¢	1835 25¢
	Fine	**Unc.**	**Fine**	**Unc.**	**Fine**	**Unc.**
1946	5.00	25.00	3.50	15.00	2.00	5.00
1949	6.50	30.00	3.50	15.00	2.00	5.00
1954	15.00	60.00	8.50	25.00	3.25	11.00
1959	30.00	150.00	12.50	65.00	4.75	18.00
1964	90.00	550.00	45.00	325.00	11.00	75.00
1969	125.00	800.00	50.00	485.00	24.00	250.00
1974	160.00	1950.00	60.00	1875.00	40.00	1200.00
Increase in value from 1946 to 1974	3100%	7700%	1614%	12,400%	1900%	23,900%

	1862 25¢	1862 25¢	1853 A & R 25¢	1853 A & R 25¢	1854 25¢	1854 25¢
	Unc.	**Proof**	**Fine**	**Unc.**	**Fine**	**Unc.**
1946	2.75	8.50	1.00	3.50	.65	2.00
1949	2.75	7.50	1.00	4.50	.75	2.75
1954	4.00	10.00	3.00	9.00	1.75	5.00
1959	7.00	30.00	4.25	22.50	3.75	18.00
1964	20.00	60.00	9.00	55.00	6.50	40.00
1969	45.00	140.00	12.00	275.00	7.00	75.00
1974	275.00	300.00	16.00	800.00	11.00	500.00
Increase in value from 1946 to 1974	9900%	3429%	1500%	22,757%	1592%	24,900%

Selected Coin Prices, 1946–1974

	1875 25¢	1875 25¢	1873 Arrows 25¢	1873 Arrows 25¢	1894 25¢	1894 25¢
	Unc.	**Proof**	**Unc.**	**Proof**	**Unc.**	**Proof**
1946	1.75	5.00	3.50	12.00	3.50	6.00
1949	2.50	4.50	4.00	10.50	3.50	5.75
1954	4.00	7.50	20.00	30.00	6.00	9.00
1959	6.00	30.00	50.00	125.00	9.50	32.50
1964	15.00	55.00	125.00	250.00	19.00	55.00
1969	45.00	95.00	200.00	375.00	45.00	100.00
1974	230.00	300.00	425.00	500.00	190.00	275.00
Increase in value from 1946 to 1974	13,043%	5900%	12,043%	4067%	5329%	4483%

	1917 T-1 25¢	1917 T-1 25¢	1929 25¢	1929 25¢	1942 25¢	1942 25¢
	Fine	**Unc.**	**Fine**	**Unc.**	**Unc.**	**Proof**
1946	1.25	2.75	.50	1.50	.75	2.00
1949	1.00	2.75	.60	2.50	.75	2.00
1954	1.75	5.00	.85	4.00	.85	4.00
1959	3.00	8.00	1.00	6.50	1.90	8.00
1964	5.00	30.00	1.85	15.00	3.00	25.00
1969	5.75	47.50	1.75	35.00	2.25	30.00
1974	7.75	150.00	2.75	60.00	2.75	35.00
Increase in value from 1946 to 1974	520%	5355%	450%	3900%	267%	1650%

	1795 50¢	1795 50¢	1797 50¢	1797 50¢	1805 50¢	1805 50¢
	Good	**Fine**	**Good**	**Fine**	**Good**	**Fine**
1946	6.00	17.50	125.00	200.00	2.50	5.50
1949	7.50	18.50	135.00	225.00	2.50	6.00
1954	13.50	27.50	150.00	275.00	4.00	8.00
1959	25.00	55.00	235.00	485.00	9.00	16.00
1964	105.00	185.00	1000.00	2100.00	20.00	40.00
1969	135.00	275.00	1400.00	3500.00	30.00	65.00
1974	130.00	285.00	1850.00	4250.00	35.00	75.00
Increase in value from 1946 to 1974	2067%	1529%	1380%	2025%	1300%	1264%

Selected Coin Prices, 1946–1974

	1831 50¢	1831 50¢	1837 50¢	1837 50¢	1838 50¢	1838 50¢
	Fine	**Unc.**	**Fine**	**Unc.**	**Fine**	**Unc.**
1946	1.75	3.25	2.50	6.00	2.50	5.00
1949	1.50	3.50	2.50	6.50	2.50	6.50
1954	2.00	5.50	4.50	11.50	4.75	12.50
1959	3.25	11.00	10.00	37.50	10.00	37.50
1964	7.00	22.50	27.50	80.00	23.50	75.00
1969	12.00	60.00	30.00	190.00	30.00	175.00
1974	25.00	350.00	45.00	550.00	45.00	550.00
Increase in value from 1946 to 1974	1329%	10,669%	1700%	9067%	1700%	10,900%

	1862 50¢	1862 50¢	1853 A & R 50¢	1853 A & R 50¢	1854 50¢	1854 50¢
	Unc.	**Proof**	**Fine**	**Unc.**	**Fine**	**Unc.**
1946	3.50	12.00	2.75	6.50	1.50	3.00
1949	4.50	11.00	2.25	7.00	1.50	4.00
1954	6.00	15.00	4.00	15.00	2.50	8.00
1959	10.00	55.00	8.00	37.50	5.00	16.50
1964	30.00	100.00	14.50	80.00	8.00	40.00
1969	65.00	170.00	22.00	370.00	8.50	90.00
1974	325.00	375.00	35.00	1500.00	16.00	500.00
Increase in value from 1946 to 1974	9186%	3025%	1173%	22,977%	967%	16,567%

	1875 50¢	1875 50¢	1873 Arrows 50¢	1873 Arrows 50¢	1902 50¢	1902 50¢
	Unc.	**Proof**	**Unc.**	**Proof**	**Unc.**	**Proof**
1946	3.50	10.00	5.00	20.00	3.50	8.50
1949	4.00	9.00	5.50	18.00	4.50	7.75
1954	5.50	13.00	20.00	40.00	7.50	12.00
1959	10.00	50.00	70.00	150.00	14.00	55.00
1964	22.00	75.00	135.00	300.00	27.50	80.00
1969	52.50	135.00	250.00	500.00	90.00	145.00
1974	300.00	350.00	500.00	600.00	375.00	400.00
Increase in value from 1946 to 1974	8471%	3400%	9900%	2900%	10,614%	4606%

Selected Coin Prices, 1946–1974

	1942 50¢	1942 50¢	1950 50¢	1950 50¢	1964 50¢	1964 50¢
	Unc.	**Proof**	**Unc.**	**Proof**	**Unc.**	**Proof**
1946	1.25	2.50	—	—	—	—
1949	1.00	2.50	—	—	—	—
1954	1.50	5.00	1.75	10.00	—	—
1959	2.00	11.00	4.00	10.00	—	—
1964	3.50	35.00	14.00	50.00	—	—
1969	6.50	60.00	18.50	65.00	1.00	3.50
1974	12.00	110.00	18.00	70.00	1.25	8.00
					3.00	4.00
Increase in value from 1946 to 1974	860%	4300%				

	1795 Flowing Hair 3L. $1	1795 Flowing Hair 3L. $1	1795 Draped Bust $1	1795 Draped Bust $1	1802 $1	1802 $1
	Fine	**V.F.**	**Fine**	**V.F.**	**Fine**	**V.F.**
1946	20.00	35.00	20.00	30.00	12.50	17.50
1949	22.50	35.00	22.50	32.50	12.50	17.50
1954	37.50	47.50	35.00	47.50	25.00	40.00
1959	60.00	90.00	65.00	95.00	32.50	50.00
1964	185.00	310.00	165.00	250.00	70.00	100.00
1969	285.00	450.00	300.00	485.00	160.00	225.99
1974	375.00	650.00	375.00	575.00	275.00	350.00
Increase in value from 1946 to 1974	1775%	1757%	1775%	1817%	2100%	1900%

	1836 Gobrecht $1	1860 $1	1860 $1	1871 $1	1871 $1	1882 $1
	Proof	**Unc.**	**Proof**	**Unc.**	**Proof**	**Unc.**
1946	150.00	17.50	30.00	7.50	13.00	2.50
1949	150.00	20.00	30.00	9.50	14.50	2.50
1954	185.00	31.00	45.00	17.50	27.50	3.00
1959	690.00	50.00	90.00	26.00	55.00	2.75
1964	1350.00	65.00	125.00	35.00	90.00	2.00
1969	1900.00	135.00	275.00	110.00	300.00	4.00
1974	2700.00	530.00	700.00	500.00	700.00	10.00
Increase in value from 1946 to 1974	1700%	2929%	2233%	6567%	5285%	300%

Selected Coin Prices, 1946–1974

	1882 $1	1922 $1	1876 Trade $1	1876 Trade $1	1853 Gold $1	1853 Gold $1
	Proof	**Unc.**	**Unc.**	**Proof**	**Fine**	**Unc.**
1946	9.00	2.00	4.50	12.50	5.00	7.50
1949	10.00	2.00	5.00	15.00	5.00	7.50
1954	13.00	2.00	12.50	27.50	8.50	10.00
1959	50.00	2.50	22.50	57.50	16.00	24.00
1964	75.00	2.50	32.50	100.00	—	60.00
1969	220.00	4.00	110.00	340.00	42.50	70.00
1974	345.00	10.00	360.00	600.00	95.00	250.00
Increase in value from 1946 to 1974	3733%	400%	7900%	4700%	1800%	3233%

	1855 Gold $1	1855 Gold $1	1857 $1 Gold	1857 Gold $1	1796 Gold $2½ No Stars	1807 $2½
	Fine	**Unc.**	**Fine**	**Unc.**	**Fine**	**Fine**
1946	7.50	12.50	6.00	9.00	150.00	40.00
1949	6.50	12.50	6.00	10.00	150.00	40.00
1954	8.50	15.00	8.50	11.00	190.00	55.00
1959	18.00	45.00	16.00	26.00	575.00	110.00
1964	—	220.00	—	55.00	2000.00	400.00
1969	110.00	425.00	50.00	85.00	2900.00	475.00
1974	250.00	1750.00	95.00	250.00	3200.00	600.00
Increase in value from 1946 to 1974	3233%	13,900%	1483%	2678%	2033%	1400%

	1808 $2½	1808 $2½	1830 $2½	1830 $2½	1836 $2½	1836 $2½
	Fine	**Unc.**	**Fine**	**Unc.**	**Fine**	**Unc.**
1946	100.00	250.00	37.50	75.00	9.00	18.00
1949	150.00	250.00	35.00	75.00	10.00	17.50
1954	160.00	300.00	45.00	75.00	12.00	17.50
1959	500.00	1200.00	65.00	130.00	17.50	29.00
1964	1450.00	6000.00	300.00	800.00	52.50	100.00
1969	2000.00	7000.00	400.00	1000.00	65.00	175.00
1974	2400.00	10000.00	600.00	2600.00	120.00	850.00
Increase in value from 1946 to 1974	2300%	3900%	1500%	3367%	1233%	4622%

Selected Coin Prices, 1946–1974

	1907 $2½	1907 $2½	1910 $2½	1910 $2½	1889 $3	1889 $3
	Unc.	**Proof**	**Unc.**	**Proof**	**Unc.**	**Proof**
1946	12.50	20.00	10.00	20.00	25.00	45.00
1949	15.00	35.00	9.00	20.00	30.00	50.00
1954	15.00	25.00	11.00	20.00	47.50	60.00
1959	24.00	115.00	18.00	45.00	120.00	150.00
1964	55.00	250.00	35.00	450.00	325.00	850.00
1969	65.00	400.00	60.00	525.00	460.00	1100.00
1974	150.00	1000.00	125.00	1000.00	1100.00	2150.00
Increase in value from 1946 to 1974	1100%	4900%	1150%	4900%	4300%	4678%

	1879 $4 Flowing Hair	1795 Small Eagle $5	1795 Small Eagle $5	1803/2 $5	1803/2 $5	1812 $5
	Proof	**Fine**	**Unc.**	**Fine**	**Unc.**	**Unc.**
1946	550.00	100.00	150.00	25.00	50.00	55.00
1949	500.00	75.00	150.00	25.00	50.00	50.00
1954	800.00	135.00	225.00	45.00	65.00	65.00
1959	2000.00	215.00	435.00	70.00	115.00	115.00
1964	6000.00	800.00	1750.00	225.00	500.00	450.00
1969	—	1400.00	2400.00	450.00	750.00	650.00
1974	15000.00	1500.00	4500.00	550.00	1250.00	1150.00
Increase in value from 1946 to 1974	2627%	1400%	2900%	2100%	2400%	1991%

	1813 $5	1818 $5	1836 $5	1836 $5	1861 $5	1861 $5
	Fine	**Unc.**	**Fine**	**Unc.**	**Unc.**	**Proof**
1946	30.00	60.00	15.00	30.00	22.50	100.00
1949	25.00	57.50	12.50	25.00	25.00	85.00
1954	55.00	90.00	11.00	25.00	25.00	85.00
1959	90.00	145.00	18.00	37.50	22.50	265.00
1964	230.00	650.00	55.00	110.00	55.00	550.00
1969	350.00	825.00	65.00	200.00	85.00	850.00
1974	450.00	1300.00	125.00	850.00	200.00	1400.00
Increase in value from 1946 to 1974	1400%	2067%	733%	2733%	789%	1300%

Selected Coin Prices, 1946–1974

	1900 $5	1900 $5	1912 $5	1912 $5	1795 $10	1795 $10
	Unc.	**Proof**	**Unc.**	**Proof**	**Fine**	**Unc.**
1946	20.00	40.00	17.50	35.00	135.00	200.00
1949	17.50	50.00	12.50	30.00	125.00	200.00
1954	17.50	50.00	15.00	32.50	175.00	300.00
1959	19.00	85.00	19.00	110.00	300.00	500.00
1964	32.50	350.00	35.00	650.00	700.00	2450.00
1969	60.00	475.00	80.00	800.00	1100.00	2900.00
1974	115.00	900.00	160.00	1800.00	1300.00	7000.00
Increase in value from 1946 to 1974	475%	2150%	814%	5043%	863%	3400%

	1801 $10	1801 $10	1861 $10	1861 $10	1901 $10	1901 $10
	Fine	**Unc.**	**Unc.**	**Proof**	**Unc.**	**Proof**
1946	75.00	100.00	50.00	125.00	37.50	70.00
1949	60.00	100.00	55.00	110.00	37.50	70.00
1954	80.00	135.00	55.00	110.00	35.00	75.00
1959	130.00	210.00	52.50	375.00	35.00	185.00
1964	350.00	725.00	75.00	1000.00	47.50	600.00
1969	600.00	1200.00	95.00	1500.00	70.00	850.00
1974	750.00	2500.00	350.00	2500.00	200.00	1500.00
Increase in value from 1946 to 1974	900%	2400%	600%	1900%	433%	2043%

	1908 $10 No Motto	1910 $10	1910 $10	1864 $20	1864 $20	1876 $20
	Unc.	**Unc.**	**Proof**	**Unc.**	**Proof**	**Unc.**
1946	37.50	37.50	50.00	85.00	350.00	75.00
1949	35.00	37.50	50.00	80.00	300.00	70.00
1954	35.00	35.00	60.00	80.00	300.00	70.00
1959	49.00	36.00	160.00	100.00	825.00	80.00
1964	70.00	50.00	1200.00	200.00	1900.00	95.00
1969	125.00	100.00	1350.00	300.00	2350.00	125.00
1974	550.00	250.00	3000.00	600.00	5000.00	375.00
Increase in value from 1946 to 1974	1367%	567%	5900%	606%	1329%	400%

Selected Coin Prices, 1946–1974

	1876 $20	1904 $20	1904 $20	1907 High Relief $20	1908 No Motto $20	1911 $20
	Proof	**Unc.**	**Proof**	**Unc.**	**Unc.**	**Unc.**
1946	250.00	75.00	200.00	120.00	75.00	75.00
1949	225.00	75.00	200.00	—	70.00	70.00
1954	275.00	75.00	250.00	145.00	75.00	65.00
1959	700.00	65.00	600.00	260.00	77.50	62.50
1964	1800.00	85.00	1600.00	850.00	87.50	85.00
1969	2500.00	110.00	2400.00	950.00	110.00	135.00
1974	5000.00	375.00	3750.00	3000.00	375.00	375.00
Increase in value from 1946 to 1974	1900%	400%	1775%	2400%	400%	400%

	1911 $20
	Proof
1946	110.00
1949	100.00
1954	110.00
1959	500.00
1964	2000.00
1969	2500.00
1974	4350.00
Increase in value from 1946 to 1974	3855%

APPENDIX B

Numismatic Magazines and Newspapers

The following leading numismatic publications contain information of general interest to coin collectors as well as news of coin club activities throughout the world.

COINage Magazine
16250 Ventura Blvd
Encino, CA 91316

Coins Magazine
Iola, WI 54945

Coin World
P. O. Box 150
Sidney, OH 45365

Numismatic News Weekly
Iola, WI 54945

Numismatic Scrapbook Magazine
P. O. Box 150
Sidney, OH 45365

The Canadian Numismatic Journal
Published by the Canadian Numismatic Assoc.
P. O. Box 226
Barrie, Ontario, Canada

The Numismatist
Published by the American Numismatic Assoc.
P. O. Box 2366
Colorado Springs, CO 80901

The two leading dealers' organizations are:

Professional Numismatists Guild
John J. Smies, Executive Secretary
Box 371
Courtland, KS 66939
(membership directory on request)

International Association of Professional Numismatists
Emile Bourgey,
7, rue Drouot
75009 Paris
France
(free membership directory on request)

The American Numismatic Association maintains a coin authentication and certification service. Persons desiring to avail themselves of this service must write first to request a schedule of fees and mailing instructions. All inquiries should be accompanied by a self-addressed stamped envelope. This is a service of the American Numismatic Association, the world's largest nonprofit organization devoted to coin collecting. The American Numismatic Association Certification Service is located separately from the main ANA headquarters. The address is:

Charles Hoskins, Director
ANA Certification Service
Box 87, Ben Franklin Station
Washington, D.C. 20044

Glossary

The following glossary includes terms which the coin collector and investor is apt to encounter in the field of United States coins. The listing defines terms which have special meaning for the coin collector, as opposed to general or ordinary meanings. All coin grades are capitalized in general usage.

About Uncirculated. Coin grading or condition term referring to a piece in nearly Uncirculated (Mint) condition. *See* Chapter 12, Coin Grading.

adjustment marks. Small file marks or striations found on early United States gold and silver coins, particularly issues from about 1794 to 1810. During these years it was important that gold and silver coins had the correct weight of metal. Slightly overweight planchets were filed at the Mint until the desired amount of metal was removed, thus bringing them to the required legal standard.

alloy. A mixture or combination of two or more basic metals. For example, bronze is an alloy composed of copper, zinc, and tin.

alteration. Changing of a feature of a coin to give it the false appearance of being rare or more valuable than it actually is. For example, the last digit of a coin's date might be altered to give it the appearance of another date, a rarer one. Or a mintmark might be affixed to a coin by solder. Purchasing coins from a reputable firm precludes such possibilities.

arrows at date. During 1853–1855 and again during 1873 and 1874 arrowheads were placed to the left and right of the date of certain varieties of dimes, quarters, and half dollars to indicate a change in the coin's authorized weight.

assay. Process by which the metallic content of a mineral ore is determined. During the Gold Rush in California, for example, the United States Government maintained an assay office at which miners could make deposits of gold dust or bullion. The assay office determined the gold content of the various deposits made and gave payment based upon the gold content.

bit. One-eighth of a Spanish milled dollar, equivalent in value to 12½¢. The term two bits comes from the use of this phrase in America over a century ago.

blundered die. Coinage die containing an error or blunder made by the engraver—the misplacement of a letter, the punching of a date upside down, and so on. Many examples occur throughout numismatics.

branch mint. In United States coinage, a mint other than the Philadelphia Mint. The Philadelphia Mint, established in 1792, was known as the "mother mint." Beginning in 1838, branch mints were opened in other areas.

broken bank note. A piece of currency issued by a privately owned bank during the early 19th century. Many of these banks went broke during the Panic of 1837 and other unfortunate financial times of this era, hence the term.

bronze. Alloy composed of copper, zinc, and tin metal. Bronze has been used to produce United States cents since 1864 except for some years in which other alloys were used.

capped-bust design. A popular design used on United States silver and gold coins during the early 18th century; for example, the dimes of 1809 through 1837.

cent. Term for the denomination representing the value of 1/100th of one dollar. The popular term penny, which has no official status in the American coinage system, is sometimes used to describe cents, a holdover from the early 19th century when English pennies circulated in America.

choice. An adjective used to describe an especially select Uncirculated or Proof coin—one which is exceedingly well struck, which has a minimum of handling marks, and which is an outstanding example of its type.

chopmark. A small punch mark or counterstamp applied to a coin, usually silver, by an Oriental merchant through whose hands the coin passed. This chopmark indicates that the merchant accepted the coin as being genuine and of full weight and fineness. Chopmarks are frequently found on United States trade dollars of the 1873–1878 era.

Civil War token. Small privately issued tokens, usually the size of a one-cent piece, issued mainly during 1862–1864 to fill the need for a medium of exchange during a time when official government coins were being hoarded by the public. Designs and motifs divide themselves into two main categories: those of a political nature and those with advertising.

clad metal. Special coinage material used to make United States dimes, quarters, and half dollars, since 1965 (dollar coinage commenced in 1971). A center core has copper-nickel or silver bonded to both sides, thus giving modern United States coins the appearance of traditional silver metal.

classic head design. Motif used on various United States coin issues during the early 19th century; large cents of 1808–1814, for example.

colonial coins. Coins issued by the thirteen colonies, coins issued in Europe for specific circulation in the American colonies, merchants' tokens, and other issues which circulated in the United States prior to the establishment of the United States Government Mint in 1792. Medals and tokens honoring George Washington are sometimes also included in this general category (although these were struck in most instances after 1792) as are coinages of various individual states such as Connecticut, Vermont, and New Jersey.

colonial currency. Paper money issued by the various American colonies, primarily during the 18th century. The category is sometimes broadened to include Continental currency—currency issued under authority of the Continental Congress during the American Revolution.

commemorative. Coin of a special design issued for a limited time to honor or observe a specific event or person. United States commemorative coins were first issued in 1892 for the Columbian Exposition.

Continental currency. Paper money issued by the authority of the Continental Congress in the 1770's.

copper. Popular coinage metal for lower denomination coins. Among United States coins, half cents and cents were made of copper in the early years. After 1864, bronze, an alloy containing copper, was generally used to produce cents and two-cent pieces.

copper-nickel. Alloy composed of copper and nickel and having a silvery appearance. Certain varieties of United States one-cent pieces were made of copper-nickel from 1856 through 1864. In recent years copper-nickel alloy has furnished the outside surfaces for clad-metal coins from dimes through dollars.

counterfeit. Not genuine.

counterstamp. A special mark—a design, series of letters, or numbers—stamped on the surface of a coin by a small punch or die. Counterstamps have been used for many reasons over the years, including advertising and political messages. For example, in 1824 when Marquis de Lafayette revisited the United States, many United States coins were counterstamped with the portraits of Washington and Lafayette, heroes of the American Revolution.

crown. Coin the size of a silver dollar. The general term "crowns of the world" covers silver-dollar-size coins issued by various countries over the years. Crowns are a popular collecting field.

decimal coins. Coins issued under the decimal system as fractional parts of 100 units. United States and Canadian coins are of the decimal system. Britain adopted the decimal system in 1971.

designer. Creator of a coin's design. The designer may be an artist not connected with the mint. For example, artist Felix Schlag designed the Jefferson nickel in 1938. Mr. Schlag, a Michigan resident, sent his design to the United States Mint. At the Mint various engravers translated his design into coin dies.

die. Cylindrical piece of metal at the end of which is engraved the design of a coin. To strike a coin two dies, one for the obverse and one for the reverse, are positioned in a coining press.

die variety. A design slightly different from the standard design of a given year or type. For example, several dozen die varieties of 1794 United States one-cent pieces are known. All the designs are basically the same, but each die variety differs from the other in some slight respect.

dime. Name for the United States ten-cent piece; one-tenth of a dollar.

disme. Early spelling of the word dime. Used for pattern issues of 1792. Later the silent "s" was dropped.

double die. An error in die preparation caused by a coining die receiving one blow from the hub die (which is used to make coining dies), and then a second blow but slightly misaligned from the hub die. The result is a doubling or a blurring of features on coins struck from such a die. An example is the 1955 Double Die cent.

double eagle. United States twenty-dollar gold piece.

doubloon. Gold coin of the Spanish Empire equal in value to 8 escudos; approximately $16 in United States funds at the time. Popular during the 18th and early 19th centuries.

draped-bust design. Design for United States coinage of certain denominations during the late 17th and early 18th centuries. An example is the series of large cents from 1796 through 1807.

eagle. United States ten-dollar gold piece.

eagle. Popular motif for United States coin designs. Adopted from the official United States Seal. In early years several motifs were considered, including the turkey. The eagle was adopted and has been used on various coins since 1792.

electrotype. A counterfeit coin made by electro-depositing metal.

engraver. One who cuts or engraves coinage dies or dies associated with coinage. The engraver may work from designs, models provided by artists, or other inspiration.

experimental piece. A coin classified as part of the general United States pattern series but made specifically to test a concept. For example, during the 1850's several patterns were made with holes in the center to see if this concept, popular in certain Oriental coinage, would meet with favor in the United States.

Extremely Fine. A coin grading term, capitalized in numismatic usage. *See* Chapter 12, Coin Grading.

field. Generally the blank area of a coin not used for letters or designs.

Fine. A coin grading term, capitalized in numismatic usage. *See* Chapter 12, Coin Grading.

fineness. Degree of pureness of a metal, expressed in thousandths. For example, United States trade dollars (1873–1885) have 900 FINE. on the reverse to indicate that they are 900 parts pure silver and 100 parts alloy.

first strike. Coin struck shortly after a new die is put into use. Such coins are often of unusual sharpness and sometimes possess a prooflike surface.

flowing hair design. Early design used on United States silver coins. Half dimes, half dollars, and silver dollars of 1794 and 1795 are examples.

fractional currency. United States paper money in various values ranging from 3¢ to 50¢ issued during the 1860's and 1870's. During the early part of this period silver coins were scarce in circulation due to public hoarding, and fractional currency helped to fill the need for a medium of exchange in commerce.

gem. A coin which is one of the very finest of its kind; the piece which is virtually perfect.

gold. Precious metal generally used to strike high-denomination coins. In the

United States, from 1795 through 1933, many denominations ranging in value from $1 to $20 were struck from time to time. In addition fifty-dollar gold pieces were struck in California during the 1850's and, in 1915, as commemoratives for the Panama Pacific International Exposition.

Good. A coin grading term, capitalized in numismatic usage. *See* Chapter 12, Coin Grading.

grade. The condition or amount of wear that a coin has received. Generally, the higher the grade the more valuable the coin is. Grades are expressed by terms of specific definitions to numismatists. Such terms are capitalized in numismatic usage. Standard coin grades include Good, Very Good, Fine, Very Fine, Extremely Fine, About Uncirculated, Uncirculated, and Proof. *See* Chapter 12, Coin Grading.

half dime. United States silver five-cent piece. Half dimes were struck from 1794–1873.

half disme. United States 1792 pattern half dime. When half dimes were first made of regular design beginning in 1794, the silent "s" was dropped in the terminology.

half dollar. United States fifty-cent piece.

half eagle. United States five-dollar gold piece.

Hard Times token. Privately issued token with either a political or advertising motif issued during the 1833–1844 "hard times" era. Such pieces, usually the size of an American cent, served as an unofficial medium of exchange.

heraldic eagle design. Motif used for the reverse of certain United States silver and gold coins during the late 18th and early 19th centuries. Half dollars from 1801 through 1807 used this style.

incuse. Opposite of relief. Coin design which appears to be incised or intaglio or recessed in the field. Examples are provided by gold quarter eagles and half eagles of the 1908–1929 years. Most other coin designs are in relief.

ingot. Bar of silver or gold metal on which information such as the weight, fineness (sometimes), and value are stamped.

legend. Principal lettering or inscription on a coin.

lettered edge. Lettered inscription on the edge of a coin. For example, United States half dollars of the 1794–1836 era have FIFTY CENTS OR HALF A DOLLAR lettered on the edge.

Liberty. Name given to the allegorical feminine portrait or figure on many American coins. Sometimes called Miss Liberty. For example, Liberty seated silver coins of the 19th century portray a seated woman.

Liberty cap design. The Liberty cap appears as part of many United States coin designs. The Liberty cap, a headpiece given to slaves in ancient times when they secured their freedom, was emblematic of America as a free country. The Liberty cap design appears on many coins including half cents of 1793–1797, large cents of 1793–1796, and Liberty seated silver coins.

Liberty seated design. Design used on American half dimes, dimes, twenty-cent pieces, quarters, half dollars, and silver dollars during the mid-19th century. The obverse depicts the seated figure of a woman, an allegorical representation of Liberty.

Matte Proof. Special type of Proof produced at the Philadelphia Mint (inspired by the Paris Mint) during the years before World War I. The finish is produced by a special pickling process which gives a grainy surface to the issues. Used on certain types of copper, nickel, and gold coins. Collectors, who prefer "brilliant" Proofs, were not enthusiastic about Matte Proofs, so the mint discontinued their production.

medal. A piece struck to commemorate a specific person, place, or event. Such pieces have no face value or legal tender status and are thus different from coins.

minor coins. Coins of low denomination. In the United States, the term covers pieces made of copper, nickel, and alloys of these metals; excluded are silver and gold coins. Among coins of the world the term refers to pieces smaller than crown or silver-dollar size, including lower-denomination copper and silver coins.

mint. Facility for striking coins. A modern mint contains coining presses, assaying and refining equipment, machinery for preparing planchets, and devices for attending to other operations for coinage production.

mint error. Defective or misstruck coin. Such a coin might be struck off-center or struck on a defective planchet.

mintmark. Letter or design which indicates where a coin was struck. Among United States mints, all but the Philadelphia Mint use representative letters for mintmarks. For example, coins struck at the San Francisco Mint bear a small s mintmark.

motto. Philosophical phrase used on a coin. Among American coins the mottos E PLURIBUS UNUM and IN GOD WE TRUST are important.

mule. A coin produced by combining two illogical dies, dies not originally intended for use with each other. For example, the obverse of a five-cent piece in combination with the reverse of a five-dollar gold piece would be a mule. During the 19th century, the United States Mint occasionally produced such pieces as curiosities for collectors.

nickel. Popular metal used in alloy form to produce three-cent pieces from 1865–1889 and five-cent pieces from 1866 to date. Nickel is also an ingredient of copper-nickel alloy.

nickel. United States five-cent piece made of nickel alloy. Such coins have been produced since 1866.

numismatist. Coin collector.

obverse. Front or "heads" side of a coin. Usually the obverse bears the date and the main coin design.

original. Coin was struck during the year indicated on it. Sometimes used to describe coins for which restrikes (which see) also exist.

ornamented edge. Special design such as circles and squares, series of leaves, etc., placed along the edge of a coin.

overdate. Coin date made by punching one or more numerals over an earlier-dated die to update it. For example, in 1799, silver dollar dies of 1798 were overcut with a new 9 digit to make them current. Such a coin is described as 1799/8.

overmintmark. Superimposition of one mintmark over another. An example is the 1938-D/S buffalo nickel.

overstrike. Coin produced by using a previously struck coin as a planchet. For example, certain coins of colonial New Jersey were produced by using Connecticut copper coins for planchets. Traces of the Connecticut design can be seen on some of these pieces.

pattern. Coin made to try a new design, test a new coinage concept, or to otherwise ascertain what a coin will look like before such coin is officially authorized and produced for circulation.

penny. English coin equal in value to 1/12 shilling. Usually made of copper. Often incorrectly used to designate the United States one-cent piece.

pioneer gold coins. Territorial gold coins (which see).

plain edge. Edge of a coin without reeding, lettering, or any design. The edges on modern United States cents and nickels are examples.

planchet. Circular blank piece of metal from which a coin is struck.

Proof. Coin struck from highly polished coin dies and using specially-prepared planchets. Such pieces have a mirrorlike surface. *See* Chapter 12, Coin Grading.

prooflike. Describes an Uncirculated piece which has a partial Proof surface but which was not struck as a Proof.

pseudo-coin. A fantasy coin or other piece struck in modern times to create a scarcity for collectors. Such pieces often have face value and/or legal tender status and are issued by governments of small nations. However, like souvenir postage stamps, most such coins do not actively circulate within the issuing countries but are sold in quantity to American and European collectors. This term was originated by the International Association of Professional Numismatists to differentiate pseudo-coins from legitimate coin issues.

punctuated date. A date to which a die flaw or other characteristic gives an appearance of punctuation. Examples are the 1,795 half cent and the 18.11 half dollar. Both examples of "punctuation" were caused by die defects.

quarter dollar. United States twenty-five-cent piece.

quarter eagle. United States two-and-a-half-dollar gold piece.

recut date. Coin date strengthened by overpunching the original date with the same date (when a different date is used it becomes an overdate). Many examples of recut dates and other recut features such as letters and mintmarks exist.

reeded edge. Edge of a coin bearing a series of alternating grooves and ridges. For example, 20-century United States dimes, quarters, half dollars, and dollars all have reeded edges.

relief. Portions of a coin's edge which are raised above the field. Coin designs which are extremely raised and have an almost sculptured appearance are said to be in high relief, the 1907 MCMVII twenty-dollar gold piece, for example.

restrike. Coin struck from an official coinage die but at a later date than that indicated.

reverse. Back or "tails" side of a coin.

rim. Raised portion of a coin around the periphery of the obverse and reverse. Protects the design features of a coin from excessive wear.

Sandblast Proof. Special type of Proof coin, produced occasionally by the Philadelphia Mint during the early 20th century for certain limited issues. Made by impinging fine particles of sand at high velocity against a coin's surface. The appearance is somewhat like that of a Matte Proof (which see).

silver. Precious metal used to strike various coin denominations. United States coins include three-cent pieces, half dimes, and all denominations from the dime through the dollar of years ago. In 1965, the Mint stopped using silver for general coinage due to its high cost. Now silver coins are produced only occasionally for collectors.

silver dollar. United States one-dollar silver piece. Silver dollars made of silver were struck from 1794 through 1935, inclusive. Modern Eisenhower "silver" dollars (1971 to date) are mostly made of clad metal, although some silver pieces have been made for collectors.

slug. Octagonal fifty-dollar gold piece produced in California during the 1850's.

small eagle design. Reverse design used on certain United States silver and gold coins of the late 18th and early 19th centuries. Half dollars of 1796 and 1797 use the small eagle design on the reverse, for example.

stella. United States four-dollar gold piece. Stellas were made in pattern form in 1879 and 1880. No pieces were ever struck for general circulation.

store card. Privately issued token bearing an advertisement. A trade token.

token. Small piece issued for use as a medium of exchange or to facilitate commerce but without having an official face value or currency status. In the United States privately issued tokens have been produced by many individuals and firms. No longer in general circulation, tokens are still used in subways and similar turnstiles and in vending machines.

toning. Patination or natural coloration formed on a coin over a period of years due to the effect of the atmosphere upon its surface. Toning can be very attractive, and most advanced collectors and museums prefer coins which exhibit this feature.

trade dollar. United States silver-dollar-size coin but slightly heavier in weight than the usual silver dollar. Issued from 1873 through 1885 and designated specifically for use in commerce with Oriental countries.

transportation token. Token of private issue used for passage on a streetcar, railroad, or other form of transportation.

trial piece. Coin struck specifically to test dies. Usually struck in metal less valuable than that officially used to produce coins of a given denomination for circulation. For example, trial pieces of gold coins were often struck in copper.

trime. United States silver three-cent piece issued from 1851 through 1873.

Uncirculated. Grading term referring to a coin which has never seen circulation and which retains full original sharpness, although such piece was originally produced for use in the channels of commerce (as opposed to Proof coins which are especially struck for collectors). Term is capitalized in numismatic usage. *See* Chapter 12, Coin Grading.

Very Fine. A coin grading term, capitalized in numismatic usage. *See* Chapter 12, Coin Grading.

Very Good. A coin grading term, capitalized in numismatic usage. *See* Chapter 12, Coin Grading.

Washington pieces. Coins, tokens, and medals issued to honor George Washington. Most were struck from about 1783 until 1810.

Bibliography

Adams, Edgar H., and Woodin, William H., *United States Pattern, Trial and Experimental Pieces.* New York: American Numismatic Society, 1913.

Bancroft, Hubert Howe, *History of California, Vol. VI, 1848–1859.* San Francisco: The History Company, 1888.

Beistle, M. L., *A Register of Half Dollar Die Varieties.* Shippensburg, Pa.: Beistle Co., 1929.

Bowers, Q. David, *Coins and Collectors.* Johnson City, N.Y.: Windsor Research Publications, 1964.

———, *High Profits from Rare Coin Investment.* Los Angeles: Bowers and Ruddy Galleries, 1974.

———, "How to Be a Successful Coin Dealer." *Coin World.* Sidney, Ohio, 1973.

———, *How to Start a Coin Collection.* Los Angeles: Petersen Publishing Co., 1973.

Bressett, Kenneth E., *A Guide Book of English Coins.* 1966–67 ed. Racine, Wis.: Western Publishing Co., 1966.

Buttrey, T. V., and Hubbard, Clyde, *A Guide Book of Mexican Coins.* Racine, Wis.: Western Publishing Co., 1971.

Charlton, J. E., *Standard Catalogue of Canadian Coins, Tokens & Paper Money.* Toronto: Charlton International Publishing Co., 1973.

Craig, W. D., *Coins of the World, 1750–1850.* Racine, Wis.: Western Publishing Co., 1971.

Criswell, Grover C., *Confederate and Southern State Currency.* Pass-A-Grille Beach, Florida: privately printed, 1957.

———, *North American Currency.* Citra, Fla.: Criswell's Publications, 1969.

Davenport, John S., *German Talers, 1700–1800.* London: Spink & Son, Ltd., 1967.

Donlon, William P., *United States Large Size Paper Money, 1861 to 1923.* Utica, N.Y.: privately printed, 1973.

Forman, Harry J., *How You Can Make Big Profits Investing in Coins.* Flushing, N.Y.: Nummus Press, 1972.

Friedberg, Robert, *Coins of the British World.* New York: Coin and Currency Institute, 1962.

———, *Paper Money of the United States.* New York: Coin and Currency Institute, 1972.

Fuld, George, and Fuld, Melvin, *United States Civil War Store Cards.* Baltimore, Md.: privately printed, 1972.

Hibler, Harold E., and Kappen, Charles V., *So-Called Dollars.* New York: Coin and Currency Institute, 1963.

Judd, J. Hewitt, *United States Pattern, Experimental and Trial Pieces.* Racine, Wis.: Western Publishing Co., 1970.

Linecar, Howard W. A., *The Crown Pieces of Great Britain.* London: Ernest Benn, Ltd., 1969.

Low, Lyman H., *Hard Times Tokens.* New York: privately printed, 1899.

Maris, Edward, *Varieties of the Copper Issues of the U.S. Mint in the Year 1794.* 2nd ed. Philadelphia: privately printed, 1870.

Newman, Eric P., *The Early Paper Money of America.* Racine, Wis.: Western Publishing Co., 1967.

——— and Bressett, Kenneth E., *The Fantastic 1804 Dollar.* Racine, Wis.: Western Publishing Co., 1962.

Noe, Sydney P. *The Pine Tree Coinage of Massachusetts.* New York: American Numismatic Society, 1952.

Remick, Jerome; James, Somer; Doyle, Anthony and Finn, Patrick. *The Guidebook & Catalogue of British Commonwealth Coins, 1649–1971.* Winnepeg, Canada: Regency Coin and Stamp Co., 1971.

Ruddy, James F., *Photograde.* Los Angeles: Bowers and Ruddy Galleries, 1974.

Scott, Kenneth C., *Counterfeiting in Colonial Connecticut.* New York: American Numismatic Society, 1957.

Sheldon, William H., *Penny Whimsy.* New York: Harper & Row, 1958.

Taxay, Don, *The Comprehensive Catalogue and Encyclopedia of United States Coins.* 1971 ed. Omaha, Nebr.: Scott Publishing Co., 1970.

———, *United States Mint and Coinage.* New York: Arco Publishing Co., 1966.

Yeoman, Richard S., *A Guide Book of United States Coins.* Racine, Wis.: Western Publishing Co., 1946–1974.

Index

Adams, Edgar H., 144, 155
aluminum patterns, 149, 153
American Numismatic Association, 18, 61, 62, 174, 176, 183, 196, 238, 258–9, 307
Ancient World, 9–10, 22
associations, 258–9
  dealer, 240, 258, 306
Atlantic Garden token, 187–9
auctions, 258, 260

Bailey & Co., 171
Baldwin & Co., 166, 168
Bancroft, Hubert Howe, 162
bank notes
  broken banks, 197–200
  national banks, 201–2
Barber, Charles E., 69, 76, 80
Barber, William, 153–4
Bashlow, Robert, 173–4
Bechtler, August, 159–60
Bechtler, Christopher, Jr., 159–60
Bechtler, Christopher, Sr., 159–60
Beebe, Aubrey, 62
Beistle, M. L., 174–6
Bergen, Henry, 283
Bickford, Dana, 156–7
Birch, Thomas, 45, 151
Blake & Co., 168
Brasher, Ephraim, 40
brass threepence, 229
Breen, Walter, 31, 47
Brenner, Victor David, 56–8
Bressett, Kenneth, 64–5, 83, 261
Broderick & Kohler, 166
bronze alloy coins, 55–6
Brown, Samuel, 61
"Bryan money," 190, **191**
Buttrey, T. V., 218
Byrne, Ray, 183

Calendar, Joseph, 37
California
  coinage, 159, 160–1, 163–8
    authenticity, 168
    mined gold as money, 158
  gold industry, 158, 164, 166
  gold rush, 162–3
  U.S. Assay Office, 164–5
Canada, 207–15
  commemoratives, 211–14
  decimal coins, 210
  mint mark, 211
  Proofs, 249, 250
  provincial issues, 214
  Royal Canadian mint, **208–9**, 210–14
  tokens, 208–10
Carson City (Nev.) Mint, **49**, 50
catalogs, 258–9
cents, *see* One-cent piece
Charlotte (N.C.) Mint, **48**, 50
Charlton, J. E., 214–15
Clark, Gruber & Co., 169
Clark, Murray, 200
cleaning coins, 252–3
Cliff House token, **187**, 189–90
clipping, 23
Cohen, Jerry, 71
coinage (*see also* Mints; *denominations, subjects*), 22–34, 77

Page numbers in **boldface** *denote illustrations.*

coinage (*cont'd*)
adjustment marks, 65–6
Ancient World, 22
Canada, **208–9**, 210–14
colonial, 22–3
commemoratives, *see* Commemoratives
contractors, 25–7, 42–3, 53–4
dating, 31
decimal system, 42, 220
denominations
foreign, *see countries*
United States, 42, 44–5, 50
designs, 52, 65, 144–58
dies, 24–34, 149
early, 24–7, 37–42
firsts, U.S., 29–30, 42–3, 44–50
foreign, status in U. S., 52
intrinsic-value concept, 22–3
metric, 156–7
motto, 132, 148, 152
pattern coins, 144–58
planchets, 22
Proofs, 248–50
restrikes, 52, 149–51
security edge, 23–4
types, major, 89–03, **94–121**
varieties, *see* Rare pieces; *denominations*
Coinage, 257, 306
Coins Magazine, 257, 306
Coin World, 257, 264, 306
collecting coins (*see also* Investment, coins as), 8–21, 54–60
buying, 136, 241, 256–8, 260, 264
cleaning coins, 252–3
clubs, 258
dealers, selecting, 240, 253
exhibitions, etc., 18–19, 258
grading coins, 238–51, 253
Great Britain, 41–2, 218–20
handling and storing, 259
information sources, 257–8, 264, 265, 306–7
insurance, 259
number of collectors, 8–9
prices, *see* Investment, coins as; Prices; Rare pieces; *denominations*
romance of coins, 1–7
selling coins, 260
unreleased coins, 135
varieties of collections, 17, 254–6
world coins, 236–7, 283
collections, notable, 18
Caldwell, 67–8, 283
Champa, 73–4, 154, 270
Eliasberg, 127, 129
Fairbanks, 6
Farouk, 135
collections (*cont'd*)
Herstal, 131, 192
Keusch, 158
Lohr, 145
National, 82
Nickel, 229
Rothert, 283
St. Oswald, 4–6, 81
Schilke, 17
Smithsonian, 129, 132, 155, 159
Terrell, 71–2
U. S. Mint, 193
Colonial Period
coinage, 22, 23, 36–7, **38**, **39**, 40–2
European coins, 25, 35, **38**, **39**, 40, 41
grading coins of, 251
paper money, 195–6
St. Oswald Collection, 4–6
tokens, 42
Colorado, **161**, 169
commemoratives
coins, British, 219–20, 225–6, 229–30
coins, Canadian, 211
coins, German, **233**, 234
coins, Swiss, 234–5, 236
coins, United States, 52, 137–44
Alabama centennial, 138, **140**
bicentennial, 11, 139
Carver, George W., 138, 142
Cincinnati, 138, **140–1**
circulated at face value, 139–40
Columbian Expo, 11, 137, 139, **140**
Delaware founding, 139
Eisenhower, 3, 88
first U. S., 10–11
gold, 143–4
Grant, 138, **140–1**, 143, 158
Kennedy, 3, 80–1
Lafayette, **46**, 137
Lewis and Clark, 143
Lincoln, 56–7
Missouri centennial, 138
Panama Pacific International Expo, 122, **140–1**, 143–4
Peace, 3, 87
Roosevelt, 72
silver (*see also names*), 137–43, 144
suspension, 138–9
Washington, Booker T., 138, 142
Washington, George, **46**, 76–7, 137, 142
tokens and medals, 191–4
Erie Canal, 183, 190, 192
fairs and expositions, 193–4
Louisiana Purchase Expo, 193
Washington, 3, **46**, 193
Confederate States of America, 56, 171–6, 200–1

Connecticut, 24–7, 37, 251
Continental Currency, 42, 197
Conway (J. J.) & Co., 169
copper coins (*see also denominations*)
  Great Britain, 220
  United States, 42, 44, 45, 47
    patterns, 149, 153, 155, 156
    states, early, 24–7, 37–41
counterfeiting, 7, 27, 40, 64, 196, 277
counterstamped coins, 194, **223**, 226
Cox, R. E., Jr., 269
Criswell, Grover C., Jr., 198, 200
crowns, British, 220, 225–30
  counterstamped, 226
  Edward VIII, **228**, 229
  George V, **223–4**, 227–8
  LIMA, 226
  "Petition," 225
  Victoria, **223–4**, 227
  VIGO, 205–6

Dahlonega (Ga.) Mint, **49**, 50, 174
dealers, 240, 257–58, 264
decimal system, 42, 220
Defrancisci, Anthony, 87
Denver Mint, 50
Deseret, **161**, 168–69
designs (*see also denominations*), 11–12, 52, 144–58
dime (*see also* Ten-cent coins), 45
disme, silver, 45
dollar token (so-called), 190, **191**
dollars, *see denominations, as* One dollar
Donlon, William T., 18, 204
Dorscher, Dora, 76
double eagles (twenty-dollar pieces), 1, 93, 120–21, 132–35
doubloon, 40
Dubosq & Co., 166

eagles (ten-dollar pieces), 44, 47, 93, **118**, **118–19**
Eglit, Nathan, 194

farthings, 220, 230–1
Feuchtwanger, Louis, 184–5
fifty-dollar pieces (slugs) (half unions), **160–1**, 164–5, 167
  patterns, **147**, 154–6
five-cent pieces, 60–5, 90, **99–100**
  alloy, wartime, 64
  buffalo or Indian head, 62–3, **244**
  CENTS-less 1883, 61
  counterfeit, 64
  half disme, 44–7
  Jefferson, 11, 64–5
  Liberty
    1883, 7

five-cent pieces (*cont'd*)
    1913, 19, 61–2
    1938-D/S, 63–4
    grading, example of, **242–3**
  patterns, 146–7, 148, 149, 157
    Hawaii, **178**
five-dollar pieces (half eagles), 45, 47, 93, **116–18**, **129–31**
  California, **160–1**, 164, 165, 166, 167
  Colorado, 169
  Georgia, 159, **160–1**, 162
  Mormon (Deseret) (Utah), **161**, 168–9
  North Carolina, 162
  Oregon, **161**, 168
Flanagan, John, 76
Ford, John L., Jr., 175
Forman, Harry J., 262–3
four-dollar pieces (Stellas), 93, **116**, 128, 156
France, **38**, 41, 43, 52, 55, 236
Franklin Mint, 192
Fraser, James E., 62
Fraser, Laura Gardin, 158
Friberg, Claes O., 20
Friedberg, Jack, 204
Friedberg, Robert, 204
Fuld, George, 185
Fuld, Melvin H., 185

Garroway, David, 70
Gasparro, Frank, 81, 88
Georgia, 158, 159
Germany, 232–4
Gobrecht, Christian, 83–4, 151–2
gold coins (*see also denominations*)
  Canada, 212–14
  common date, investment in, 286–7
  Great Britain, 220–1
  Mexico, 215, 217
  United States, 44, 45, 122–36, 131
    commemoratives, 143–4
    doubloon, colonial, 40
    gold price, 136
    gold standard, 122–3, 136
    last minting, 10
    melted down, 129–30, 131, 132, 135
    ownership regulation, 1, 122, 123
    patterns, *see* Patterns
    Proofs, 249
    shipment abroad, 136
    territorial, 158–70
    Union series proposal, 155
grading coins, 238–53
  abbreviations, 250
  About Good, **242**, **244**, 245
  About Uncirculates, **243**, 246
  authenticity, 240, 276–7, 307
  Brilliant Uncirculated, 246–7

grading coins (*cont'd*)
Choice Uncirculated, 247
different grades in one coin, 250–1
Extremely (Extra) Fine, **243**, 246
Fine, **243**, **244**, 246
Gem Uncirculated, 247
Good, **242**, **244**, 245–6
in research, 241
investment and, 274–6
"on the average," 251
overgrading, 239–40
Photograde system, 238–51
pricing and, 239–40, 241
Proof, 248–50
treating or processing, 252–3
Uncirculated, 246–8
Very Fine, **243**, 246
Very Good, **242**, **244**, 246
Great Britain (*see also denominations*), 42, 52, 54, 55, 219–32
collecting in, 41–2, 218–20
colonial coins, **25**, **35**, **38**, **39**, 40–1, 43, 231–2
commemoratives, 219–20
Commonwealth countries, 232
counterstamped coins, 194, **223**, 226
denominations, 220–1
farthing, Queen Anne, 230–1
imitations of coins, 27
mints, 221
monarchs, reigning, 221–5
Proofs, 249, 250
rarities, 219, **223**, **223–4**, 227
tokens, 41–2, 219
Greece, Ancient, 9, **10**, 22
Green, E. H. R., 62
Guide Book of United States Coins, 258, 261, 264
guinea, British, 220
Gwin, Senator, 155

half cent, 44, 47, 51, 52, 89, **94**
half crown, **228**, 229, 230
half dime (disme), 44–7, 65–8, 90, **100–1**
half dollar, 45, 47, 77–81, 91–2, **107–10**
California, 167–8
commemoratives, 3, 11, 52, 80–1, 137–42, 144
Confederate, 174–6
Hawaii, 179
Liberty seated, 79–80
Liberty walking, 80
patterns, **146–7**, 153–4, 158
rare, 78, 79, 154, 269–70, **272**
half eagle, 45, 47, 93, **116–18**, 129–31
half union, *see* Fifty-dollar pieces
Hamrich, John, 34

handling coins, 259
Harmon, Ruben, Jr., 38–40
Harper, John, 53
Haseltine, John W., 155, 172–3
Hawaii, 177–80
Henry, W. Howard, 74
Hewitt, Lee, 241
Hibernia, **39**, 41
Hibler, Harold E., 193
Humbert, Augustus, 164
Hydeman, Edwin, 70

Idler, William, 89
information sources, 257–58, 264, 265, 306–7
insuring coins, 259
International Association of Professional Numismatists, 240, 306
intrinsic-value concept, 10, 22–3
investment, coins as, 13–17, 261–7
advantages, 264–5
authenticity of coins, 276–7
bulk coins, 285–6
Collection/Investment Program, 284–5
common coins, 271–3
gold coins, common-date, 286–7
grade of coins, 274–6
holding time, 281–2
information sources, 257–8, 264, 265
market expansion, 273–4
quantity vs. quality, 268–9
prices, 270–1, 273–4
marketability and, 269–70
information, 258, 261
profitability record, 265–7, 280
questions and answers, 268–79
rare coins, 271–3, 280–7
timing, 277–8
type sets, 256, 282–4
Ireland, **39**, 41, 232

Jarvis, James, **39**, 43
Jeffrey, Fred J., 219–20, 230
Jenks, Joseph, 23
Johnson, B. G., 62
Judd, J. Hewitt, 47, 144–5, 152

Kalakaua, King David, 179, 180
Kappen, Charles V., 193
Kasson, John A., 128
Kellogg & Co., 167
Kohler, Frederick D., 166
Kosoff, Abe, 18, 70
Krause, Chester R., 207
Krider, Peter L., 172

Linderman, Henry, 156–7

Linecar, Howard W. A., 226
Longacre, James B., 31, 55, 79, 132, 166
Lovett, Robert, Jr., 171–3
Lovi, Art, 18
Low, Lyman H., 181, 183–4

Machin's Mill, 26–7, 40
MacNeil, Herman A., 76
Marcy, W. L., 125–6
Maris, Edward, 27–8, 53
Marshall, John, 162–3
Maryland, 40–1
Mason, E. B. Jr., 174, 175
Massachusetts, 37, **39**
  Bay Colony, 22, 36–7, 195, 196
McClintock, J. R., 47
McDermott, J. V., 19, 62
Medallic Art Co., 193
medals, *see* Commemoratives, tokens and medals
Mehl, B. Max, 19–20, 62, 83
Merkin, Lester, 75
Merriweather, George A., 283
metric coinage, 156–7
Mexico, 215–18
  decimal system, 217
  devaluation, 217–18
  mints, 215–17, 218
  Spanish monetary system, 35, 215
Mickley, J. J., 75
Miller, Don, 181–2
Miner's Bank (San Francisco), 159
mints (*see also* Coinage; *denominations*)
  Canada, **208–9**, 210–14
  France, 236
  Great Britain, 221
  Mexico, 215–17, 218
  United States, 27, 44–5, 50, 174
    mintmarks, **48–50**, 50, 64
    overmintmark, 63–4
Mishler, Clifford, 207
Moffat & Co., 159, 164–5
Morgan, George T., 86, 154
Mormon coinage, **161**, 168–9
Morris, Gouverneur, 42
Moskowitz, Irving, 18
Murbach, John, 168, 180

Nagy, Steven K., 155–6
New Brunswick, 214
Newfoundland, 214
New Jersey, 26, 38, 196
Newman, Eric P., 26, 82, 195, 196
New Orleans Mint, **48**, 50, 174
New York, 26, 40, 200
nickel coins, *see* Five-cent pieces; Three-cent pieces

Noe, Sydney P., 36–7
Norris, Grieg & Norris, 164
North Carolina, 158, 159–62, 196
Numismatic News, 257
Numismatist, The, 257, 264, 306

one-cent pieces, 44, 45, 47, 50–1, 52–9, 89–90, **95–8**
  1794, 5
  1799, 54
  Birch, 45, 151
  Booby Head, 54
  bronze, 56–9
  commemoratives, **46**
  Confederate, 171–4
  Connecticut, 24–7
  Double Die, 31–4
  first U. S., 29–30, 42–3
  Fugio, 26, **39**
  Hawaii, 177, **178**
  Indian head, 55–6
  Jefferson Head, 53
  large, 54, 89, **95–6**, 151
  Lincoln, 56, 56–9, 150
  omitted in 1815, 54
  patterns, 151, 152
  restrikes, 150–1
  Silly Head, 54
  steel, 10, 58
  varieties, early, 27–31, 53–4
one-dollar pieces
  California, 167–8
  gold, 92, **114**, 123
    commemoratives, 143–4
    Georgia, 162
    North Carolina, 162
    patterns, **148–9**
  metric, pattern, **146–7**
  silver, Canadian, 211–14
  silver, Hawaii, 179
  silver, Spanish, 35, **39**, 42
  silver, United States, 45, 47, 50, 81–8, 92, **111–14**
    alloy, 87–8
    auction, Government, 86
    Bland-Allison Act, 85–6
    commemoratives (*see also* Commemoratives), 137–43, 144
    Continental, 42
    1804, 6, **18–19**, 19–21, 82–3
    Gobrecht, 83–4, 151–2
    Liberty seated, 84–5
    melted down, 85–7
    Morgan, 86–7
    patterns, **146–7**, 151–4, 156
    perched eagle, 84
    restrikes, 150

one dollar pieces (*cont'd*)
1794, 5–6, 81
trade dollars, 88–9, 92, **114**, 249
Oregon, **161**, 168
Oregon Exchange Co., 168
Ormsby (J. S.) & Co., 165

Pacific Co., 166
Paget, T. H., 229
paper money
Confederate and Southern, 56, 200–1
Hawaii, 180
United States, 195–206
bank notes, broken banks, 197–200
bank notes, national banks, 201–2
Colonial Period, 195–6
Continental Currency, 42, 197
Demand Notes, 201
denominations, 195, 204, 206
fractional currency, 206
large-size, **202–3**, 204
motto, 204–5
Silver Certificates (1896), 204
Paquet, Anthony C., 132–3, 154
Parsons (John) & Co., 169
patterns, 144–58
basic pattern issues, 148
Champa collection, 154
experimental, 148–9
fifty-dollar, **147**, 154–6
first, 151
five-cent, 146–7, 148, 149, 157
half-dollar, 146–7, 153–4, 158
Lohr Collection, 145
metric, **146–7**, 156–7
motto, 152
one-dollar, 148–9, 151–4
piece de caprice, 149
restrikes, 149–51
Standard Silver, 152–3
ten-cent, 158
trial pieces, 149
twenty-dollar, **147**, 156, 157
twenty-five cent, **146–7**, 153–4, 158
Patterson, A. M. H., 175
Patterson, DuBois, 145
Patterson, R. M., 125–6
Peck, C. Wilson, 230–1
pennies
Great Britain, 219, 220
United States (*see also* One-cent pieces), 40–1, 52
Perkins, Jacob, 37, **46**
Peuch & Co., 183
Philadelphia Mint, 45, **48**, 50, 64
Canadian coinage, 210–11
Double Die cents, 31–4

Philadelphia Mint (*cont'd*)
Liberty 1913 nickels, 61
Proofs, 248–50
restrikes, 52, 150
varieties, early, 27–31
Photograde system, 238–51
pioneer issues, *see* Territorial coins, gold
prices (*see also* Investment, coins as; Rare pieces; *denominations*), 270–1, 291–305
grades and (*see also* Grading coins), 239–40, 241
marketability and, 269–70
reference sources, 258, 261
Prince Edward Island, 214
Professional Numismatists Guild, 240, 306
Proof coins, 16, 18, 248–50
Proskey, David, 175–6
publications, 257–8, 264, 265, 306

quarter dollar, *see* Twenty-five-cent pieces
quarter eagles, 45, 92–3, **115–16**, 123–6, 144
1848 CAL., 125–6, 142–3
Indian head, 124, 126

Randall, J. Colvin, 172
rare pieces
California, **161**, 165, 166, 167
Colorado, 169
fifty-dollar gold, 155–6, 165, 167
five-cent, 61–2, 148
four-dollar, 128
five-dollar, 129–31
Georgia, 159
grading, *see* Grading coins
Great Britain, 219, 223–4, 227
half-cent, 51
half-dime, 65, 66, 67–8
half-dollar, 78, 79, 154, 269–70, **272**
Hawaii, **178**, 179
investing in, 271–3, 280–7
Newfoundland, 214
one-cent, 31–4, 53, 54, 56, **57**, 58, 150, 151
one-dollar, silver, 6, **18–19**, 19–21, 81, 82–3, 84
Oregon, 168
quarter eagle, 124–6
patterns, 148, 150, 151, 155–6
restrikes, 52, 150–1, 172–6
ten-cent, 69–72
ten-dollar, 132
territorial, **161**, 169–70
three-dollar, 127

rare pieces (*cont'd*)
  tokens, 183
  trade dollars, 89
  twenty-cent, 73–4, 270
  twenty-dollar, 1–3, 133–5
  twenty-five-cent, 75
Raymond, Wayte, 15, 263
Reich, John, 51
Reid, Templeton, 159
Remick, Jerome, 232
restrikes, 52, 149–51, 172–6
Rittenhouse, David, 45
Roberts, Gilroy, 81
Robinson, Frank S., 71
Roettier, Jan, 225
Roman coins, 9–10, 22
Roosevelt, Theodore, 11–12, 132
Rosa Americana issues, **39**, 41
Rothert, Matt, 204–5, 283
Ruddy, James F., 5–6, 16–17, 33, 69–70, 145, 220, 229, 256, 268, 269, 282, 284
  Photograde system, 238–51
Ruddy, Nancy, 200

Saint-Gaudens, Augustus, 11–12, **13**, 131, 134, 157
Saltus, J. Sanford, 174, 175–6
San Francisco Mint, **49**, 50, 56, 249, 250
Schilke, Oscar G., 14–17, 149
Schlag, Felix, 11, 64
Schultz & Co., 166
Scotland, 232
Scott, J. W., 175–6
Scott, Kenneth, 196
Sheldon, William H., 29, 53, 255
shilling, 226
  Pine Tree, 36–7
silver coins (*see also denominations*)
  Canada, 211, **212–13**
  Great Britain, 220, **222–4**, 225–30
  Mexico, 215, 217–18
  United States, 44–5, 47, 60, 65
    adjustment marks, 65–6
    Bland-Allison Act, 85–6
    coinage, 22–4
    colonial, 22–3
    commemorative (*see also* Commemoratives), 137–43, 144, 211
    last heavy silver-content, 10
    patterns, see Patterns
    Proofs, 249
    Standard Silver patterns, 152–3
Simon, Thomas, 225
Sinnock, John R., 72, 80
Smith, Elliott, 176
"so-called dollars," 190, **191**
South Carolina, 196
Spangenberger, Henry G., 193–4
Spanish coinage, 35, **39**, 42, 43, 52
Spink & Son, 201, 219
Spreckels, Claus, 179
state coinages (*see also* Territorial coins, *gold; state names*), 24–7, 37–42
steel cent, 10, 58
Stellas (four-dollar gold pieces), 93, **116**, 128
Stickney, Matthew A., 82–3
store cards, *see* Tokens, trademan's
storing coins, 259
Sutter, John, 162–3
Swiss Credit Bank, 136
Switzerland, **234–5**, 236

talers
  German, **232–3**, 234
  Swiss, **234–5**, 236
Taxay, Don, 29, 45, 47, 53, 159–60
Taylor, B. F., 174, 175
ten-cent pieces
  Canadian, 210
  Hawaii, **178**, 179
  United States, 68–72, 91, **101–3**
    disme, 45
    Liberty, 68–71
    Mercury, 71–2, 158
    Roosevelt, 72
ten-dollar pieces (eagles), 44, 47, 93, **118–19**, 131
  California, 158, 160–1, 165–8
  Colorado, **161**, 169
  Deseret (Mormon) (Utah), 168
  Georgia, 159
  Indian, 131–2
  Oregon, 168
terms, glossary of, 309–16
territorial coins, gold, 158–70
  California, 158–9, **160–1**, 163–8
  Colorado, **161**, 169
  Deseret (Mormon) (Utah), **161**, 168–9
  Georgia, 158, 159, **160–1**, 162
  mined gold, 158
  North Carolina, 158, 159–62
  Oregon, **161**, 168
three-cent pieces
  nickel, 59–60, 90, **98**
  silver, 60, 90, **98**, 152
three-dollar pieces, 93, **116**, 126–7, paper, 197, 198–200
three pence, Edward VIII, 229
Token and Medal Society, 181
tokens
  Canada, 208–10
  for coin-operated instruments, 186–90
  commemorative, *see* Commemoratives
  counterstamped, 194

tokens (*cont'd*)
"dollars, so-called," 190, **191**
Great Britain, 41–2, 219
political, 181, 182, 190, **191**, 194
trademan's, 180–91
colonial, 42
Civil War, 56, 185–6
Hard Times, 181–5
Mott, William and John, 39, 181
Talbot, Allum & Lee, 15
trade dollars, 88–9, 92, **114**, 249
Trotter, P. B., 237
Tucker, Warren, 34
twelve-and-a-half cent, **178**, 179
twenty-cent pieces
Canada, 210, **213–14**
United States, 72–4, 91, **103**
twenty-dollar pieces (double eagles), 1, 93, **120–1**, 132–5
1859-O, 1–3
1907 Saint Gaudens, 11–12, **13**, 134
California, **160**, 165, 166, 167
Canada, 212–14
Colorado, 169
Deseret (Mormon) (Utah), 168
Paquet reverse, 132–4
patterns, **147**, 156, 157
twenty-five-cent pieces
Canada, 210
Hawaii, **178**, 179
United States, 45, 74–7, 91, **104–6**
twenty-five-cent pieces (*cont'd*)
California, 167–8
commemoratives, 11, 76–7, 137, **140**, 144
Liberty seated, 75–6
Liberty standing, 76, 272–3
patterns, **146–7**, 153–4, 158
"two bits," 35
twenty-five-dollar pieces, 159
two-and-a-half-dollar pieces (quarter eagles), 45, 92–3, **115–16**, 123–6
territorial, 159, **161**, 162, 168
two-cent pieces, 59, 90, **98**, 152
two-dollar pieces, 204

Uncirculated coins, 246–8
Utah (Deseret) coinage, **161**, 168–9

varieties, *see* Rare pieces; *denominations*
Vermont, 26, 27, 38–40

Walsh, Alexander, 183, 192
Washington, George, 44, 45, 46
Wass, Molitor & Co., 167
Weinman, Adolph A., 71, 80
Witherle, Joshua, 37
Wolfson, Samuel, 6
Wood, William, **39**, 41
Woodin, William H., 144, 155, 156, 157

Zerbe, Farran, 9

75 10 9 8 7 6 5 4 3 2 1